# BERLITZ®

# SPANISH
## for travellers

By the staff of Berlitz Guides

# How best to use this phrase book

● We suggest that you start with the **Guide to pronunciation** (pp. 6–8), then go on to **Some basic expressions** (pp. 9–15). This gives you not only a minimum vocabulary, but also helps you get used to pronouncing the language. The phonetic transcription throughout the book enables you to pronounce every word correctly.

● Consult the **Contents** pages (3–5) for the section you need. In each chapter you'll find travel facts, hints and useful information. Simple phrases are followed by a list of words applicable to the situation.

● Separate, detailed contents lists are included at the beginning of the extensive **Eating out** and **Shopping guide** sections (Menus, p. 39, Shops and services, p. 97).

● If you want to find out how to say something in Spanish, your fastest look-up is via the **Dictionary** section (pp. 164–189). This not only gives you the word, but is also cross-referenced to its use in a phrase on a specific page.

● If you wish to learn more about constructing sentences, check the **Basic grammar** (pp. 159–163).

● Note the **colour margins** are indexed in Spanish and English to help both listener and speaker. And, in addition, there is also an **index in Spanish** for the use of your listener.

● Throughout the book, this symbol ☞ suggests phrases your listener can use to answer you. If you still can't understand, hand this phrase book to the Spanish-speaker to encourage pointing to an appropriate answer. The English translation for you is just alongside the Spanish.

Second revised edition—6th printing 1988
Printed in Yugoslavia

# Contents

## Guide to pronunciation — 6

## Some basic expressions — 9

## Arrival — 16

16 Passport control
16 Customs
18 Baggage—Porters
18 Changing money

19 Where is…?
19 Hotel reservation
20 Car hire (rental)
21 Taxi

## Hotel—Accommodation — 22

23 Checking in—Reception
25 Registration
26 Hotel staff
26 General requirements
28 Telephone—Post (mail)

28 Difficulties
29 Laundry—Dry cleaner's
30 Hairdresser—Barber
31 Checking out
32 Camping

## Eating out — 33

34 Meal times
34 Spanish cuisine
36 Asking and ordering
38 Breakfast
39 What's on the menu?
41 Starters (appetizers)
43 Salads
43 Soups
44 Omelets
45 Paella
45 Fish and seafood
47 Meat
48 Poultry and game
49 Sauces

50 Vegetables
51 Herbs and spices
52 Cheese
53 Fruit
54 Dessert
55 Aperitifs
56 Wine
58 Sangria
59 Beer
59 Spirits and liqueurs
60 Nonalcoholic drinks
61 Complaints
62 The bill (check)
63 Snacks—Picnic

4

## Travelling around 65

| | | | |
|---|---|---|---|
| 65 | Plane | 73 | Underground (subway) |
| 66 | Train | 74 | Boat service |
| 68 | Inquiries | 75 | Car |
| 69 | Tickets | 76 | Asking the way |
| 69 | Reservation | 77 | Parking |
| 70 | On the train | 78 | Breakdown—Road |
| 71 | Baggage—Porters | | assistance |
| 72 | Coach (long-distance bus) | 78 | Accident—Police |
| 72 | Bus | 79 | Road signs |

## Sightseeing 80

| | | | |
|---|---|---|---|
| 81 | Where is...? | 84 | Religious services |
| 82 | Admission | 85 | Countryside |
| 83 | Who—What—When? | 85 | Landmarks |

## Relaxing 86

| | | | |
|---|---|---|---|
| 86 | Cinema (movies)—Theatre | 89 | Bullfight |
| 87 | Opera—Ballet—Concert | 90 | Sports |
| 88 | Nightclubs—Disco | 92 | On the beach |

## Making friends 93

| | | | |
|---|---|---|---|
| 93 | Introductions | 95 | Invitations |
| 94 | The weather | 95 | Dating |

## Shopping guide 97

| | | | |
|---|---|---|---|
| 98 | Shops and services | 119 | Electrical appliances |
| 100 | General expressions | 120 | Grocery |
| 104 | Bookshop—Stationer's | 121 | Jeweller's—Watch- |
| 106 | Camping equipment | | maker's |
| 108 | Chemist's (drugstore) | 123 | Optician |
| 112 | Clothing | 124 | Photography |
| 112 | Colour | 126 | Tobacconist's |
| 113 | Material | 127 | Souvenirs |
| 114 | Size | 127 | Records—Cassettes |
| 116 | Shoes | 128 | Toys |
| 117 | Clothes and accessories | | |

## Your money: banks—currency     129

| 130 | At the bank | 131 | Business terms |

## At the post office     132

| 133 | Telegrams | 134 | Telephoning |

## Doctor     137

| 137 | General | 143 | Prescription—Treatment |
| 138 | Parts of the body | | |
| 139 | Accidents—Injury | 144 | Fee |
| 140 | Illness | 144 | Hospital |
| 141 | Women's complaints | 145 | Dentist |

## Reference section     146

| 146 | Countries | 152 | Greetings |
| 147 | Numbers | 153 | Time |
| 149 | Year and age | 154 | Abbreviations |
| 149 | Seasons | 155 | Signs and notices |
| 150 | Months | 156 | Emergency |
| 150 | Dates | 156 | Lost property |
| 151 | Days | 157 | Conversion tables |
| 152 | Public holidays | | |

## Basic Grammar     159

## Dictionary and index (English-Spanish)     164

## Spanish index     190

## Map of Spain     192

Acknowledgments
We are particularly grateful to José Carasa for his help in the preparation of this book, and to Dr. T.J.A. Bennett who devised the phonetic transcription.

# Guide to pronunciation

This and the following chapter are intended to make you familiar with the phonetic transcription we devised and to help you get used to the sounds of Spanish.

As a minimum vocabulary for your trip, we've selected a number of basic words and phrases under the title "Some Basic Expressions" (pages 9–15).

### An outline of the spelling and sounds of Spanish

You'll find the pronunciation of the Spanish letters and sounds explained below, as well as the symbols we're using for them in the transcriptions. Note that Spanish has some diacritical letters—letters with special markings—which we don't know in English.

The imitated pronunciation should be read as if it were English except for any special rules set out below. It is based on Standard British pronunciation, though we have tried to take into account General American pronunciation as well. Of course, the sounds of any two languages are never exactly the same; but if you follow carefully the indications supplied here, you'll have no difficulty in reading our transcriptions in such a way as to make yourself understood.

Letters written in bold should be stressed (pronounced louder).

### Consonants

| Letter | Approximate pronunciation | Symbol | Example | |
|--------|---------------------------|--------|---------|---|
| f, k, l, m, n, p, t, x, y | as in English | | | |
| b | 1) generally as in English | b | **bueno** | **bway**noa |
| | 2) between vowels, a sound between b and v | bh | **bebida** | bay**bhee**dhah |

| c | 1) before **e** and **i** like **th** in thin | th | **centro** | **thay**ntroa |
| | 2) otherwise, like **k** in kit | k | **como** | **ko**amoa |
| ch | as in English | ch | **mucho** | **moo**choa |
| d | 1) generally as in dog, although less decisive | d | **donde** | **doan**day |
| | 2) between vowels and at the end of a word, like **th** in this | dh | **edad** | ay**dhahdh** |
| g | 1) before **e** and **i**, like **ch** in Scottish loch | kh | **urgente** | oor**khayn**tay |
| | 2) between vowels and sometimes inside a word, a weak, voiced version of the **ch** in loch | g | **agua** | **ah**gwah |
| | 3) otherwise, like **g** in go | g | **ninguno** | neen**goo**noa |
| h | always silent | | **hombre** | **om**bray |
| j | like **ch** in Scottish loch | kh | **bajo** | **bah**khoa |
| ll | like **lli** in million | ly | **lleno** | **lyay**noa |
| ñ | like **ni** in onion | ñ | **señor** | say**ñor** |
| qu | like **k** in kit | k | **quince** | **keen**thay |
| r | more strongly trilled (like a Scottish **r**), especially at the beginning of a word | r | **río** | **ree**oa |
| rr | strongly trilled | rr | **arriba** | ah**rreeb**hah |
| s | always like the **s** in sit, often with a slight lisp | s/ss | **vista** **cuantos** | **bees**tah **kwahn**toass |
| v | 1) tends to be like **b** in bad, but less tense | b | **viejo** | **byay**khoa |
| | 2) between vowels, more like English **v** | bh | **rival** | ree**bhahl** |
| z | like **th** in thin | th | **brazo** | **brah**thoa |

## Vowels

| a | like **ar** in cart, but fairly short | ah | **gracias** | **grahth**yahss |
| e | 1) sometimes like **a** in late | ay | **de** | day |
| | 2) less often, like **e** in get | eh | **llover** | lyoa**bhehr** |
| i | like **ee** in feet | ee | **sí** | see |

| o | 1) like oa in boat, but pronounced without moving tongue or lips | oa | sopa | soapah |
|---|---|---|---|---|
| | 2) sometimes like o in got | o | dos | doss |
| u | like oo in loot | oo | una | oonah |
| y | only a vowel when alone or at the end of a word; like ee in feet | ee | y | ee |

**N.B.** 1) In forming diphthongs, **a**, **e**, and **o** are strong vowels, and **i** and **u** (pronounced before a vowel like **y** in yes and **w** in was) are weak vowels. This means that in diphthongs the strong vowels are pronounced more strongly than the weak ones. If two weak vowels form a diphthong, the second one is pronounced more strongly.

2) The acute accent (′) is used to indicate a syllable that is stressed, e.g., *río* = **ree**oa.

3) In words ending with a consonant, the last syllable is stressed, e.g., *señor* = say**ñor**.

4) In words ending with a vowel, the next to last syllable is stressed, e.g., *mañana* = mah**ñah**nah.

| Pronunciation of the Spanish alphabet | | | | | |
|---|---|---|---|---|---|
| A | ah | J | khoatah | R | ayrray |
| B | bay | K | kah | S | ayssay |
| C | thay | L | ayllay | T | tay |
| CH | chay | LL | aylyay | U | oo |
| D | day | M | aymmay | V | bhay |
| E | ay | N | aynnay | W | bhay doablay |
| F | ayffay | Ñ | aynyay | X | aykheess |
| G | gay | O | oa | Y | ee gryaygah |
| H | ahchay | P | pay | Z | thaytah |
| I | ee | Q | koo | | |

# Some basic expressions

| Yes. | **Sí.** | see |
| No. | **No.** | noa |
| Please. | **Por favor.** | por fahbhor |
| Thank you. | **Gracias.** | grahthyahss |
| No, thank you. | **No, gracias.** | noa grahthyahss |
| Yes, please. | **Sí, por favor.** | see por fahbhor |
| Thank you very much. | **Muchas gracias.** | moochahss grahthyahss |
| That's all right/ Don't mention it. | **No hay de qué.** | noa igh day kay |
| You're welcome. | **De nada.** | day nahdhah |

## Greetings *Saludos*

| Good morning. | **Buenos días.** | bwaynoass deeahss |
| Good afternoon. | **Buenas tardes.** | bwaynahss tahrdayss |
| Good evening. | **Buenas tardes.** | bwaynahss tahrdayss |
| Good night. | **Buenas noches.** | bwaynahss noachayss |
| Good-bye. | **Adiós.** | ahdhyoss |
| See you later. | **Hasta luego.** | ahstah lwaygoa |
| This is Mr. ... | **Este es el Señor ...** | aystay ayss ayl sayñor |
| This is Mrs. ... | **Esta es la Señora ...** | aystah ayss lah sayñoarah |
| This is Miss ... | **Esta es la Señorita ...** | aystah ayss lah sayñoareetah |
| How do you do? (Pleased to meet you.) | **Encantado(a)\* de conocerle.** | aynkahntahdhoa(ah) day koanoathayrlay |

---

\* A woman would say *encantada*

SOME BASIC EXPRESSIONS

| How are you? | ¿Cómo está usted? | koamoa aystah oostaydh |
| Very well. And you? | Muy bien. ¿Y usted? | mwee byayn. ee oostaydh |
| How's it going? | ¿Cómo le va? | koamoa lay bah |
| Fine, thanks. And you? | Muy bien, gracias. ¿Y usted? | mwee byayn grahthyahss. ee oostaydh |
| I beg your pardon? | ¿Perdóneme? | payrdoanaymay |
| Excuse me. (May I get past?) | Perdóneme. | payrdoanaymay |
| Sorry! | Lo siento. | loa syayntoa |
| You're welcome. | Está bien. | aystah byayn |

## Questions *Preguntas*

| Where? | ¿Dónde? | doanday |
| How? | ¿Cómo? | koamoa |
| When? | ¿Cuándo? | kwahndoa |
| What? | ¿Qué? | kay |
| Why? | ¿Por qué? | por kay |
| Who? | ¿Quién? | kyayn |
| Which? | ¿Cuál/Cuáles? | kwahl/kwahlayss |
| Where is ...? | ¿Dónde está ...? | doanday aystah |
| Where are ...? | ¿Dónde están ...? | doanday aystahn |
| Where can I find/ get ...? | ¿Dónde puedo encontrar/con-seguir ...? | doanday pwaydhoa aynkontrahr/konsaygeer |
| How far? | ¿A qué distancia? | ah kay deestahnthyah |
| How long? | ¿Cuánto tiempo? | kwahntoa tyaympoa |
| How much? | ¿Cuánto? | kwahntoa |
| How many? | ¿Cuántos? | kwahntoass |
| How much does it cost? | ¿Cuánto cuesta? | kwahntoa kwaystah |
| How do I get to ...? | ¿Cómo puedo llegar a ...? | koamoa pwaydhoa lyaygahr ah |

Expresiones generales

| When does ... open/close? | ¿Cuándo abren/cierran ...? | kwahndoa ahbrayn/thyayrrahn |
| What do you call this/that in Spanish? | ¿Cómo se llama esto/eso en español? | koamoa say lyahmah aystoa/ayssoa ayn ayspahñol |
| What do you call these/those in Spanish? | ¿Cómo se llaman estos/esos en español? | koamoa say lyahmahn aystoass/ayssoass ayn ayspahñol |
| What does this/that mean? | ¿Qué quiere decir esto/eso? | kay kyayray daytheer aystoa/ayssoa |
| Is that correct? | ¿Es correcto? | ayss koarrayktoa |
| Why are you laughing? | ¿Por qué se ríe? | poar kay say reeay |
| Is my pronunciation that bad? | ¿Es mala mi pronunciación? | ayss mahlah mee proanoon-thyahthyon |

**Do you speak ...?** *¿Habla usted ...?*

| Do you speak English? | ¿Habla usted inglés? | ahblah oostaydh eenglayss |
| Is there anyone here who speaks ...? | ¿Hay alguien aquí que hable ...? | igh ahlgyayn ahkee kay ahblay |
| I don't speak much Spanish. | No hablo mucho español. | noa ahbloa moochoa ayspahñol |
| Could you speak more slowly? | ¿Puede usted hablar más despacio? | pwaydhay oostaydh ahblahr mahss dayspahthyoa |
| Could you repeat that? | ¿Podría usted repetir eso? | poadreeah oostaydh raypayteer ayssoa |
| Please write it down. | Por favor, escríbalo. | por fahbhor ayskreebhahloa |
| Can you translate this for me? | ¿Puede usted traducírmelo? | pwaydhay oostaydh trahdhootheermayloa |
| Can you translate this for us? | ¿Puede usted traducírnoslo? | pwaydhay oostaydh trahdhootheernoasloa |
| Please point to the word/phrase/sentence in the book. | Por favor, señale la palabra/la expresión/la frase en el libro. | por fahbhor sayñahlay lah pahlahbrah/lah aykspraysyon/lah frahssay ayn ayl leebroa |

| | | |
|---|---|---|
| Just a minute. I'll see if I can find it in this book. | **Un momento. Veré si lo puedo encontrar en este libro.** | oon moamayntoa. bayray see loa **pway**dhoa aynkoan**trahr** ayn **ays**tay **lee**broa |
| I understand. | **Comprendo/ Entiendo.** | koam**prayn**doa/ aynt**yayn**doa |
| I don't understand. | **No comprendo.** | noa koam**prayn**doa |
| Do you understand? | **¿Comprende usted?** | koam**prayn**day oo**staydh** |

## Can/May ...? *¿Puede ...?*

| | | |
|---|---|---|
| Can I have ...? | **¿Puede darme ...?** | **pway**dhay **dahr**may |
| Can we have ...? | **¿Puede darnos ...?** | **pway**dhay **dahr**noass |
| Can you show me ...? | **¿Puede usted enseñarme ...?** | **pway**dhay oo**staydh** aynsay**ñahr**may |
| I can't. | **No puedo.** | noa **pway**dhoa |
| Can you tell me ...? | **¿Puede usted decirme ...?** | **pway**dhay oo**staydh** day**theer**may |
| Can you help me? | **¿Puede usted ayudarme?** | **pway**dhay oo**staydh** ahyoo**dhar**may |
| Can I help you? | **¿Puedo ayudarle?** | **pway**dhoa ahyoo**dhar**lay |
| Can you direct me to ...? | **¿Puede usted indicarme la dirección a ...?** | **pway**dhay oo**staydh** eendee**kahr**may lah doorohk**thyon** ah |

## Wanting *Deseos*

| | | |
|---|---|---|
| I'd like ... | **Quisiera ...** | kee**ssyay**rah |
| We'd like ... | **Quisiéramos ...** | kee**ssyay**rahmoass |
| What do you want? | **¿Qué desea usted?** | kay day**ssay**ah oo**staydh** |
| Please give me ... | **Por favor, déme ...** | por fah**bhor daymay** |
| Give it to me, please. | **Démelo, por favor.** | **day**mayloa por fah**bhor** |
| Bring me ... | **Tráigame ...** | **trigh**gahmay |
| Bring it to me. | **Tráigamelo.** | **trigh**gahmayloa |

| Show me ... | **Enséñeme ...** | aynsay**ñay**may |
| Show it to me. | **Enséñemelo.** | aynsay**ñay**mayloa |
| I'm hungry. | **Tengo hambre.** | **tayn**goa ahmbray |
| I'm thirsty. | **Tengo sed.** | **tayn**goa saydh |
| I'd like something to eat/drink. | **Quisiera algo para comer/beber.** | kee**ssyay**rah **ahl**goa **pah**rah ko**amayr**/bay**bhayr** |
| I'm tired. | **Estoy cansado(a).*** | ay**stoy** kahn**sah**dhoa(ah) |
| I'm lost. | **Me he perdido.** | may ay payr**dee**dhoa |
| I'm looking for ... | **Estoy buscando ...** | ay**stoy** boo**skahn**doa |
| It's important. | **Es importante.** | ayss eempoar**tahn**tay |
| It's urgent. | **Es urgente.** | ayss oor**khayn**tay |
| Hurry up! | **¡Dése prisa!** | **day**ssay **pree**ssah |

## It is/There is ...   Es/Está/Hay ...

| It is/It's ... | **Es ...** | ayss |
| Is it ...? | **¿Es ...?** | ayss |
| It isn't ... | **No es ...** | noa ayss |
| Isn't it ...? | **¿No es ...?** | noa ayss |
| Here it is. | **Aquí está.** | ah**kee** ay**stah** |
| Here they are. | **Aquí están.** | ah**kee** ay**stahn** |
| There it is. | **Ahí está.** | a**hee** ay**stah** |
| There they are. | **Ahí están.** | a**hee** ay**stahn** |
| There is/There are ... | **Hay ...** | igh |
| Is there/Are there ...? | **¿Hay ...?** | igh |
| There isn't/There aren't ... | **No hay ...** | noa igh |
| Isn't there/Aren't there ...? | **¿No hay ...?** | noa igh |
| There isn't/There aren't any ... | **No hay ninguno(a)/ No hay ningunos(as) ...** | noa igh neen**goo**noa(ah)/noa igh neen**goo**noass(ahss) |

---

* A woman would say *cansada*

## It's ...   Es/Está ...

| | | |
|---|---|---|
| big/small | **grande/pequeño*** | grahnday/paykayñoa |
| quick/slow | **rápido/lento** | rahpeedhoa/layntoa |
| early/late | **temprano/tarde** | taymprahnoa/tahrday |
| cheap/expensive | **barato/caro** | bahrahtoa/kahroa |
| near/far | **cerca/lejos** | thehrkah/lehkhoss |
| hot/cold | **caliente/frío** | kahlyayntay/freeoa |
| full/empty | **lleno/vacío** | lyaynoa/bahtheeoa |
| easy/difficult | **fácil/difícil** | fahtheel/deefeetheel |
| heavy/light | **pesado/ligero** | payssahdhoa/leekhayroa |
| open/shut | **abierto/cerrado** | ahbhyehrtoa/thehrrahdhoa |
| free (vacant)/ occupied | **libre/ocupado** | leebray/oakoopahdhoa |
| right/wrong | **correcto/incorrecto** | koarrehktoa/eenkoarrehktoa |
| old/new | **viejo/nuevo** | byaykhoa/nwaybhoa |
| old/young | **viejo/joven** | byaykhoa/khoabhehn |
| next/last | **próximo/último** | proakseemoa/oolteemoa |
| beautiful/ugly | **bonito/feo** | boaneetoa/fehoa |
| good/bad | **bueno/malo** | bwaynoa/mahloa |
| better/worse | **mejor/peor** | mehkhor/pehor |

## Quantities   Cantidades

| | | |
|---|---|---|
| a little/a lot | **un poco/mucho** | oon poakoa/moochoa |
| few/a few | **pocos/(alg)unos** | poakoass/(ahlg)oonoass |
| much/many | **mucho/muchos** | moochoa/moochoass |
| more than/less than | **más que/menos que** | mahss kay/maynoass kay |
| enough/too | **bastante/demasiado** | bahstahntay/daymah-ssyahdhoa |
| some | **unos/unas** | oonoass/oonahss |
| any | **alguno/alguna** | ahlgoonoa/ahlgoonah |

* For feminine and plural forms, see grammar section page 159 (adjectives).

**Some more useful words** *Algunas palabras útiles*

| | | |
|---|---|---|
| at | **a/en** | ah/ayn |
| on | **sobre/en** | soabray/ayn |
| in | **en** | ayn |
| to | **a/para** | ah/pahrah |
| for | **por/para** | por/pahrah |
| from | **de/desde** | day/daysday |
| inside | **dentro** | dayntroa |
| outside | **fuera** | fwayrah |
| up/upstairs | **arriba** | ahreebha |
| down/downstairs | **abajo** | ahbhahkhoa |
| above | **encima** | ayntheemah |
| below | **debajo** | daybhahkhoa |
| under | **debajo** | daybhahkhoa |
| next to | **junto a** | khoontoa ah |
| between | **entre** | ayntray |
| with/without | **con/sin** | kon/seen |
| since | **desde** | daysday |
| and | **y** | ee |
| or | **o** | oa |
| not | **no** | noa |
| nothing | **nada** | nahdhah |
| never | **nunca** | noonkah |
| none | **ninguno/ninguna** | neengoonoa/neengoonah |
| very | **muy** | mwee |
| too (also) | **también** | tahmbyayn |
| soon | **pronto** | proantoa |
| perhaps | **quizá/tal vez** | keethah/tahl bayth |
| here | **aquí** | ahkee |
| there | **allí** | ahlyee |
| now | **ahora** | ahoarah |
| then | **entonces** | ayntoanthayss |
| yet | **todavía** | toadahbheeah |

# Arrival

**CONTROL DE PASAPORTES**
PASSPORT CONTROL

| | | |
|---|---|---|
| Here's my passport. | **Aquí está mi pasaporte.** | ahkee aystah mee pahssahportay |
| I'll be staying … | **Me quedaré …** | may kaydahray |
| a few days | **unos días** | oonoas deeahss |
| a week | **una semana** | oonah saymahnah |
| I don't know yet. | **No lo sé todavía.** | noa loa say toadhahbheeah |
| I'm here on holiday/business. | **Estoy aquí de vacaciones/negocios.** | aystoy ahkee day bahkahthyoanayss/naygothyoass |
| I'm just passing through. | **Estoy sólo de paso.** | aystoy soaloa day pahssoa |

## If things become difficult:

| | | |
|---|---|---|
| I'm sorry, I don't understand. | **Lo siento, no comprendo.** | loa syayntoa noa komprayndoa |
| Is there anyone here who speaks English? | **¿Hay alguien aquí que hable inglés?** | igh ahlgyayn ahkee kay ahblay eenglayss |

**ADUANA**
CUSTOMS

After collecting your baggage at the airport (*el aeropuerto* —ayl ahehroa**pwayr**toa) you have a choice: follow the green arrow if you have nothing to declare. Or leave via a doorway marked with a red arrow if you have items to declare (in excess of those allowed).

**artículos para declarar**
goods to declare

**nada que declarar**
nothing to declare

The chart below shows what you can bring in duty-free.*

| | Cigarettes | | Cigars | | Tobacco | Spirits (Liquor) | | Wine |
|---|---|---|---|---|---|---|---|---|
| 1) | 200 | or | 50 | or | 250 g. | 1 l. | or | 2 l. |
| 2) | 300 | or | 75 | or | 400 g. | 1.5 l. | and | 5 l. |
| 3) | 400 | or | 100 | or | 500 g. | 1 l. | or | 2 l. |

1) Visitors arriving from EEC countries with tax-free items, and visitors from other European countries
2) Visitors arriving from EEC countries with non-tax-free items
3) Visitors arriving from countries outside Europe

| I've nothing to declare. | **No tengo nada que declarar.** | noa **tayngoa nahdhah** kay dayklah**rahr** |
|---|---|---|
| I've a ... | **Tengo ...** | **tayngoa** |
| carton of cigarettes | **un cartón de cigarrillos** | oon kahr**ton** day theegahr-**reel**yoass |
| bottle of whisky | **una botella de whisky** | oonah boa**tay**lyah day **wees**kee |
| bottle of wine | **una botella de vino** | oonah boa**tay**lyah day **bee**noa |
| It's for my personal use. | **Es de mi uso personal.** | ayss day mee **oos**soa pehrso**a**nahl |
| It's a gift. | **Es un regalo.** | ayss oon ray**gah**loa |

---

| **Su pasaporte, por favor.** | Your passport, please. |
|---|---|
| **¿Tiene usted algo que declarar?** | Do you have anything to declare? |
| **Por favor, abra esta bolsa.** | Please open this bag. |
| **Tendrá que pagar impuestos por esto.** | You'll have to pay duty on this. |
| **¿Tiene usted más equipaje?** | Do you have any more luggage? |

## Baggage—Porters  *Equipaje—Mozos*

You'll find porters to carry your luggage to taxi ranks or bus stops. Major airports have self-service luggage carts which can be found in the baggage claim area.

| | | |
|---|---|---|
| Porter! | ¡Mozo! | moathoa |
| Please take this luggage. | Por favor, lleve este equipaje. | por fahbhor lyaybhay aystay aykeepahkhay |
| That's mine. | Eso es mío. | ayssoa ayss meeoa |
| That's my bag/ suitcase. | Esa es mi bolsa/ maleta. | ayssay eyss mee bolsah/ mahlaytah |
| There is one piece missing. | Falta un bulto. | fahltah oon booltoa |
| Please take this/my luggage to the ... | Por favor, lleve este/ mi equipaje ... | por fahbhor lyaybhay aystay/mee aykeepahkhay |
| bus | al autobús | ahl owtoabhooss |
| luggage lockers | a la consigna automática | ah lah konseegnah owtoamahteekah |
| taxi | al taxi | ahl tahksee |
| How much is that? | ¿Cuánto es? | kwahntoa ayss |
| Where are the baggage trolleys (carts)? | ¿Dónde están los carritos de equipaje? | doanday aystahn los kahrreetoss day aykeepahkhay |

## Changing money  *Cambio de moneda*

| | | |
|---|---|---|
| Where's the nearest currency exchange office? | ¿Dónde está la oficina de cambio más cercana? | doanday aystah lah oafeetheenah day kahmbyoa mahss thayrkahnah |
| Can you change these traveller's cheques (checks)? | ¿Puede cambiarme estos cheques de viajero? | pwaydhay kahmbyahrmay aystoass chaykayss day byahkhayroa |
| I want to change some ... | Quiero cambiar ... | kyayroa kahmbyahr |
| dollars | dólares | doalahrayss |
| pounds | libras | leebrahss |
| Can you change this into pesetas? | ¿Puede cambiarme esto en pesetas? | pwaydhay kahmbyahrmay aystoa ayn payssaytahss |
| What's the exchange rate? | ¿A cuánto está el cambio? | ah kwahntoa aystah ayl kahmbyoa |

TIPPING, see inside back-cover

## Where is ...? ¿Dónde está ...?

| | | |
|---|---|---|
| Where is/are the ...? | **¿Dónde está/ están ...?** | doanday aystah/aystahn |
| booking office | **la oficina de reservas** | lah oafeetheenah day rayssayrbahss |
| car hire | **la agencia de alquiler de coches** | lah ahkhaynthyah day ahl- keelayr day koachayss |
| currency-exchange office | **la oficina de cambio de moneda** | lah oafeetheenah day kahm- byoa day moanaydhah |
| duty-free shop | **la tienda libre de impuestos** | lah tyayndah leebray day eempwaysstoass |
| luggage lockers | **la consigna automática** | lah konseegnah owto- mahteekah |
| newsstand | **el quiosco de periódicos** | ayl kyoskoa day payryodheekoass |
| restaurant | **el restaurante** | ayl raystowrahntay |
| toilets | **los servicios** | loss sehrbeethyoass |
| How do I get to ...? | **¿Cómo podría ir a ...?** | koamoa poadreeah eer ah |
| Is there a bus into town? | **¿Hay un autobús que va al centro?** | igh oon owtoabhooss kay bah ahl thayntroa |
| Where can I get a taxi? | **¿Dónde puedo coger un taxi?** | doanday pwaydhoa koakhayr oon tahksee |

## Hotel reservation  *Reserva de hotel*

| | | |
|---|---|---|
| Do you have a hotel guide? | **¿Tiene una guía de hoteles?** | tyaynay oonah geeah day oatehlayss |
| Could you please reserve a room for me at a hotel/ boarding-house? | **¿Podría reservarme una habitación en un hotel/una pensión, por favor?** | poadreeah rayssayrbahr- may oonah ahbheetahthyon ayn oon oatehl/oonah paynsyon por fahbor |
| in the centre | **en el centro** | ayn ayl thayntroa |
| near the railway station | **cerca de la estación de ferrocarril** | thayrkah day lah aystah- thyon day fehrrokahrreel |
| a single room | **una habitación sencilla** | oonah ahbheetahthyon sayntheelyah |
| a double room | **una habitación doble** | oonah ahbheetahthyon doablay |
| not too expensive | **no muy cara** | noa mwee kahrah |
| Where is the hotel/ boarding-house? | **¿Dónde está el hotel/ la pensión?** | doanday aystah ayl oatehl/ lah paynsyon |

HOTEL, see page 22

### Car hire (rental) *Alquiler de coches*

Normally you must be over 21 and hold an international driving licence. In practice, British, American and European licences are accepted in almost all situations.

| I'd like to hire (rent) a ... | Quisiera alquilar un ... | keessyayrah ahlkeelahr oon |
| car | coche | koachay |
| small car | coche pequeño | koachay paykayñoa |
| medium-sized car | coche no de lujo | koachay noa day lookhoa |
| large car | coche grande | koachay grahnday |
| automatic car | coche automático | koachay owtoamahteekoa |
| I'd like it for ... | Lo quisiera para ... | loa keessyayrah pahrah |
| a day | un día | oon deeah |
| a week | una semana | oonah saymahnah |
| Are there any weekend arrangements? | ¿Hay condiciones especiales para los fines de semana? | igh koandeethyonayss ayspaythyahlayss pahrah loass feenayss day saymahnah |
| Do you have any special rates? | ¿Tienen tarifas especiales? | tyaynayn tahreefahss ayspaythyahlayss |
| What's the charge per day/week? | ¿Cúanto cobran por día/semana? | kwahntoa koabrahn por deeah/saymahnah |
| Is mileage included? | ¿Está incluido el kilometraje? | aystah eenklooeedhoa ayl keeloamaytrahkhay |
| Is petrol (gasoline) included? | ¿Está incluida la gasolina? | aystah eenklooeedhah lah gahssoaleenah |
| What's the charge per kilometre? | ¿Cuánto cobran por kilómetro? | kwahntoa koabrahn por keeloamaytroa |
| I want to hire the car here and leave it in ... | Quiero alquilar un coche aquí y entregarlo en ... | kyayroa ahlkeelahr oon koachay ahkee ee ayntraygahrloa ayn |
| I want full insurance. | Quiero un seguro a todo riesgo. | kyayroa oon saygooroa ah toadhoa ryaysgoa |
| What's the deposit? | ¿Cuál es el depósito? | kwahl ayss ayl daypoasseetoa |
| I've a credit card. | Tengo una tarjeta de crédito. | tayngoa oonah tahrkhaytah day krayddheetoa |
| Here's my driving licence. | Este es mi permiso de conducir. | aystay ayss mee pehrmeessoa day kondootheer |

CAR, see page 75

## Taxi *Taxi*

Taxis in major towns are fitted with meters. The figure displayed at the end of your trip may not be the full price. Legitimate added charges are compounded for night and holiday travel, pickups at railway stations, theatres or bullrings, and for baggage. It's usually best to ask the approximate fare beforehand.

| Where can I get a taxi? | ¿Dónde puedo coger un taxi? | doanday pwaydhoa koakhehr oon tahksee |
|---|---|---|
| Please get me a taxi. | Pídame un taxi, por favor. | peedhahmay oon tahksee por fahbhor |
| What's the fare to ...? | ¿Cuánto es la tarifa a ...? | kwahntoa ayss lah tahreefah ah |
| How far is it to ...? | ¿Cuánto se tarda a ...? | kwahntoa say tahrdah ah |
| Take me to ... | Lléveme ... | lyaybhaymay |
| this address | a estas señas | ah aystahss sayñahss |
| the airport | al aeropuerto | ahl ahehropwayrto |
| the air terminal | a la terminal aérea | ah lah tehrmeenahl ahayrayah |
| the railway station | a la estación de ferrocarril | ah lah aystahthyon day fehrrokahrreel |
| the town centre | al centro de la ciudad | ahl thayntroa day lah thyoodhahdh |
| the ... Hotel | al hotel ... | ahl oatehl |
| Turn ... at the next corner. | Doble ... en la próxima esquina. | doablay ... ayn lah prokseemah ayskeenah |
| left | a la izquierda | ah lah eethkyayrdah |
| right | a la derecha | ah lah dayraychah |
| Go straight ahead. | Siga derecho. | seegah dayraychoa |
| Please stop here. | Pare aquí, por favor. | pahray ahkee por fahbhor |
| I'm in a hurry. | Tengo mucha prisa. | tayngoa moochah preessah |
| Could you drive more slowly? | ¿Puede usted ir más despacio? | pwaydhay oostaydh eer mahss dayspahthyoa |
| Could you help me carry my bags? | ¿Podría ayudarme a llevar mi equipaje? | poadreeah ahyoodhahr-may ah lyaybhahr mee aykeepahkhay |
| Would you please wait for me? | ¿Puede esperarme, por favor? | pwaydhay ayspay-rahrmay poi fahbhor |

TIPPING, see inside back-cover

# Hotel—Other accommodation

Early reservation (and confirmation) is essential in most major tourist centres in the high season. Most towns and arrival points have a tourist information office, and that's the place to go if you're stuck without a room.

**Hotel**
(oatehl)

There are five official categories of hotels: luxury, first class A, first class B, second class and third class. There may be price variations within any given category, depending on the location and the facilities offered. There are also, of course, plenty of unclassified hotels where you will find clean, simple accommodation and good food.

**Hostal**
(oastahl)

Modest hotels, often family concerns, graded one to three stars.

**Residencia**
(rayssee-daynthyah)

When referred to as *hostal-residencia* or *hotel-residencia,* this term indicates a hotel without a restaurant.

**Pensión**
(paynsyon)

This roughly corresponds to a boarding house. Usually divided into four categories, it offers *pensión completa* (full board) or *media pensión* (half board). Meals are likely to be from a set menu.

**Albergue**
(ahlbehrgay)

Modern country inns, catering especially to the motorist.

**Parador**
(pahrahdhor)

Palaces, country houses or castles that have been converted into hotels and are under government supervision.

**Refugio**
(rehfookhyoa)

Small inns in remote and mountainous regions. They're often closed in winter.

**Apartamento amueblado**
(ahpahrtah-mayntoa ah-mwayblahdhoa)

A furnished flat (apartment) mainly in resorts. Available from specialized travel agents or directly from the landlord (look for the sign *se alquila*— to let, for rent).

**Albergue de juventud**
(ahlbehrgay day khoobhehntoodh)

Youth hostel. Foreign tourists wishing to use them should be members of the international Youth Hostels Association.

CAMPING, see page 32

## Checking in—Reception  *Recepción*

| | | |
|---|---|---|
| My name is ... | **Mi nombre es ...** | mee **noam**bray ayss |
| I've a reservation. | **He hecho una reserva.** | eh aychoa oonah rayssayrbah |
| We've reserved two rooms. | **Hemos reservado dos habitaciones.** | ehmoass rayssayr**bah**dhoa doss ahbheetahth**yo**nayss |
| Here's the confirmation. | **Aquí está la confirmación.** | ahkee aystah lah konfeermahth**yon** |
| Do you have any vacancies? | **¿Tiene habitaciones libres?** | tyay**nay** ahbheetahth**yo**nayss leebhrayss |
| I'd like a single/ double room. | **Quisiera una habitación sencilla/ doble.** | keess**yay**rah oonah ahbheetahth**yon** sayn**thee**lyah/**doa**blay |
| I'd like a room ... | **Quisiera una habitación ...** | keess**yay**rah oonah ahbheetahth**yon** |
| with twin beds | **con dos camas** | kon doss **kah**mahss |
| with a double bed | **con una cama matrimonial** | kon oonah **kah**mah mah-treemoa**nyahl** |
| with a bath | **con baño** | kon **bah**ñoa |
| with a shower | **con ducha** | kon **doo**chah |
| with a balcony | **con balcón** | kon bahl**kon** |
| with a view | **con vista** | kon **bees**tah |
| in the front | **en la parte delantera** | ayn lah **pahr**tay daylahn**tay**rah |
| at the back | **en la parte trasera** | ayn lah **pahr**tay trah**ssay**rah |
| facing the sea | **con vista al mar** | kon **bees**tah ahl mahr |
| facing the courtyard | **con vista al patio** | kon **bees**tah ahl **pah**tyoa |
| It must be quiet. | **Tiene que ser tranquila.** | tyay**nay** kay sayr trahn**kee**lah |
| Is there ...? | **¿Hay ...?** | igh |
| air conditioning | **aire acondicionado** | **igh**ray ahkondeethyoa-**nah**dhoa |
| heating | **calefacción** | kahlayfahk**thyon** |
| a radio/a television in the room | **radio/televisión en la habitación** | **rah**dhyoa/taylaybhee**ssyon** ayn lah ahbheetahth**yon** |
| laundry/room service | **servicio de lavado/ de habitación** | sehr**bee**thyoa day lahbhah**dhoa**/day ahbheetahth**yon** |
| hot water | **agua caliente** | **ah**gwah kahl**yayn**tay |
| running water | **agua corriente** | **ah**gwah korr**yayn**tay |
| a private toilet | **water particular** | **wah**tayr pahrteekoo**lahr** |

CHECKING OUT, see page 31

## How much? *¿Cuánto cuesta?*

| What's the price ...? | **¿Cuánto cuesta ...?** | kwahntoa kwaystah |
| per night/per week | **por noche/por semana** | por noachay/por saymahnah |
| for bed and breakfast | **por dormir y desayunar** | por dormeer ee dayssahyoonahr |
| excluding meals | **excluyendo las comidas** | aykslooyayndoa lahss koameedhahss |
| for full board (A.P.) | **por pensión completa** | por paynsyon komplaytah |
| for half board (M.A.P.) | **por media pensión** | por maydhyah paynsyon |
| Does that include service/breakfast? | **¿Está incluido el servicio/el desayuno?** | aystah eenklooeedhoa ayl sehrbeethyoa/ayl dayssahyoonoa |
| Is tax included? | **¿Están incluidos los impuestos?** | aystahn eenklooeedhoass loss eempwaystoass |
| Is there any reduction for children? | **¿Hay algún descuento para los niños?** | igh ahlgoon dayskwayntoa pahrah loss neeñoass |
| Do you charge for the baby? | **¿Cobran ustedes por el bebé?** | koabrahn oostaydhayss por ayl baybay |
| That's too expensive. | **Eso es demasiado caro.** | ayssoa ayss daymahssyahdhoa kahroa |
| Haven't you anything cheaper? | **¿No tiene usted nada más barato?** | noa tyaynay oostaydh nahdhah mahss bahrahtoa |

## Decision *Decisión*

| May I see the room? | **¿Puedo ver la habitación?** | pwaydhoa behr lah ahbheetahthyon |
| No, I don't like it. | **No, no me gusta.** | noa noa may goostah |
| It's too ... | **Es demasiado ...** | ayss daymahssyahdhoa |
| cold/hot | **fría/caliente** | freeah/kahlyayntay |
| dark/small | **oscura/pequeña** | oskoorah/paykayñah |
| noisy | **ruidosa** | rweedhoassah |
| I asked for a room with a bath. | **Yo había pedido una habitación con baño.** | yoa ahbheeah paydheedhoa oonah ahbheetahthyon kon bahñoa |

NUMBERS, see page 147

| Do you have anything ...? | ¿Tiene usted algo ...? | tyaynay oostaydh ahlgoa |
| better/bigger | mejor/más grande | mehkhor/mahss grahnday |
| cheaper | más barato | mahss bahrahtoa |
| quieter | más tranquilo | mahss trahnkeeloa |
| higher up/lower down | más arriba/más abajo | mahss ahrreebhah/mahss ahbhahkhoa |
| Do you have a room with a better view? | ¿Tiene usted una habitación con una vista mejor? | tyaynay oostaydh oonah ahbheetahthyon kon oonah beestah mehkhor |
| That's fine, I'll take it. | Muy bien, la tomaré. | mwee byayn lah toamahray |

## Registration  *Inscripción*

Upon arrival at a hotel or boarding house you'll be asked to fill in a registration form *(una ficha)*.

| Apellido/Nombre | Name/First name |
| Domicilio/Calle/nº | Home address/Street/No. |
| Nacionalidad/Profesión | Nationality/Profession |
| Fecha de nacimiento | Date of birth |
| Lugar | Place |
| Fecha | Date |
| Firma | Signature |

| What does this mean? | ¿Qué quiere decir esto? | kay kyayray daytheer aystoa |

| ¿Me deja ver su pasaporte? | May I see your passport? |
| ¿Le importa llenar esta ficha? | Would you mind filling in this registration form? |
| Firme aquí, por favor. | Please sign here. |
| ¿Cuánto tiempo va a quedarse? | How long will you be staying? |

| We'll be staying ... | Nos quedaremos ... | noss kaydhahraymoass |
| overnight only | sólo una noche | soaloa oonah noachay |
| a few days | algunos días | ahlgoonoass deeahss |
| a week (at least) | una semana (por lo menos) | oonah saymahnah (por loa maynoass) |
| I don't know yet. | No lo sé todavía. | noa loa say toadhahbheeah |

## Hotel staff  *Personal del hotel*

| hall porter | el conserje | ayl koansayrkhay |
| maid | la camarera | lah kahmahrayrah |
| manager | el director | ayl deerehktoar |
| page (bellboy) | el botones | ayl boatoanayss |
| porter | el mozo | ayl moathoa |
| receptionist | el recepcionista | ayl raythaypthyoneestah |
| switchboard operator | la telefonista | lah taylayfoaneestah |
| waiter | el camarero | ayl kahmahrayroa |
| waitress | la camarera | lah kahmahrayrah |

## General requirements  *Peticiones generales*

| What's my room number? | ¿Cuál es el número de mi habitación? | kwahl ayss ayl noomayroa day mee ahbheetahthyon |
| The key, please. | La llave, por favor. | lah lyahbhay por fahbhor |
| Where can I park my car? | ¿En dónde puedo aparcar mi coche? | ayn doanday pwaydhoa ahpahrkahr mee koachay |
| Does the hotel have a garage? | ¿Tiene garaje el hotel? | tyaynay gahrahkhay ayl oatehl |
| Will you have our luggage sent up? | ¿Puede usted encargarse de que suban nuestro equipaje? | pwaydhay oostaydh aynkahrgahrsay day kay soobhahn nwaystroa aykeepahkhay |
| Is there a bath on this floor? | ¿Hay baño en este piso? | igh bahñoa ayn aystay peessoa |
| Where's the socket (outlet) for the shaver? | ¿Dónde está el enchufe para la máquina de afeitar? | doanday aystah ayl aynchoofay pahrah lah mahkeenah day ahfaytahr |

| Can we have breakfast in our room? | ¿Podemos desayunar en nuestra habitación? | poadhaymoass dayssahyoonahr ayn nwaystrah ahbheetahthyon |
| I'd like to leave this in your safe. | Me gustaría dejar esto en su caja fuerte. | may goostahreeah daykhahr aystoa ayn soo kahkhah fwehrtay |
| Can you find me a ...? | ¿Podría buscarme ...? | poadreeah booskahrmay |
| baby-sitter | una niñera | oonah neeñayrah |
| secretary | una secretaria | oonah saykraytahryah |
| typewriter | una máquina de escribir | oonah mahkeenah day ayskreebheer |
| Will you please wake me up at ... | Por favor, ¿puede despertarme a las ...? | por fahbhor pwaydhay dayspayrtahrmay ah lahss |
| May I have a/an/some ...? | ¿Me puede dar ...? | may pwaydhay dahr |
| ashtray | un cenicero | oon thayneethayroa |
| bath towel | una toalla de baño | oonah toaahlyah day bahñoa |
| (extra) blanket | una manta (más) | oonah mahntah (mahss) |
| envelopes | unos sobres | oonoass soabrayss |
| hot-water bottle | una botella de agua caliente | oonah bhoataylyah day ahgwah kahlyayntay |
| (more) hangers | (más) perchas | (mahss) pehrchahss |
| ice cubes | cubitos de hielo | koobheetoass day yayloa |
| needle and thread | una aguja e hilo | oonah ahgookha ay eeloa |
| (extra) pillow | una almohada (más) | oonah ahlmoaahdhah (mahss) |
| reading-lamp | una lámpara para leer | oonah lahmpahrah pahrah layehr |
| soap | jabón | khahbhon |
| writing-paper | papel de escribir | pahpehl day ayskreebheer |
| Where's the ...? | ¿Dónde está ...? | doanday aystah |
| beauty salon | el salón de belleza | ayl sahlon day baylyaythah |
| dining-room | el comedor | ayl koamaydhor |
| emergency exit | la salida de emergencia | lah sahleedhah day aymayrkhaynthyah |
| hairdresser's | la peluquería | lah paylookayreeah |
| lift (elevator) | el ascensor | ayl ahsthaynsoar |
| restaurant | el restaurante | ayl raystowrahntay |
| television room | la sala de televisión | lah sahlah day taylaybheessyon |
| toilet | el servicio | ayl sayrbeethyoa |

BREAKFAST, see page 38

### Telephone—Post (mail) *Teléfono – Correo*

| Can you get me Madrid 123-45-67? | ¿Puede comunicarme con el número 123-45-67 de Madrid? | pwaydhay komoonee-kahrmay kon ayl noomayroa 123-45-67 day mahdreedh |
| Do you have any stamps? | ¿Tiene usted sellos? | tyaynay oostaydh saylyoass |
| Would you please mail this for me? | Por favor, ¿mandaría usted esto por correo? | por fahbhor mahndahreeah oostaydh aystoa por korrehoa |
| Are there any messages for me? | ¿Hay algún recado para mí? | igh ahlgoon raykahdhoa pahrah mee |
| How much are my telephone charges? | ¿Cuánto debo de llamadas telefónicas? | kwahntoa dayboa day lyahmahdahss taylayfoa-neekahss |

### Difficulties *Dificultades*

| The ... doesn't work. | ... no funciona. | ... noa foonthyoanah |
| air conditioner | el acondicionador de aire | ayl ahkondeethyoanah-dhor day ighray |
| fan | el ventilador | ayl baynteelahdhor |
| heating | la calefacción | lah kahlayfahkthyon |
| light | la luz | lah looth |
| radio | la radio | lah rahdhyoa |
| toilet | los servicios | loss sehrbeethyoass |
| television | el televisor | ayl taylaybheessoar |
| The window is jammed. | La ventana está atrancada. | lah bayntahnah aystah ahtrahnkahdha |
| The curtain is stuck. | La cortina está atrancada. | lah koarteenah aystah ahtrahnkahdhah |
| There's no (hot) water. | No hay agua (caliente). | noa igh ahgwah (kahlyayntay) |
| The wash-basin is clogged. | El lavabo está atascado. | ayl lahbhahbhoa aystah ahtahskahdhoa |
| The tap (faucet) is dripping. | El grifo está goteando. | ayl greefoa aystah goatayahndhoa |
| My bed hasn't been made up yet. | Aún no me han hecho la cama. | ahoon noa may ahn aychoa lah kahmah |

POST OFFICE AND TELEPHONE, see page 132–135

| The bulb is burnt out. | La bombilla está fundida. | lah bombeelyah aystah foondeedhah |
| The ... is broken. | ... está roto (rota). | ... aystah rotoa (rotah) |
| blind | la persiana | lah pehrsyahnah |
| lamp | la lámpara | lah lahmpahrah |
| plug | una clavija de enchufe | oonah klahbheekhah day aynchoofay |
| shutter | el postigo | ayl posteegoa |
| switch | el interruptor | ayl eentehrrooptor |
| Can you get it repaired? | ¿Puede usted arreglarlo(la)? | pwaydhay oostaydh ahrrayglahrloa(lah) |

## Laundry—Dry cleaner's  *Lavandería—Tintorería*

| I want these clothes ... | Quiero que ... esta ropa. | kyairoa kay ... aystah roapah |
| cleaned | limpien | leempyayn |
| ironed/pressed | planchen | plahnchayn |
| washed | laven | lahbhayn |
| When will it be ready? | ¿Cuándo estará lista? | kwahndoa aystahrah leestah |
| I need it ... | La necesito para ... | lah naythaysseetoa pahrah |
| today | hoy | oy |
| tonight | esta noche | aystah noachay |
| tomorrow | mañana | mahñahnah |
| before Friday | antes del viernes | ahntayss dayl byehrnayss |
| Can you mend/sew this? | ¿Puede usted remendar/coser esto? | pwaydhay oostaydh rehmayndahr/koassayr aystoa |
| Can you sew on this button? | ¿Puede usted coser este botón? | pwaydhay oostaydh koassayr aystay boaton |
| Can you get this stain out? | ¿Puede usted quitar esta mancha? | pwaydhay oostaydh keetahr aystah mahnchah |
| This isn't mine. | Esto no es mío. | aystoa noa ayss meeoa |
| There's one piece missing. | Falta una prenda. | fahltah oonah prayndah |
| There's a hole in this. | Hay un hoyo aquí. | igh oon oayoa ahkee |
| Is my laundry ready? | ¿Está lista mi ropa? | aystah leestah mee roapah |

## Hairdresser's — Barber's   *Peluquería — Barbería*

| Is there a hairdresser/ beauty salon in the hotel? | ¿Hay una peluquería/ un salón de belleza en el hotel? | igh oonah paylookayreeah/ oon sahlon day baylyaythah ayn ayl oatehl |
| Can I make an appointment for this afternoon? | ¿Puedo pedir hora para esta tarde? | pwaydhoa paydheer oarah pahrah aystah tahrdhay |
| I want a haircut, please. | Quiero un corte de pelo, por favor. | kyayroa oon kortay day pehloa por fahbhor |
| I'd like a shave. | Quisiera que me afeitaran. | keessyayrah kay may ahfaytahrahn |

| I want (a) ... | Quiero ... | kyayroa |
|---|---|---|
| bleach | un aclarado | oon ahklahrahdhoa |
| blow dry | un modelado | oon moadaylahdhoa |
| colour rinse | unos reflejos | oonoass rehflaykhoass |
| dye | una tintura | oonah teentoorah |
| fringe (bangs) | un flequillo | oon flaykeelyoa |
| manicure | una manicura | oonah mahneekoorah |
| parting (part) | una raya | oonah rahyah |
| left/right/ in the middle | a la izquierda/ derecha/en medio | a lah eethkyayrdhah/ dayraychah/ayn maydhyoa |
| permanent wave | una permanente | oonah pehrmahnayntay |
| setting lotion | un fijador | oon feekhadhoar |
| shampoo and set | lavado y marcado | lahbhahdhoa ee mahrkahdhoa |

| I'd like a shampoo for ... hair. | Quisiera un champú para cabello ... | keessyayrah oon chahmpoo pahrah kahbhaylyoa |
|---|---|---|
| dry | seco | saykoa |
| greasy (oily) | graso | grahssoa |
| normal | normal | normahl |

| Do you have a colour chart? | ¿Tiene usted un muestrario? | tyaynay oostaydh oon mwaystrahryoa |
| Don't cut it too short. | No me lo corte mucho. | noa may loa koartay moochoa |
| That's enough off. | Eso es bastante. | ayssoa ayss bahstahntay |
| A little more off the ... | Un pocco más ... | oon poakoa mahss |

| back | por detrás | por daytrahss |
| neck | en el cuello | ayn ayl kwaylyoa |
| sides | en los lados | ayn loss lahdhoass |
| top | arriba | ahrreebhah |

DAYS OF THE WEEK, see page 151

| | | |
|---|---|---|
| Please don't use any oil/hairspray. | Por favor, no me dé ningún aceite/laca. | por fah**bhor** noa may day neen**goon** ah**thay**tay/**lah**kah |
| Would you please trim my ...? | ¿Quiere usted recortarme ...? | **kyay**ray oos**taydh** rehkor**tahr**may |
| beard | la barba | lah **bahr**bah |
| moustache | al bigote | ayl bee**goa**tay |
| sideboards (sideburns) | las patillas | lahss pah**teel**yahss |

## Checking out  *Al marcharse*

| | | |
|---|---|---|
| May I have my bill, please? | Por favor, ¿puede darme mi cuenta? | por fah**bhor** **pway**dhay **dahr**may mee **kwayn**tah |
| I'm leaving early in the morning. Please have my bill ready. | Me marcho por la mañana, temprano. Por favor, tenga mi cuenta preparada. | may **mahr**choa por lah mah**ñah**nah taym**prah**noa. por fah**bhor** **tayn**gah mee **kwayn**tah praypah**rah**dhah |
| What time must I check out? | ¿A qué hora debo desocupar la habitación? | ah kay **oa**rah **day**bhoa dayssoakoo**pahr** lah ahbheetah**thyon** |
| Would you call a taxi, please? | ¿Quiere llamar un taxi, por favor? | **kyay**ray lyah**mahr** oon **tahk**see por fah**bhor** |
| I must leave at once. | Debo marcharme ahora mismo. | **day**bhoa mahr**chahr**may a**hoa**rah **mees**moa |
| Is everything included? | ¿Está todo incluido? | ays**tah** **toa**dhoa eenkloo**eed**hoa |
| Do you accept credit cards? | ¿Acepta tarjetas de crédito? | ah**thayp**tah tahr**khay**tahss day **kray**dheetoa |
| You've made a mistake in this bill, I think. | Creo que se ha equivocado usted en esta cuenta. | **kreh**oa kay say ah aykee-bhoakahdhoa oos**taydh** ayn **ays**tah **kwayn**tah |
| Would you send someone to bring down our luggage? | ¿Quiere usted mandar a alguien para bajar nuestro equipaje? | **kyay**ray oos**taydh** mahn**dahr** ah **ahl**gyayn **pah**rah bah**khahr** **nways**troa aykee**pah**khay |
| Here's my forwarding address. | Remita mis cartas a esta dirección. | ray**mee**tah meess **kahr**tahss ah **ays**tah deerayk**thyon** |
| It's been a very enjoyable stay. | Ha sido una estancia muy agradable. | ah **seed**hoa **oo**nah ays**tahn**thyah mwee ahgrah**dhah**blay |

TAXI, see page 21

## Camping *Camping*

Camping facilities vary, but most sites have electricity and running water. Many have shops and children's playgrounds, and some even laundrettes and restaurants. For a complete list of camp sites consult any Spanish National Tourist Office.

| | | |
|---|---|---|
| Is there a camp site near here? | **¿Hay algún camping cerca de aquí?** | igh algoon kahmpeeng thehrkah day ahkee |
| Can we camp here? | **¿Podemos acampar aquí?** | poadhaymoass ahkahmpahr ahkee |
| Have you room for a caravan (trailer)/ tent? | **¿Tiene sitio para una tienda/caravana?** | tyaynay seetyo pahrah oonah tyayndah/kahrahbhahnah |
| What's the charge ...? | **¿Cuál es el precio ...?** | kwahl ayss ayl praythyoa |
| per day/person | **por día/persona** | por deeah/pehrsoanah |
| for a car/tent | **por coche/tienda** | por koachay/tyayndah |
| for a caravan (trailer) | **por caravana** | por kahrahbhahnah |
| May we light a fire? | **¿Podemos encender una hoguera?** | poadhaymoass aynthayndehr oonah oagehrah |
| Is there/Are there (a) ...? | **¿Hay ...?** | igh |
| drinking water | **agua potable** | ahgwah poatahblay |
| electricity | **electricidad** | aylayktreetheedhahd |
| playground | **un campo de juego** | oon kahmpoa day khwaygoa |
| restaurant | **un restaurante** | oon raystowrahntay |
| shopping facilities | **tiendas** | tyayndahss |
| swimming pool | **una piscina** | oonah peestheenah |
| Where are the showers/toilets? | **¿Dónde están las duchas/los servicios?** | doanday aystahn lahss doochahss/loass sayrbeethyoass |
| Where can I get butane gas? | **¿Dónde puedo conseguir gas butano?** | doanday pwaydhoa konsaygeer gahss bootahnoa |

| | |
|---|---|
| **PROHIBIDO ACAMPAR** | **PROHIBIDO ACAMPAR CON CARAVANA** |
| NO CAMPING | NO CARAVANS (TRAILERS) |

CAMPING EQUIPMENT, see page 106

# Eating out

There are many different places where you can eat and drink in Spain.

**Albergue de carretera**
(ahl**behr**gay day kahrreh**tay**rah)
Motel; strategically located on main roads; snacks and full meals offered, quick service

**Bar**
(bahr)
Bar; drinks and *tapas* (see page 63) served, sometimes hot beverages, too

**Café**
(kah**fay**)
As in all Mediterranean countries, *cafés* can be found on virtually every street corner. An indispensable part of everyday life, the *café* is where people get together for a chat over a coffee, soft drink or glass of wine.

**Cafetería**
(kahfaytay**ree**ah)
Coffee shop; not to be confused with the English word cafeteria; there's counter service or —for a few pesetas extra—you can choose a table. The set menu is often very good.

**Casa de comidas**
(**kahs**sah day koamee**dhahss**)
Simple inn serving cheap meals

**Fonda**
(**fon**dah)
Typical Spanish inn

**Hostería**
(ostay**ree**ah)
Restaurant; often specializing in regional cooking

**Merendero**
(mayraynd**ayr**oa)
Seaside fish restaurant; you can usually eat out-of-doors

**Parador**
(pahrah**dhor**)
A government-supervised establishment located in a historic castle, palace or former monastery. A *parador* is usually noted for excellent regional dishes served in a dining room with handsome Spanish decor.

**Pastelería/ Confitería**
(pahstaylay**ree**ah/ konfeetay**ree**ah)
Pastry shop; some serve coffee, tea and drinks

**Posada**
(poassahd**hah**)
A humble version of a *fonda;* the food is usually simple but good

| | |
|---|---|
| **Refugio**<br>(rehfookhyoa) | Mountain lodge serving simple meals |
| **Restaurante**<br>(raystowrahntay) | Restaurant; these are classified by the government but the official rating has more to do with the decor than with the quality of cooking |
| **Salón de té**<br>(sahlon day tay) | Tearoom; at bit exclusive |
| **Taberna**<br>(tahbhehrnah) | Similar to an English pub or American tavern in atmosphere; always a variety of *tapas* on hand as well as other snacks |
| **Tasca**<br>(tahskah) | Similar to a *bar*; drinks and *tapas* are served at the counter; standing only |

**Meal times**   *Horas de comida*

Breakfast (*el desayuno*—ayl dayssahyoonoa) is generally served from 7 to 10 a.m.

Lunch (*el almuerzo*—ayl ahlmwayrthoa) is generally served from around 2 or 3 p.m.

Dinner (*la cena*—lah thaynah) is served far later than at home, from about 8 p.m. in tourist areas, elsewhere from about 9.

The Spaniards like to linger over a meal, so service may seem on the leisurely side.

**Spanish Cuisine**   *Cocina española*

The history of Spain has had much to do with the wealth and variety of Spanish cuisine. The Celtic tribes which settled Galicia cooked with animal fats, in particular pork fat. The Romans introduced garlic, as well as olive oil, which is today the basic ingredient of Spanish cooking. The conquering Arabs brought lemons, oranges, saffron, dates and rice. And the discovery of America in 1492 further enriched Spanish cuisine with the potato, pimentos, pepper and cocoa.

In addition, Spain's 5,000 kilometres of coastline offer, at all seasons, a profusion of Atlantic and Mediterranean seafood.

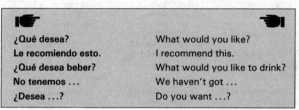

| | |
|---|---|
| **¿Qué desea?** | What would you like? |
| **Le recomiendo esto.** | I recommend this. |
| **¿Qué desea beber?** | What would you like to drink? |
| **No tenemos ...** | We haven't got ... |
| **¿Desea ...?** | Do you want ...? |

**Hungry?**   *¿Hambre?*

| | | |
|---|---|---|
| I'm hungry/I'm thirsty. | **Tengo hambre/ Tengo sed.** | tayngoa ahmbray/ tayngoa saydh |
| Can you recommend a good restaurant? | **¿Puede recomendarme un buen restaurante?** | pwaydhay raykoamayndahrmay oon bwayn raystowrahntay |
| Where can we get a typical Spanish meal? | **¿Dónde podemos encontrar comidas típicas de España?** | doanday poadhaymoass aynkontrahr koameedhahss teepeekahss day ayspahñah |
| Are there any inexpensive restaurants around here? | **¿Hay restaurantes no muy caros cerca de aquí?** | igh raystowrahntayss noa mwee kahroass thehrkah day ahkee |

If you want to be sure of getting a table in well-known restaurants, it may be better to telephone in advance. Some of them close one day a week (usually a Monday).

| | | |
|---|---|---|
| I'd like to reserve a table for 4. | **Quiero reservar una mesa para 4.** | kyayroa rehssayrbahr oonah mayssah pahrah 4 |
| We'll come at 8. | **Vendremos a las 8.** | bayndraymoass ah lahss 8 |

TIPPING, see inside back-cover

## Asking and ordering  *Preguntando y pidiendo*

| | | |
|---|---|---|
| Good evening, I'd like a table for 3. | **Buenas tardes, quisiera una mesa para 3.** | bwaynahss tahrdayss keessyayrah oonah mayssah pahrah 3 |
| Could we have a table ...? | **¿Nos puede dar una mesa ...?** | noss pwaydhay dahr oonah mayssah |
| in the corner | **en el rincón** | ayn ayl reenkon |
| by the window | **al lado de la ventana** | ahl lahdhoa day lah behntahnah |
| in a non-smoking area | **en la sección de no fumadores** | ayn lah sekthyon day noa foomahdhorayss |
| outside/on the patio | **fuera/en el patio** | fwayrah/ayn ayl pahtyoa |
| Waiter!/ Waitress! | **¡Camarero!/ ¡Camarera!** | kahmahrayroa/ kahmahrayrah |
| I'd like something to eat/drink. | **Quisiera algo de comer/beber.** | keessyayrah ahlgoa day koamayr/behbhayr |
| What do you recommend? | **¿Qué me aconseja?** | kay may ahkoansehkhah |
| May I please have the menu? | **¿Puedo ver la carta, por favor?** | pwaydhoa behr lah kahrtah por fahbhor |
| What's this? | **¿Qué es esto?** | kay ayss aystoa |
| Do you have ...? | **¿Tienen ...?** | tyaynayn |
| a set menu/local dishes | **platos combinados/ especialidades locales** | plahtoass koambeenah-dhoass/ayspaythyahlee-dhahdhayss loakahlayss |
| I'd like a supplement. | **Quisiera otra ración.** | keessyayrah oatrah rahthyon |
| Nothing more, thanks. | **Nada más, gracias.** | nahdhah mahss grahthyahss |
| Can we have a/an ..., please? | **¿Puede darnos ..., por favor?** | pwaydhay dahrnoass ... por fahbhor |
| ashtray | **un cenicero** | oon thayneethayroa |
| (extra) chair | **una silla (más)** | oonah seelyah (mahss) |
| cup | **una taza** | oonah tahthah |
| fork | **un tenedor** | oon taynaydhoar |
| glass | **un vaso** | oon bahssoa |
| knife | **un cuchillo** | oon koocheelyoa |
| napkin (serviette) | **una servilleta** | oonah sehrbeelyaytah |
| plate | **un plato** | oon plahtoa |
| spoon | **una cuchara** | oonah koochahrah |

COMPLAINTS, see page 61

| I'd like some ... | Quisiera ... | keessyayrah |
|---|---|---|
| bread | pan | pahn |
| butter | mantequilla | mahntaykeelyah |
| ketchup | salsa de tomate | sahlsah day toamahtay |
| lemon | limón | leemon |
| mustard | mostaza | moastahthah |
| oil | aceite | athaytay |
| olive oil | aceite de oliva | athaytay day oaleebhah |
| pepper | pimienta | peemyayntah |
| rolls | panecillos | pahnaytheelyoass |
| salt | sal | sahl |
| seasoning | condimentos | kondeemyayntoass |
| sugar | azúcar | ahthookahr |
| vinegar | vinagre | beenahgray |

## Some useful expressions if you have to follow a diet:

| I have to live on a diet. | Tengo que guardar dieta. | tayngoa kay gwahrdahr dyaytah |
|---|---|---|
| I mustn't eat food containing ... | No debo comer alimentos que contengan ... | noa daybhoa koamayr ahleemayntoass kay koantayngahn |
| flour/fat | harina/grasa | ahreenah/grahssah |
| salt/sugar | sal/azúcar | sahl/ahthookahr |
| Do you have ... for diabetics? | ¿Tiene ... para diabéticos? | tyaynay ... pahrah dyahbhayteekoass |
| cakes | pasteles | pahsstaylayss |
| fruit juice | jugo de frutas | khoogoa day frootahss |
| special menus | menús especiales | maynooss aysspaythyahlyss |
| Do you have vegetarian dishes? | ¿Tiene platos vegetarianos? | tyaynay plahtoass baykhaytahryahnoass |
| Could I have ... instead of the dessert? | ¿Podría tomar ... en lugar del postre? | poadhryah toamahr ... ayn loogahr dayl poasstray |
| cheese | queso | kayssoa |
| fruit | fruta | frootah |
| Can I have an artificial sweetener? | ¿Puede darme un edulcorante? | pwaydhay dahrmay oon aydhoolkoarahntay |

## Breakfast  *Desayuno*

Most Spaniards eat continental breakfast: coffee, bread or rolls and jam. However, many of the larger hotels also provide a full breakfast (*el desayuno completo*—ayl dayssahyoonoa komplaytoa) with fruit juice and eggs.

| | | |
|---|---|---|
| I'd like breakfast, please. | **Quisiera desayunar, por favor.** | keessyayrah dayssahyoo-nahr por fahbhor |
| I'll have a/an/ some ... | **Tomaré ...** | toamahray |
| bacon and eggs | **huevos con tocino** | waybhoass kon toatheenoa |
| cereal | **cereales** | thayrayahlayss |
| boiled egg | **huevo cocido** | waybhoa koatheedhoa |
| soft | **pasado por agua** | pahssahdhoa por ahgwah |
| medium | **blando (mollet)** | blahndoa (moalyayt) |
| hard | **duro** | dooroa |
| fried eggs | **huevos fritos** | waybhoass freetoass |
| fruit juice | **un jugo de fruta** | oon khoogoa day frootah |
| grapefruit | **pomelo** | pomayloa |
| orange | **naranja** | nahrahnkhah |
| ham and eggs | **huevos con jamón** | waybhoass kon khahmon |
| jam | **mermelada** | mehrmaylahdhah |
| marmalade | **mermelada amarga de naranjas** | mehrmaylahdhah ahmahr-gah day nahrahnkhahss |
| scrambled eggs | **huevos revueltos** | waybhoass raybhwaytoass |
| toast | **tostadas** | toastahdhahss |
| May I have some ...? | **¿Podría darme ...?** | poadreeah dahrmay |
| bread | **pan** | pahn |
| butter | **mantequilla** | mahntaykeelyah |
| (hot) chocolate | **chocolate (caliente)** | choakoalahtay (kahlyayntay) |
| coffee | **café** | kahfay |
| caffein-free | **descafeinado** | dayskahfayeenahdhoa |
| black | **solo** | soaloa |
| with milk | **con leche** | kon laychay |
| honey | **miel** | myehl |
| milk | **leche** | laychay |
| cold/hot | **fría/caliente** | freeah/kahlyayntay |
| pepper | **pimienta** | peemyayntah |
| salt | **sal** | sahl |
| tea | **té** | tay |
| with milk | **con leche** | kon laychay |
| with lemon | **con limón** | kon leemon |
| (hot) water | **agua (caliente)** | ahgwah (kahlyayntay) |

**What's on the menu?**   *¿Qué hay en el menú?*

Under the headings below you'll find alphabetical lists of dishes that might be offered on a Spanish menu with their English equivalent. You can simply show the book to the waiter. If you want some fruit, for instance, let *him* point to what's available on the appropriate list. Use pages 36 and 37 for ordering in general.

|  | Page |  |
|---|---|---|
| Starters (Appetizers) | 41 | **Entremeses** |
| Salads | 43 | **Ensaladas** |
| Soups | 43 | **Sopas** |
| Omelets and other egg dishes | 44 | **Tortillas y platos a base de huevo** |
| Paella | 45 | **Paella** |
| Fish and seafood | 45 | **Pescados y mariscos** |
| Meat | 47 | **Carnes** |
| Poultry and game | 48 | **Aves y caza** |
| Sauces | 49 | **Salsas** |
| Vegetables | 50 | **Verduras** |
| Herbs and spices | 51 | **Condimentos y especias** |
| Cheese | 52 | **Quesos** |
| Fruit | 53 | **Frutas** |
| Dessert | 54 | **Postres** |
| Drinks |  | **Bebidas** |
| Aperitifs | 55 | **Aperitivos** |
| Wine | 56 | **Vino** |
| Sangria | 58 | **Sangría** |
| Beer | 59 | **Cerveza** |
| Spirits and liqueurs | 59 | **Licores** |
| Nonalcoholic drinks | 60 | **Bebidas sin alcohol** |
| Snacks – Picnics | 63 | **Tentempiés – Meriendas** |

In addition to various à la carte dishes, restaurants usually offer one or more set menus *(platos combinados)* or a dish of the day *(plato del día)* which provide a good meal at a fair price.

Comidas y bebidas

## Reading the menu *Leyendo la carta*

| | |
|---|---|
| Especialidades de la casa | Specialities of the house |
| Especialidades locales | Local specialities |
| Plato del día | Dish of the day |
| Platos fríos | Cold dishes |
| Platos típicos | Specialities |
| Recomendamos | We recommend |
| Suplemento sobre ... | ... extra |

| | | |
|---|---|---|
| agua mineral | ahgwah meenayrahl | mineral water |
| aperitivos | ahpayreeteebhoass | apéritifs |
| arroces | ahrrothayss | rice |
| asados | ahssahdhoass | roasts |
| aves | ahbhayss | poultry |
| bebidas | baybheedhahss | drinks |
| carnes | kahrnayss | meat |
| caza | kahthah | game |
| cerveza | thehrbaythah | beer |
| entremeses | ayntraymayssayss | starters (appetizers) |
| ensaladas | aynsahlahdhahss | salads |
| frutas | frootahss | fruit |
| granizados | grahneethahdhoass | iced drinks |
| helados | aylahdhoass | ice-cream |
| huevos | waybhoass | egg dishes |
| jugo | khoogoa | fresh juice |
| legumbres | laygoombrayss | vegetables |
| mariscos | mahreeskoass | seafood |
| parrilladas | pahrreelyahdhass | grills |
| pastas | pahsstahss | pastas |
| pastelería | pahsstaylayreeah | pastries |
| patatas | pahtahtahss | potatoes |
| pescados | payskahdhoass | fish |
| postres | poastrayss | dessert |
| quesos | kayssoass | cheese |
| refrescos | rayfraysskoass | cold drinks |
| sopas | soapahss | soups |
| verduras | bayrdoorahss | vegetables |
| vinos | beenoass | wine |
| zumo | thoomoa | fresh juice |

## Starters (Appetizers) *Entremeses*

If you are planning to eat a three-course meal try not to tuck into too many of the great variety of *tapas* (see page 63) over your apéritif.

| | | |
|---|---|---|
| I'd like a starter (appetizer). | **Quisiera unos entremeses.** | keessyayrah oonoass ayntraymayssayss |
| What do you recommend? | **¿Qué me aconseja?** | kay may ahkonsaykhah |
| **aceitunas (rellenas)** | ahthaytoonahss (raylyaynahss) | (stuffed) olives |
| **aguacate** | ah wahkahtay | avocado |
| **alcachofas** | ahlkahchoafahss | artichoke |
| **almejas** | ahlmehkhahss | clams |
| a la marinera | ah lah mahreenayrah | in paprika sauce |
| **anchoas** | ahnchoahss | anchovies |
| **anguila ahumada** | ahngeelah ahoomahdhah | smoked eel |
| **arenque (ahumado)** | ahrehnkay (ahoomahdhoa) | (smoked) herring |
| **atún** | ahtoon | tunny (tuna) |
| **cabeza** | kahbehthah | brawn (headcheese) |
| de cordero | day koardayroa | lamb's |
| de ternera | day tehrnayrah | calf's |
| **calamares** | kahlahmahrayss | squid |
| a la romana | ah lah roamahnah | deep-fried |
| **callos** | kahlyoass | tripe (usually in hot paprika sauce) |
| **caracoles** | kahrahkoalayss | snails |
| **carne de cangrejo** | kahrnay day kahngrehkhoa | crabmeat |
| **champiñones** | chahmpeeñoanayss | button mushrooms |
| **chorizo** | choareethoa | spicy sausage made of pork, garlic and paprika |
| **cigalas** | theegahlahss | Dublin Bay prawns (sea crayfish) |
| **entremeses variados** | ayntraymayssayss bahryahdhoass | assorted appetizers |
| **espárragos (puntas de)** | aysparrahgoass (poontahss day) | asparagus (tips) |
| **fiambres** | fyahmbrayss | cold cuts |
| **gambas** | gahmbahss | prawns (shrimps) |
| al ajillo | ahl ahkheelyoa | with garlic |
| a la plancha | ah lah plahnchah | grilled |
| **higaditos de pollo** | eegahdheetoass day poalyoa | chicken livers |

| huevos duros | waybhoass dooroass | hard-boiled eggs |
|---|---|---|
| jamón | khahmon | ham |
| en dulce | ayn doolthay | boiled |
| serrano | sayrrahnoa | cured |
| langosta | lahngoastah | spiny lobster |
| langostinos | lahngoasteenoass | prawns (shrimps) |
| mejillones | mehkheelyoanayss | mussels |
| melón | maylon | melon |
| ostras | oastrahss | oysters |
| palitos de queso | pahleetoass day kayssoa | cheese sticks (straws) |
| pepinillos | paypeeneelyoass | gherkins |
| pepino | paypeenoa | cucumber |
| percebes | pehrthaybhayss | goose barnacles |
| pimientos | peemyayntoass | peppers |
| quisquillas | keeskeelyahss | common prawns (shrimps) |
| rábanos | rahbhanoass | radishes |
| salchichón | sahlcheechon | salami |
| salmón (ahumado) | sahlmon (ahoomahdhoa) | (smoked) salmon |
| sardinas | sahrdeenahss | sardines |
| zumo de fruta | thoomoa day frootah | fruit juice |
| piña/tomate | peeñah/toamahtah | pineapple/tomato |
| pomelo/naranja | poamayloa/nahrahnkhah | grapefruit/orange |

If you feel like something more ambitious and are prepared to leave the gastronomic beaten track, some of these may tempt you:

**albóndigas**
(ahlbondee ahss)
spiced meatballs

**banderillas**
(bahndayreelyahss)
similar to *palitos* but with gherkins

**buñuelitos**
(booñwayleetoass)
small fritters made with ham, fish, egg or a wide variety of other fillings

**empanadillas**
(aympahnahdheelyahss)
small savoury pasties stuffed with meat or fish

**palitos**
(pahleetoass)
ham, cheese, pâté, smoked anchovy, trout or eel on a skewer

**pinochos, pinchitos**
(peenoachoass, peencheetoass)
grilled skewered meat

**tartaletas**
(tahrtahlaytahss)
small open tarts filled with fish, meat, vegetables or cheese

## Salads  *Ensaladas*

| | | |
|---|---|---|
| What salads do you have? | ¿Qué clase de ensaladas tienen? | kay **klahss**ay day aynsah-**lahd**hahss **tyay**nayn |
| Can you recommend a local speciality? | ¿Puede aconsejarnos una especialidad local? | **pway**dhay ahkonsay**khahr**noass oonah ayspaythyah-leed**hahdh lo**akahl |

| ensalada | aynsah**lahd**hah | salad |
|---|---|---|
| de gambas | day **gahm**bahss | shrimp |
| de lechuga | day laych**oo**gah | green |
| de patata | day pah**tah**tah | potato |
| de pepino | day pay**pee**noa | cucumber |
| del tiempo | dayl **tyay**mpoa | (in) season |
| de tomate | day toa**mah**tay | tomato |
| valenciana | balayn**thyah**nah | with green peppers, lettuce and oranges |

## Soups  *Sopas*

In Spain, soup is undoubtedly the most popular first course. There is a great variety of soups ranging from the simple *sopa de ajo* to the filling *sopa de mariscos*. Here are a few that you're sure to find on the menu during your trip.

| consomé al jerez | konsoa**may** ahl khay**rayth** | chicken broth with sherry |
|---|---|---|
| sopa de ajo | **soa**pah day **ahk**hoa | garlic soup |
| sopa de arroz | **soa**pah day ar**roth** | rice soup |
| sopa de cangrejos | **soa**pah day kahn**greh**khoass | crayfish soup |
| sopa de cebolla | **soa**pah day thay**boa**lyah | onion soup |
| sopa de cocido | **soa**pah day koa**theed**hoa | a kind of broth |
| sopa de espárragos | **soa**pah day ays**pahr**rahgoass | asparagus soup |
| sopa de fideos | **soa**pah day feed**hay**oass | noodle soup |
| sopa Juliana | **soa**pah jooly**ah**nah | bouillon of finely shredded vegetables |
| sopa de mariscos | **soa**pah day mah**rees**koass | seafood soup |
| sopa de patatas | **soa**pah day pah**tah**tahss | potato soup |
| sopa de pescado | **soa**pah day pays**kahd**hoa | fish soup |
| sopa de tomate | **soa**pah day toa**mah**tay | tomato soup |
| sopa de tortuga | **soa**pah day tor**too**gah | turtle soup |
| sopa de verduras | **soa**pah day bayr**doo**rahss | vegetable soup |

| **caldo gallego**<br>(kahldoa gahlyehgoa) | meat and vegetable broth |
| **gazpacho**<br>(gahthpahchoa) | a cold soup of cucumber, tomato, green pepper, bread, onion and garlic |

## Omelets  *Tortillas*

The Spanish omelet is more likely to be round rather than the rolled form of the classic French *omelette*. Here are the names of a few of the more common egg dishes you'll find on the menu:

| **tortilla** | toarteelyah | omelet |
| **de alcachofa** | day ahlkahchoafah | artichoke omelet |
| **de cebolla** | day thayboalyah | onion omelet |
| **de espárragos** | day ayspahrrahgoass | asparagus omelet |
| **gallega** | gahlyehgah | potato omelet with ham, chili peppers and peas |
| **de jamón** | day khamon | ham omelet |
| **paisana** | paheessahnah | omelet with potatoes, peas, prawns or ham |
| **de patatas** | day pahtahtahss | potato omelet |
| **de queso** | day kayssoa | cheese omelet |
| **al ron** | ahl ron | rum omelet |
| **de setas** | day saytahss | mushroom omelet |

... and other egg dishes:

| **huevos a la flamenca**<br>(waybhoass ah lah flahmaynkah) | eggs baked with tomato, onion and diced ham; often garnished with asparagus tips, red peppers or slices of spicy pork sausage |
| **huevos al nido**<br>(waybhoass ahl needhoa) | "eggs in the nest"; egg yolks set in small, soft rolls; fried and then covered in egg white |
| **huevos al trote**<br>(waybhoass ahl troatay) | boiled eggs filled with tunny (tuna) fish and dressed with mayonnaise |
| **huevos revueltos al pisto**<br>(waybhoass raywayltoass ahl peestoa) | scrambled eggs with vegetables |

### Paella

An immensely popular dish along Spain's Mediterranean coast, *paella* actually refers to the large metal pan traditionally used for making rice dishes in the Valencia region. Basically, the *paella* dish is made of golden saffron rice garnished with meat, fish, seafood and/or vegetables. Here are four of the most popular ways of preparing *paella* (pah**ay**lyah):

| | |
|---|---|
| **catalana** <br> (kahtah**lah**nah) | spicy pork sausages, pork, squid, tomato, chili pepper, peas; the same dish is sometimes referred to as *arroz a la catalana* |
| **marinera** <br> (mahree**nay**rah) | fish and seafood only |
| **valenciana** <br> (bahlayn**thyah**nah) | chicken, shrimp, mussels, prawns, squid, peas, tomato, chili pepper, garlic—it's the classic *paella* |
| **zamorana** <br> (thamoa**rah**nah) | ham, pork loin, pig's trotters (feet), chili pepper |

Another rice dish is called *arroz a la cubana* (ahr**roth** ah lah koo**bhah**nah) made with white rice, fried eggs and bananas and a savoury tomato sauce.

### Fish and seafood  *Pescado y mariscos*

Don't miss the opportunity to sample some of the wide variety of fresh fish and seafood in coastal areas.

| | | |
|---|---|---|
| I'd like some fish. | **Quisiera pescado.** | kee**ssyay**rah pays**kahdh**oa |
| What kind of seafood do you have? | **¿Qué tipo de mariscos tiene usted?** | kay **tee**poa day mah**reeskoass tyay**nay oo**staydh** |
| **almejas** | ahl**meh**khahss | clams |
| **arenques** | ah**rehn**kayss | herring |
| **atún** | ah**toon** | tunny (tuna) |
| **bacalao** | bahkah**lah**oa | cod |
| **besugo** | bay**ssoo**goa | (sea) bream |
| **bonito** | boa**nee**toa | tunny (tuna) |
| **boquerones** | boakay**roa**nayss | whitebait |
| **caballa** | kah**bhah**lyah | mackerel |

46

| calamares | kahlahmahrayss | squid |
|---|---|---|
| cangrejo | kahngrehkhoa | crab/crayfish |
| chipirones | cheepeeroanayss | baby squid |
| cigalas | theegahlahss | Dublin Bay prawns (sea crayfish) |
| congrio | koangryoa | conger eel |
| escarcho | ayskahrchoa | roach |
| lampreas | lahmprehahss | lamprey |
| langosta | lahngoastah | spiny lobster |
| langostinos | lahngoasteenoass | prawns (shrimps) |
| lenguado | layngwahdhoa | sole |
| merluza | mayrloothah | hake |
| mero | mehroa | seabass |
| mújol | mookhoal | mullet |
| ostras | ostrahss | oysters |
| perca | pehrkah | perch |
| percebes | pehrthaybhayss | goose barnacles |
| pescadilla | payskahdheelyah | whiting |
| pez espada | payth ayspahdhah | swordfish |
| pulpitos | poolpeetoass | baby octopus |
| pulpo | poolpoa | octopus |
| quisquillas | keeskeelyahss | common prawns (shrimps) |
| rape | rahpay | monkfish |
| rodaballo | roadhahbhahlyoa | turbot |
| salmón | sahlmon | salmon |
| salmonetes | sahlmoanaytayss | red mullet |
| sardinas | sahrdeenahss | sardines |
| pequeñas | paykayñahss | sprats |
| trucha | troochah | trout |
| veneras | baynayrah | scallops |

You'll want to try the spicy fish and seafood stew called *zarzuela* (thahr**thway**lah)—the pride of Catalonia.

| baked | al horno | ahl oarnoa |
|---|---|---|
| cured | en salazón | ayn sahlahthon |
| deep fried | a la romana | ah lah roamahnah |
| fried | frito | freetoa |
| grilled | a la parrilla | ah lah pahrreelyah |
| marinated | en escabeche | ayn ayskahbhaychay |
| poached | hervido | ayrbeedhoa |
| sautéed | salteado | sahltehahdhoa |
| smoked | ahumado | ahoomahdhoa |
| steamed | cocido al vapor | koatheedhoa ahl bahpor |

## Meat *Carne*

Although fish and rice dishes predominate, meat also has a place in the cuisine of Spain—especially pork.

| I'd like some … | Quisiera … | keessyayrah |
|---|---|---|
| beef | **carne de buey** | **kahr**nay day bway |
| lamb | **carne de cordero** | **kahr**nay day koar**day**roa |
| pork | **carne de cerdo** | **kahr**nay day **the**hrdoa |
| veal | **carne de ternera** | **kahr**nay day tehr**nay**rah |
| **biftec** | beef**tayk** | beef steak |
| **cabrito** | kah**bree**toa | kid |
| **carne picada** | **kahr**nay peekah**dhah** | minced meat |
| **carnero** | kahr**nay**roa | mutton |
| **chuletas** | choo**lay**tahss | chops |
| **corazón** | koarah**thon** | heart |
| **criadillas** | kreeah**dhee**lyahss | sweetbreads |
| **filete** | fee**lay**tay | steak |
| **hígado** | **ee**gahdhoa | liver |
| **jamón** | khah**mon** | ham |
| **lechón** | lay**chon** | suck(l)ing pig |
| **morcilla** | moar**thee**lyah | black pudding (blood sausage) |
| **paletilla** | pahlay**tee**lyah | shank |
| **patas** | **pah**tahss | trotters (feet) |
| **pierna** | **pyehr**nah | leg |
| **rabo de buey** | **rah**bhoa day bway | oxtail |
| **riñones** | ree**ñoa**nayss | kidneys |
| **salchichas** | sahl**chee**chahss | sausages |
| **sesos** | **say**ssoass | brains |
| **solomillo de cerdo** | soaloa**mee**lyoa day **ther**doa | tenderloin of pork |
| **tocino** | toa**thee**noa | bacon |

**callos a la madrileña**
(**kah**lyoass ah lah mahdree**lay**ñah)
tripe in piquant sauce with spicy pork sausage and tomatoes

**cochifrito de cordero**
(koachee**free**toa day koar**day**roa)
highly seasoned stew of lamb or kid

**cochinillo asado**
(koachee**nee**lyoa ah**ssah**dhoa)
crispy roasted Castillian suck(l)ing pig

**empanada gallega**
(aympah**nah**dhah gah**lyay**gah)
tenderloin of pork, onions and chili peppers in a pie

**magras al estilo de Aragón**
(**mah**grahss ahl ay**stee**loa day ahrah**gon**)
cured ham in tomato sauce

**pimientos a la riojana**
(peemyayntoass ah lah ryoakhahnah)
sweet peppers stuffed with minced meat

**riñones al jerez**
(reeñoanayss ahl khehrayth)
kidneys braised in sherry

| | | |
|---|---|---|
| baked | **al horno** | ahl oarnoa |
| boiled | **hervido** | ayrbheedhoa |
| braised | **estofado** | aystoafahdhhoa |
| braised in casserole | **en salsa** | ayn sahlssah |
| fried | **frito** | freetoa |
| grilled (broiled) | **a la parrilla** | ah lah pahrreelyah |
| pot roasted | **en su jugo** | ayn soo khoogoa |
| roast | **asado** | ahssahdhoa |
| sautéed | **salteado** | sahltehahdhoa |
| stewed | **estofado** | aystoafahdhoa |
| underdone (rare) | **poco hecho** | poakoa aychoa |
| medium | **regular** | rehgoolahr |
| well-done | **muy hecho** | mwee aychoa |

### Poultry and game   Aves y carne de caza

Chicken is prepared in scores of ways in Spain. In the north, rabbit is a favourite dish—sometimes even prepared with chocolate!

| | | |
|---|---|---|
| I'd like some game. | **Quisiera carne de caza.** | keessyayrah kahrnay day kahthah |
| What poultry dishes do you have? | **¿Qué tipo de ave tiene usted?** | kay teepoa day ahbhay tyaynay oostaydh |
| **becada** | baykahdhah | woodcock |
| **capón** | kahpon | capon |
| **codorniz** | koadoarneeth | quail |
| **conejo** | koanaykhoa | rabbit |
| **conejo de monte** | koanaykhoa day moantay | wild rabbit |
| **corzo** | koarthoa | deer |
| **faisán** | fighssahn | pheasant |
| **gallina** | gahlyeenah | hen |
| **ganso** | gahnsoa | goose |
| **higaditos de pollo** | eegahdheetoass day poalyoa | chicken liver |

| | | |
|---|---|---|
| **jabalí** | khahbhahlee | wild boar |
| **lavanco** | lahbhahnkoa | wild duck |
| **liebre** | lyehbray | hare |
| **pato** | pahtoa | duck/duckling |
| **pavo** | pahbhoa | turkey |
| **perdiz** | pehrdeeth | partridge |
| **pichón** | peechon | pigeon |
| **pollo** | poalyoa | chicken |
| **muslo de pollo** | moosloa day poalyoa | chicken leg |
| **pechuga de pollo** | paychoogah day poalyoa | breast of chicken |
| **pollo asado** | poalyoa ahssahdhoa | roast chicken |
| **pollo a la brasa** | poalyoa ah lah brahssah | grilled chicken |
| **venado** | baynahdhoa | venison |

**conejo al ajillo**    rabbit with garlic
(koanaykhoa ahl
ahkheelyoa)

**menestra de pollo**    casserole of chicken and vegetables
(maynaystrah day
poalyoa)

**perdices estofadas**    partridges served in a white-wine sauce
(pehrdeethayss
aystoafahdhahss)


## Sauces  *Salsas*

Many meat, fish or vegetable dishes are dressed or braised in a light, delicate sauce. Here are the names of some well-known preparations:

**salsa allioli**    garlic sauce
(sahlsah ahlyoalee)

**a la catalana**    sauce of tomatoes and green peppers
(ah lah kahtahlahnah)

**en escabeche**    sweet and sour sauce
(ayn ayskahbhaychay)

**salsa romesco**    green peppers, pimentos, garlic; popular
(sahlsah roamayskoa)    chilled dressing for fish on the east cost
around Tarragona

**a la vasca**    parsley, peas, garlic; a delicate green dress-
(ah lah bahskah)    ing for fish in the Basque country

## Vegetables  *Verduras*

| What vegetables do you recommend? | ¿Qué verduras me aconseja? | kay bayrdoorahss may ahkoansaykhah |
| --- | --- | --- |
| I'd prefer a salad. | **Prefiero una ensalada.** | prayfyayroa oonah aynsahlahdah |

| | | |
| --- | --- | --- |
| achicoria | ahcheekoaryah | endive (Am. chicory) |
| alcachofas | ahlkahchoafahss | artichoke |
| apio | ahpyoa | celery |
| arroz | ahrroth | rice |
| berenjena | bayraynkhaynah | aubergine (eggplant) |
| berza | bayrthah | cabbage |
| calabacín | kahlahbhatheen | courgette (zucchini) |
| cebolla | thayboalyah | onion |
| champiñones | chahmpeeñoanayss | button mushrooms |
| chirivías | cheereebheeahss | parsnips |
| coles de bruselas | koalayss day broossay-lahss | Brussels sprouts |
| coliflor | koleeflor | cauliflower |
| espárragos | ayspahrrahgoass | asparagus |
| espinacas | ayspeenahkahss | spinach |
| garbanzos | gahrbahnthoass | chickpeas |
| guisantes | geessahntayss | peas |
| habas | ahbhahss | broad beans |
| hinojo | eenoakhoa | fennel |
| judías blancas | khoodheeahss **blahn**kahss | white beans |
| judías verdes | khoodheeahss behrdayss | green beans |
| lechuga | laychoogah | lettuce |
| lentejas | layntaykhahss | lentils |
| lombarda | loambahrdah | red cabbage |
| macedonia de legumbres | mahthaydhoaneeah day laygoombrayss | mixed vegetables |
| maíz | maheeth | sweet corn |
| patatas | pahtahtahss | potatoes |
| pepinillos | paypeeneelyoass | gherkins |
| pepino | paypeenoa | cucumber |
| pimientos morrones | peemyayntoass moarroanayss | sweet red peppers |
| puerros | pwayrroass | leeks |
| rábanos | rahbhahnoass | radishes |
| remolacha | raymoalahchah | beetroot |
| repollo | raypoalyoa | cabbage |
| setas | saytahss | mushrooms |
| tomates | toamahtayss | tomatoes |
| trufas | troofahss | truffles |
| zanahorias | thahnahoaryahss | carrots |

Here's a savoury vegetable dish you're sure to like. It goes well with roast chicken or other roasted and grilled meats:

**pisto**
(peestoa)

a stew of green peppers, onions, tomatoes and courgettes (zucchini); in Catalonia it's called *samfaina*, and you might also see it referred to as *frito de verduras*.

## Herbs and spices  *Condimentos y especias*

| | | |
|---|---|---|
| What is it flavoured with? | ¿Con qué está condimentado? | kon kay aystah kondeemayntahdhoa |
| Is it very spicy? | ¿Tiene muchas especias? | tyaynay moochahss ayspaythyahss |
| ajo | ahkhoa | garlic |
| albahaca | ahlbahahkah | basil |
| alcaparra | ahlkahpahrrah | caper |
| anís | ahneess | aniseed |
| azafrán | ahthahfrahn | saffron |
| berro | bayrroa | cress |
| canela | kahnaylah | cinnamon |
| cebolleta | thaybhoalyaytah | chive |
| clavo | klahbhoa | clove |
| comino | koameenoa | caraway |
| eneldo | aynayldoa | dill |
| estragón | ehstrahgon | tarragon |
| guindilla | geendeelyah | chili pepper |
| hierbas finas | yayrbahss feenahss | mixture of herbs |
| hoja de laurel | oakhah day lahoorayl | bay leaf |
| jengibre | khaynkheebray | ginger |
| menta | mayntah | mint |
| mostaza | moastahthah | mustard |
| nuez moscada | nwayth moaskahdah | nutmeg |
| orégano | oaraygahnoa | oregano |
| perejil | payraykheel | parsley |
| perifollo | payreefoalyoa | chervil |
| pimentón | peemaynton | chili pepper |
| pimienta | peemyayntah | pepper |
| romero | roamayroa | rosemary |
| sal | sahl | salt |
| salvia | sahlbyah | sage |
| tomillo | toameelyoa | thyme |
| vainilla | bighneelyah | vanilla |

## Cheese  *Queso*

Spanish restaurants seldom have a cheeseboard. Some well-known Spanish cheeses are listed below. Be sure to specify the cheese you'd like, otherwise you might be given imported cheese.

| What sort of cheese do you have? | ¿Qué clases de queso tiene? | kay klahssayss day kayssoa tyaynay |
|---|---|---|
| A piece of that one, please. | Un trozo de ése, por favor. | oon troathoa day ayssay por fabhor |

| | |
|---|---|
| **burgos** (boorgoass) | A soft, creamy cheese named after the province from which it originates |
| **cabrales** (kahbrahlayss) | A tangy, veined goat cheese; its flavour varies, depending upon the mountain region in which it was produced. |
| **mahón** (mahon) | A goat cheese from Menorca in the Balearic Islands |
| **manchego** (mahnchaygoa) | Produced from ewe's milk, this hard cheese from La Mancha can vary from milky white to golden yellow. The best *manchego* is said to come from Ciudad Real. |
| **perilla** (pehreelyah) | A firm, bland cheese made from cow's milk; sometimes known as *teta* |
| **roncal** (ronkahl) | A sharp ewe's milk cheese from northern Spain; hand-pressed, salted and smoked, with leathery rind |
| **san simón** (sahn seemon) | Similar to *perilla* |
| **villalón** (beelyahlon) | A curd cheese made from ewe's milk |

| | | |
|---|---|---|
| blue | **tipo roquefort** | teepoa rokehfoart |
| cream | **cremoso** | kraymoassoa |
| hard | **duro** | dooroa |
| mild | **suave** | swahbhay |
| ripe | **añejo** | ahñaykhoa |
| soft | **blando** | blahndoa |
| strong | **fuerte** | fwayrtay |

## Fruit  *Fruta*

| | | |
|---|---|---|
| Do you have fresh fruit? | ¿Tiene usted fruta fresca? | tyaynay oostaydh frootah frehskah |
| I'd like a (fresh) fruit cocktail. | Quisiera una ensalada de fruta (fresca). | keessyayrah oonah aynsahlahdhah day frootah (frehskah) |

| | | |
|---|---|---|
| albaricoques | ahlbahreekoakayss | apricots |
| almendras | ahlmayndrahss | almonds |
| arándanos | ahrahndahnoass | blueberries |
| avellanas | ahbhaylyahnahss | hazelnuts |
| brevas | braybhahss | blue figs |
| cacahuetes | kahkahwaytayss | peanuts |
| castañas | kahstahñahss | chestnuts |
| cerezas | thayraythahss | cherries |
| ciruelas | theerwaylahss | plums |
| ciruelas pasas | theerwaylahss pahssahss | prunes |
| coco | koakoa | coconut |
| dátiles | dahteelayss | dates |
| frambuesas | frahmbwayssahss | raspberries |
| fresas | frayssahss | strawberries |
| granadas | grahnahdhahss | pomegranates |
| grosellas negras | groassaylyahss naygrahss | blackcurrants |
| grosellas rojas | groassaylyahss roakhahss | redcurrants |
| higos | eegoass | figs |
| lima | leemah | lime |
| limón | leemon | lemon |
| mandarina | mahndahreenah | tangerine |
| manzana | mahnthahnah | apple |
| melocotón | mayloakoaton | peach |
| melón | maylon | melon |
| naranja | nahrahnkhah | orange |
| nueces | nwaythayss | walnuts |
| nueces variadas | nwaythayss bahryahdhahss | assorted nuts |
| pasas | pahssahss | raisins |
| pera | pehrah | pear |
| piña | peeñah | pineapple |
| plátano | plahtahnoa | banana |
| pomelo | poamayloa | grapefruit |
| ruibarbo | rweebhahrboa | rhubarb |
| sandía | sahndeeah | watermelon |
| uvas | oobhahss | grapes |
| blancas | blahnkahss | green |
| negras | naygrahss | blue |
| zarzamoras | thahrthahmoarahss | blackberries |

## Dessert   *Postre*

| | | |
|---|---|---|
| I'd like a dessert, please. | **Quisiera un postre, por favor.** | keessyayrah oon poastray por fahbhor |
| Something light, please. | **Algo ligero, por favor.** | ahlgoa leekhayroa por fahbhor |
| Just a small portion. | **Una ración pequeña.** | oonah rahthyon paykayñah |

## If you aren't sure what to order, ask the waiter:

| | | |
|---|---|---|
| What do you have for dessert? | **¿Qué tiene de postre?** | kay tyaynay day poastray |
| What do you recommend? | **¿Qué me aconseja?** | kay may ahkoansehkhah |
| arroz con leche | ahrroth kon laychay | rice pudding |
| bizcocho | beethkoachoa | sponge cake |
| crema catalana | kraymah kahtahlahnah | caramel pudding |
| flan | flahn | caramel pudding |
| fritos | freetoass | fritters |
| galletas | gahlyaytahss | biscuits (cookies) |
| helado | aylahdhoa | ice-cream |
| de chocolate | day choakoalahtay | chocolate |
| de fresa | day frayssah | strawberry |
| de limón | day leemon | lemon |
| de moka | day moakah | mocha |
| de vainilla | day bighneelyah | vanilla |
| mantecado | mahntehkahdhoa | enriched ice-cream |
| mazapán | mahthahpahn | marzipan |
| melocotón en almíbar | mayloakoaton ayn ahlmeebhahr | peaches in syrup |
| membrillo | maymbreelyoa | quince paste |
| merengue | mayraynggay | meringue |
| nata batida | nahtah bahteedhah | whipped cream |
| pastas | pahstahss | biscuits (cookies) |
| pastel | pahstayl | cake |
| pastel de queso | pahstayl day kayssoa | cheesecake |
| tarta de almendras | tahrtah day ahlmayndrahss | almond tart |
| tarta de manzana | tahrtah day mahnthahnah | apple tart |
| tarta de moka | tahrtah day moakah | mocha cake |
| tarta helada | tahrtah aylahdhah | ice-cream cake |
| tarteletas | tahrtaylaytahss | small tarts |
| tortitas | torteetahss | waffles |
| turrón | toorron | nougat |

**Aperitifs** *Aperitivos*

For most Spaniards, a before-dinner *vermut* (behr**moot**—vermouth) or *jerez* (kheh**rayss**—sherry) is just as important as our cocktail or highball. Vermouth is rarely drunk neat (straight) but usually on the rocks or with seltzer water. Some Spaniards, on the other hand, content themselves with a glass of the local wine. You'll probably be given a dish of olives or nuts to nibble on with your sherry or vermouth. Or in a bar specializing in *tapas* (see page 63), you can order various snacks.

Without question, the country's most renowned drink is its sherry. Like marsala, madeira and port wine, sherry has a bit of alcohol or brandy added to it—to "fortify" it—during the fermentation process.

Sherry was the first fortified wine to become popular in England. Back in Shakespeare's day it was called *sack* or *sherris sack*. *Sack* was derived from the Spanish *sacar* (to export) while the English wrote *Sherris* for the name of the town, *Jerez*, where sherry wine originated. Sherry can be divided into two groups:

| | |
|---|---|
| **fino**<br>(feenoa) | These are the pale, dry sherries which make good aperitifs. The Spaniards themselves are especially fond of *amontillado* and *manzanilla*. Some of the best *finos* are *Tío Pepe* and *La Ina*. |
| **oloroso**<br>(oloarossoa) | These are the heavier, darker sherries which are sweetened before being bottled. They're fine after-dinner drinks. One exception is *amoroso* which is medium dry. Brown and cream sherries are full-bodied and slightly less fragrant than *finos*. |

**¡SALUD!**
(sahlooth)
YOUR HEALTH/CHEERS!

## Wine   *Vino*

Though Spain is one of the world's principal producers of wine, the nation's *vino*—with the exception of sherry—is among the most unpredictable in terms of quality. Using outmoded techniques in both cultivating grapes and fermenting wine, the wine of a specific vineyard can vary considerably from one year to the next.

Some restaurants list their wine in a corner of the menu while others have them posted on a wall. As much of the country's wine doesn't travel well, don't expect an *hostería* to offer more than a few types of wine. Most of the wine must be drunk young so don't look too hard for vintage labels.

A government board permits some vintners to include *denominación de origen* on a bottle as an indication of the wine's quality. However, this designation is unreliable.

Uncontestably, Spain's best wine comes from Rioja, a region of Old Castile of which Logroño is the centre. Winemakers there add *garantía de origen* to wine they feel is of above average quality, and this term is a respected one. But other regions—notably Andalusia, Aragon, Catalonia, Navarre, New Castile, Toledo and Valdepeñas—produce quality wine, too. This is your opportunity to sample local wine, some of which is surprisingly good.

The Penedés region near Barcelona is a major source of the world's best selling white sparkling wine, unofficially called Spanish *champán*.

The general rule of thumb is that white wine goes well with fish and light meats while red wine is reserved for dark meats. A good rosé goes with almost anything. The chart on the following page will help you to choose your wine if you want to do some serious wine-tasting.

If you need help in choosing a wine, don't hesitate to ask the waiter. He'll often suggest a bottle of local renown, perhaps from the *patrón*'s own wine cellar.

| Type of wine | Examples | Accompanies |
|---|---|---|
| sweet white wine | A *moscatel* | desserts, custards, cakes, rice puddings, biscuits (cookies) |
| light, dry white wine | Much local white wine falls into this category; much of the white wine of Rioja, like *Monopole* | fish, seafood, *tapas*, cold meat, boiled meat, egg dishes like *tortillas* |
| rosé | *López de Heredia, Marqués de Murrieta* | goes with almost anything but especially cold dishes, eggs, pork, lamb, *paella* |
| light-bodied red wine | Many local wines come into this group; much of the Rioja red wine classifies, including *Viña Pomal* or the Catalonian *Priorato Reserva especial* | roast chicken, turkey, veal, lamb, beef fillet, ham, liver, quail, pheasant, stews, steaks, *zarzuela*, *paella*, *tortillas* |
| full-bodied red wine | sometimes a red wine of Tarragone, Alicante or Rioja can be classed in this category | duck, goose, kidneys, most game, tangy cheese like *cabrales* — in short, any strong-flavoured preparations |
| sparkling wine | *Champán* or *Cordoniu* | goes well with desserts and custards; if it's really dry you might try some as an aperitif or with shellfish, nuts, dried fruit |

| May I please have the wine list? | ¿Puedo ver la carta de vinos, por favor? | pwaydhoa behr lah kahrtah day beenoass por fahbhor |
| I'd like ... of ... | Quisiera ... de ... | keessyayrah ... day |
| a carafe | una garrafa | oonah gahrrahfah |
| a bottle | una botella | oonah boataylyah |
| half bottle | media botella | maydhyah boatalyah |
| a glass | un vaso | oon bahssoa |
| a small glass | un chato | oon chahtoa |
| a litre | un litro | oon leetroa |
| I want a bottle of white/red wine. | Quiero una botella de vino blanco/ vino tinto. | kyayroa oonah boataylyah day beenoa blahnkoa/ beenoa teentoa |

If you enjoyed the wine, you may want to say:

| Please bring me another ... | Tráigame otro/ otra ..., por favor. | trighgahmay oatroa/oatrah ... por fahbhor |
| Where does this wine come from? | ¿De dónde viene este vino? | day doanday byaynay aystay beenoa |

| red | tinto | teentoa |
| white | blanco | blahnkoa |
| rosé | rosé | rosay |
| dry | seco | saykoa |
| full-bodied | de cuerpo | day kwehrpoa |
| light | liviano | leebhyahnoa |
| sparkling | espumoso | ayspoomoassoa |
| sweet | dulce | doolthay |
| very dry | muy seco | mwee saykoa |

### Sangria

*Sangría* (sahngreeah) is an iced, hot-weather drink that combines red wine, brandy and mineral water, with fruit juice, sliced oranges and other fruit and sugar to taste. Beware: it can pack a punch, especially when laced with rough brandy, but you can always dilute *sangría* with soda water and plenty of ice.

**Beer** *Cerveza*

Spanish beer, generally served cool, is good and cheap. Try *Aguila especial* or *San Miguel especial*.

| A beer, please. | **Una cerveza, por favor.** | oonah thayrbhaythah por fahbhor |
| light beer | **cerveza rubia** | thayrbhaythah roobhyah |
| dark beer | **cerveza negra** | thayrbhaythah naygrah |
| foreign beer | **cerveza extranjera** | thayrbhaythah aykstrahn-khayrah |

**Spirits and liqueurs** *Licores*

If you'd like to sip a brandy after dinner, try a Spanish *coñac* like *Fundador* (foondah**dhor**) or *Carlos III* (**kahr**loass tehr**thay**roa). The Spaniards are also noted for their delicious liqueurs such as *Licor 43, Calisay,* or *Aromas de Montserrat.*

| glass | **un vaso** | oon **bahs**soa |
| bottle | **una botella** | oonah boataylyah |
| double (a double shot) | **doble** | **doa**blay |
| neat (straight) | **solo** | **soa**loa |
| on the rocks | **con hielo** | kon **yay**loa |

| I'd like a glass of ..., please. | **Quisiera un vaso de ..., por favor.** | kees**syay**rah oon **bahs**soa day ... por fahbhor |
| Are there any local specialities? | **¿Tiene alguna especialidad local?** | tyaynay ahlgoonah ayspay-thyahleedhadh loakahl |
| Please bring me a ... of ... | **Tráigame un/una ... de ..., por favor.** | trighgahmay oon/oonah ... day ... por fahbhor |
| aniseed liqueur | **anís** | ahneess |
| bourbon | **whisky americano** | weeskee ahmayreekahnoa |
| brandy | **coñac** | koañahk |
| gin | **ginebra** | kheenaybrah |
| gin-fizz | **ginebra con limón** | kheenaybrah kon leemon |

| gin and tonic | ginebra con tónica | kheenaybrah kon toaneekah |
| liqueur | licor | leekor |
| port | oporto | oaportoa |
| rum | ron | ron |
| rum coke | Cuba libre | koobhah leebray |
| Scotch | whisky escocés | weeskee ayskoathayss |
| sherry | jerez | khehrayss |
| vermouth | vermut | behrmoot |
| vodka | vodka | bodkah |
| whisky | whisky | weeskee |
| whisky and soda | whisky con soda | weeskee kon soadhah |

## Nonalcoholic drinks  *Bebidas sin alcohol*

| I'd like a/an ... | Quisiera ... | keessyayrah |
| (hot) chocolate | un chocolate (caliente) | oon choakoalahtay (kahlyayntay) |
| coffee | un café | oon kahfay |
| cup of coffee | una taza de café | oonah tahthah day kahfay |
| black coffee | café solo | kahfay soaloa |
| white coffee | café con leche | kahfay kon laychay |
| coffee with cream | café con crema | kahfay kon kraymah |
| espresso coffee | café exprés | kahfay ayksprayss |
| strong coffee | un corto | oon koartoa |
| caffein-free coffee | café descafeinado | kahfay dayskahfayeenahdhoa |
| fruit juice | un jugo de fruta | oon khoogoa day frootah |
| apple/grapefruit | manzana/pomelo | mahnthahnah/poamehloa |
| lemon/orange | limón/naranja | leemon/nahrahnkhah |
| pineapple/tomato | piña/tomate | peeñah/toamahtay |
| lemonade | una limonada | oonah leemoanahdhah |
| milk | leche | laychay |
| milkshake | un batido | oon bahteedhoa |
| mineral water | agua mineral | ahgwah meenayrahl |
| orangeade | una naranjada | oonah nahrahnkhahdhah |
| soda water | una soda | oonah soadhah |
| tea | un té | oon tay |
| with milk/lemon | con leche/con limón | kon laychay/kon leemon |
| iced tea | un té helado | oon tay aylahdhoa |
| tonic water | una tónica | oonah toaneekah |
| (iced) water | agua (helada) | ahgwah (aylahdhah) |

**Complaints** *Reclamaciones*

| That's not what I ordered. | **Esto no es lo que he pedido.** | aystoa noa ayss loa kay ay pehdheedhoa |
| I asked for ... | **He pedido ...** | ay pehdheedhoa |
| I asked for a small portion (for the child). | **He pedido una porción pequeña (para el niño).** | ay pehdheedhoa oonah porthyon paykayñah (pahrah ayl neeñoa) |
| There must be some mistake. | **Debe haber algún error.** | daybhay ahbhayr ahlgoon ayrroar |
| May I change this? | **¿Puede cambiarme eso?** | pwaydhay kahmbyahrmay ayssoa |
| The meat is ... | **Esta carne está ...** | aystah kahrnay aystah |
| overdone | **demasiado hecha** | daymahssyahdhoa ehchah |
| underdone | **poco hecha** | poakoa ehchah |
| too rare | **demasiado cruda** | daymahssyahdhoa kroodhah |
| too tough | **demasiado dura** | daymahssyahdhoa doorah |
| This is too ... | **Esto está ...** | aystoa aystah |
| bitter/salty/sweet | **amargo/salado/dulce** | ahmahrgoa/sahlahdhoa/doolthay |
| The food is cold. | **La comida está fría.** | lah koameedhah aystah freeah |
| This isn't fresh. | **Esto no está fresco.** | aystoa noa aystah frayskoa |
| What's taking you so long? | **¿Por qué se demora tanto?** | por kay say daymoarah tahntoa |
| Where are our drinks? | **¿Dónde están nuestras bebidas?** | doanday aystahn nwaystrahss baybheedhahss |
| There's a plate/glass missing. | **Falta un plato/vaso.** | fahltah oon plahtoa/bahssoa |
| The wine is too cold. | **El vino está demasiado frío.** | ayl beenoa aystah daymahssyahdhoa freeoa |
| The wine is corked. | **El vino sabe al corcho.** | ayl beenoa sahbhay ahl korchoa |
| This isn't clean. | **Esto no está limpio.** | aystoa noa aystah leempyoa |
| Would you ask the head waiter to come over? | **¿Quiere usted decirle al jefe que venga?** | kyayray oostaydh daytheerlay ahl khehfay kay bayngah |

## The bill (check) *La cuenta*

The service charge (*el servicio*—ayl sehr**bee**thyoa) is generally included. On some set menus you'll notice that wine is included in the price *(vino incluido).*

| I'd like to pay. | **Quisiera pagar.** | kee**ss**yayrah pah**gah**r |
| We'd like to pay separately. | **Quisiéramos pagar separadamente.** | kee**ss**yayrahmoass pah**gah**r saypahrahdhahmayntay |
| I think you made a mistake in this bill. | **Creo que se ha equivocado usted en esta cuenta.** | kre**ho**a kay say ah aykeebhoakahdhoa oostaydh ayn **ay**stah kwayntah |
| What's this amount for? | **¿Para qué es esta cantidad?** | pahrah kay ayss **ay**stah kahnteedhahdh |
| Is service included? | **¿Está el servicio incluido?** | aystah ayl sehr**bee**thyoa eenklooeedhoa |
| Is the cover charge included? | **¿Está el cubierto incluido?** | aystah ayl koobyehrtoa eenklooeedhoa |
| Is everything included? | **¿Está todo incluido?** | aystah toadhoa eenklooeedhoa |
| Do you accept traveller's cheques? | **¿Acepta usted cheques de viajero?** | ahthayptah oostaydh chaykayss day byah**khay**roa |
| Do you accept this credit card? | **¿Acepta esta tarjeta de crédito?** | ahthayptah **ay**stah tahr**khay**tah day **kray**dheetoa |
| Thank you, this is for you. | **Gracias, esto es para usted.** | **grah**thyahss **ay**stoa ayss pahrah oostaydh |
| That was a very good meal. | **Ha sido una comida excelente.** | ah seedhoa oonah koa**mee**dhah aykthay**layn**tay |
| We enjoyed it, thank you. | **Nos ha gustado, gracias.** | noss ah goostahdhoa **grah**thyahss |

---

**SERVICIO INCLUIDO**
SERVICE INCLUDED

---

TIPPING, see inside back-cover

**Snacks – Picnic**   *Tentempiés – Meriendas*

*Tapas* (**tah**pahss) are snacks, served with drinks in cafés and *tapa* bars. The variety is enormous. A *tapa* can be anything that tastes good and fits on a cocktail stick: smoked mountain ham, spicy sausages, cheese, olives, sardines, mushrooms, mussels, squid, octopus, meat balls, fried fish, plus sauces and exotic-looking specialities of the house. *Una tapa* is a mouthful, *una ración* is half a plateful, and *una porción* a generous amount.

| | | |
|---|---|---|
| I'll have one of those, please. | **Déme uno de ésos, por favor.** | daymay oonoa day ayssoass por fahbhor |
| Give me two of these and one of those. | **Déme dos de éstos y uno de ésos, por favor.** | daymay doss day aystoass ee oonoa day ayssoass por fahbhor |
| to the left | **a la izquierda** | ah lah eethkyayrdah |
| to the right | **a la derecha** | ah lah dayraychah |
| above | **encima** | ayntheemah |
| below | **debajo** | daybhahkhoa |
| Please give me a/an/some ... | **Déme ... por favor.** | daymay ... por fahbhor |
| It's to take away. | **Es para llevar.** | ayss pahrah lyaybhahr |
| How much is that? | **¿Cuánto es?** | kwahntoa ayss |

Here's a basic list of food and drinks that might come in useful for a light meal or when shopping for a picnic.

| | | |
|---|---|---|
| apples | **manzanas** | mahnthahnahss |
| bananas | **unos plátanos** | oonoass plahtahnoass |
| biscuits (Br.) | **unas galletas** | oonahss gahlyaytahss |
| bread | **pan** | pahn |
| butter | **mantequilla** | mahntaykeelyah |
| cake | **unos bollos/ pasteles** | oonoass boalyoass/ pahstaylayss |
| candy | **unos caramelos** | oonoass kahrahmayloass |
| cheese | **queso** | kayssoa |
| chicken | **pollo** | poalyoa |
| half a roasted chicken | **medio pollo asado** | maydhyoa poalyoa ahssahdhoa |
| chips (Am.) | **patatas fritas/chips** | pahtahtahss freetahss |
| chips (Br.) | **patatas fritas** | pahtahtahss freetahss |
| chocolate | **chocolate** | choakoalahtay |

| | | |
|---|---|---|
| coffee | **café** | kahfay |
| cold cuts | **unos fiambres** | oonoass fyahmbrayss |
| cookies | **unas galletas** | oonahss gahlyaytahss |
| crackers | **unas galletas saladas** | oonahss gahlyaytahss sahlahdhahss |
| cream | **nata** | nahtah |
| crisps (Br.) | **patatas fritas/chips** | pahtahtahss freetahss |
| cucumber | **un pepino** | oon paypeenoa |
| eggs | **huevos** | waybhoass |
| french fries | **patatas fritas** | pahtahtahss freetahss |
| fried eggs | **huevos fritos** | waybhoass freetoass |
| fried fish | **pescado frito** | payskahdhoa freetoa |
| gherkins | **unos cohombrillos** | oonoass kombreelyoass |
| grapes | **unas uvas** | oonahss oobhahss |
| ham | **jamón** | khahmon |
| ham and eggs | **jamón y huevos** | khahmon ee waybhoass |
| ham sandwich | **un bocadillo de jamón** | oon boakahdheelyoa day khahmon |
| ketchup | **salsa de tomate** | sahlsah day toamahtay |
| hamburger | **una hamburguesa** | oonah ahmboorgayssah |
| ice-cream | **helado** | aylahdhoa |
| lemons | **unos limones** | oonoass leemoanayss |
| lettuce | **una lechuga** | oonah laychoogah |
| melon | **melón** | maylon |
| milk | **leche** | laychay |
| mustard | **mostaza** | moastahthah |
| oranges | **naranjas** | nahrahnkhahss |
| pastry | **pasteles** | pahstaylayss |
| pâté | **paté** | pahtay |
| pepper | **pimienta** | peemyayntah |
| pickles | **unos pepinillos** | oonoass paypeeneelyoass |
| potatoes | **unas patatas** | oonahss pahtahtahss |
| rolls | **unos panecillos** | oonoass pahnaytheelyoass |
| salad | **una ensalada** | oonah aynsahlahdhah |
| salami | **salchichón** | sahlcheechon |
| salt | **sal** | sahl |
| sandwich | **un bocadillo** | oon boakahdheelyoa |
| sausages | **unas salchichas** | oonahss sahlcheechahss |
| spaghetti | **espaguetis** | ayspahgayteess |
| sugar | **azúcar** | ahthookahr |
| sweetener | **un edulcorante** | oon aydoolkoarahntay |
| sweets | **unos caramelos** | oonoass kahrahmayloass |
| tea | **té** | tay |
| tomatoes | **unos tomates** | oonoass toamahtayss |
| toast | **unas tostadas** | oonahss toastahdhahss |
| yoghurt | **un yogur** | oon yoagoor |

# Travelling around

**Plane** *Avión*

| | | |
|---|---|---|
| Is there a flight to Madrid? | ¿Hay algún vuelo a Madrid? | igh ahl**goon** bwayloa ah mah**dreedh** |
| Is it a nonstop flight? | ¿Es un vuelo sin escalas? | ayss oon **bway**loa seen ays**kah**lahss |
| Do I have to change planes? | ¿Tengo que cambiar de avión? | **tayn**goa kay kahm**byahr** day ah**bhyon** |
| Can I make a connection to Alicante? | ¿Puedo hacer conexión con un vuelo a Alicante? | **pway**dhoa ah**thayr** koa**nayk**syon kon oon **bway**loa ah ahlee**kahn**tay |
| I'd like a ticket to London. | Quisiera un billete para Londres. | kee**ssyay**rah oon beel**yay**tay **pah**rah **loan**drayss |
| What's the fare to París? | ¿Cuál es la tarifa a París? | kwahl ayss lah tah**ree**fah ah pah**reess** |
| single (one-way) | ida | **ee**dhah |
| return (roundtrip) | ida y vuelta | **ee**dhah ee **bweh**ltah |
| What time does the plane take off? | ¿A qué hora despega el avión? | ah kay **oa**rah days**pay**gah ayl ah**bhyon** |
| What time do I have to check in? | ¿A qué hora debo presentarme? | ah kay **oa**rah **day**bhoa prayssayn**tahr**may |
| Is there a bus to the airport? | ¿Hay un autobús que va al aeropuerto? | igh oon owtoa**bhooss** kay bah ahl ahehroa**pwayr**toa |
| What's the flight number? | ¿Cuál es el número del vuelo? | kwahl ayss ayl **noo**mayroa day **bway**loa |
| At what time do we arrive? | ¿A qué hora llegaremos? | ah kay **oa**rah lyaygah**ray**moass |
| I'd like to ... my reservation. | Quisiera ... mi reserva. | kee**ssyay**rah ... mee ray**ssayr**bah |
| cancel | anular | ahnoo**lahr** |
| change | cambiar | kahm**byahr** |
| confirm | confirmar | konfeer**mahr** |

| | |
|---|---|
| **LLEGADA** <br> ARRIVAL | **SALIDA** <br> DEPARTURE |

### Train   *Tren*

A nationalized company, the Red Nacional de los Ferro-carriles Españoles (R.E.N.F.E.—**rayn**fay) handles all rail services. While local trains are very slow, stopping at almost all stations, long-distance services are fast and reasonably punctual. First-class coaches are comfortable; second-class, adequate. Tickets can be purchased at travel agencies as well as at railway stations. Seat reservations are recommended.

| | |
|---|---|
| **EuroCity**<br>(ayooroatheetee) | International express, first and second classes |
| **Talgo, Ter, Intercity, Electrotren, Tren Estrella**<br>(**tahl**goa, tehr, "intercity", aylayktroatrayn, trayn aystraylyah) | Luxury diesel, first and second classes; supplementary charge over regular fare |
| **Expreso, Rápido**<br>(aykssprayssoa, rah-peedhoa) | Direct trains; stop at all main towns |
| **Omnibus, Tranvía, Automotor**<br>(omneebhooss, trahn-weeah, owtoamoator) | Local trains (frequent stops) |
| **Auto Expreso**<br>(owtoa aykssprayssoa) | Car train |

| PRIMERA CLASE<br>FIRST CLASS | SEGUNDA CLASE<br>SECOND CLASS |
|---|---|

| | |
|---|---|
| **Coche comedor**<br>(koachay koamaydhor) | Dining-car |
| **Coche cama**<br>(koachay kahmah) | Sleeping-car; compartments with wash basins and 1, 2 or 3 berths. |
| **Litera**<br>(leetayrah) | Berths (with sheets, blankets and pillows) |
| **Furgón de equipajes**<br>(foorgon day aykee-pahkhayss) | Luggage van (baggage car); only registered luggage permitted |

## To the railway station    *A la estación*

| | | |
|---|---|---|
| Where's the railway station? | ¿Dónde está la estación de ferrocarril? | doanday aystah lah aystahthyon day fehrrokahrreel |
| Taxi, please! | ¡Taxi! por favor. | tahksee por fahbhor |
| Take me to the railway station. | Lléveme a la estación de ferrocarril. | lyaybhaymay ah lah aystahthyon day fehrrokahrreel |
| What's the fare? | ¿Cuál es la tarifa? | kwahl ayss lah tahreefah |

---

| | |
|---|---|
| **INFORMACION TURISTICA** | TOURIST INFORMATION |
| **CAMBIO DE MONEDA** | CURRENCY EXCHANGE |

---

## Where's ...?    *¿Dónde está ...?*

| | | |
|---|---|---|
| Where is/are the ...? | ¿Dónde está/están ...? | doanday aystah/aystahn |
| booking office | la oficina de reservas | lah oafeetheenah day rayssayrbahss |
| buffet | el buffet | ayl boofay |
| currency-exchange office | la oficina de cambio de moneda | lah oafeetheenah day kahmbyoa day moanaydhah |
| information office | la oficina de información | lah oafeetheenah day eenformahthyon |
| left-luggage office (baggage check) | la oficina de equipaje | lah oafeetheenah day aykeepahkhay |
| lost property (lost and found) office | la oficina de objetos perdidos | lah oafeetheenah day obkhaytoass pehrdeedhoass |
| luggage lockers | la consigna automatica | lah konseegnah owtoamahteekah |
| newsstand | el quiosco de periódicos | ayl kyoskoa day payrryodheekoass |
| platform 7 | el andén 7 | ayl ahndayn 7 |
| restaurant | el restaurante | ayl raystowrahntay |
| ticket office | la taquilla | lah tahkeelyah |
| toilets | los servicios | loss sehrbeethyoass |
| waiting room | la sala de espera | lah sahlah day ayspayrah |

TAXI, see page 21

## Inquiries *Información*

| What time does the ... train for Granada leave? | ¿A qué hora sale el ... tren para Granada? | ah kay oarah sahlay ayl ... trayn pahrah grahnahdhah |
| first/last/next | primer/último/ próximo | preemayr/oolteemoa/ prokseemoa |
| Is it a direct train? | ¿Es un tren directo? | ayss oon trayn deerehktoa |
| Is there a connection to ...? | ¿Hay transbordo en ...? | igh trahnsbordoa ayn |
| Do I have to change trains? | ¿Tengo que cambiar de tren? | tayngoa kay kahmbyahr day trayn |
| Is there sufficient time to change? | ¿Hay tiempo sufi- ciente para trans- bordar? | igh tyaympoa soofeethyayntay pahrah trahnsbordahr |
| Will the train leave on time? | ¿Saldrá el tren a su hora? | sahldrah ayl trayn ah soo oarah |
| What time does the train arrive at Santander? | ¿A qué lora llega el tren a Santander? | ah kay oarah lyaygah ayl trayn ah sahntahndayr |
| Is there a sleeping- car/dining-car on the train? | ¿Hay coche cama/ coche restaurante en el tren? | igh koachay kahmah/ koachay raystowrahntay ayn ayl trayn |
| Does the train stop at Gerona? | ¿Para el tren en Gerona? | pahrah ayl trayn ayn khayroanah |
| What platform does the train for Barce- lona leave from? | ¿De qué andén sale el tren para Barcelona? | day kay ahndayn sahlay ayl trayn pahrah bahrthayloanah |
| What platform does the train from ... arrive at? | ¿A qué andén llega el tren de ...? | ah kay ahndayn lyaygah ayl trayn day |
| I'd like to buy a timetable. | Quisiera comprar una guía de ferrocarriles. | keessyayrah komprahr oonah geeah day fehrrokahrreelayss |

| ENTRADA | ENTRANCE |
| SALIDA | EXIT |
| A LOS ANDENES | TO THE PLATFORMS |

| | |
|---|---|
| Es un tren directo. | It's a through train. |
| Usted tiene que cambiar de tren en ... | You have to change at ... |
| Cambie de tren en ... y tome un tren de cercanías. | Change at ... and get a local train. |
| El andén ... está ... | Platform ... is ... |
| allí/arriba a la izquierda/a la derecha | over there/upstairs on the left/on the right |
| Hay un tren para Barcelona a las ... | There's a train to Barcelona at ... |
| Su tren sale del andén ... | Your train will leave from platform ... |
| Habrá una demora de ... minutos. | There'll be a delay of ... minutes. |
| Primera clase está al frente/ en medio/al final. | First class is in the front/ in the middle/at the end. |

## Tickets  *Billetes*

| | | |
|---|---|---|
| I want a ticket to Bilbao. | Quiero un billete para Bilbao. | kyayroa oon beelyaytay pahrah beelbahoa |
| single (one-way) | ida | eedhah |
| return (roundtrip) | ida y vuelta | eedhah ee bwehltah |
| first class | primera clase | preemayrah klahssay |
| second class | segunda clase | saygoondah klahssay |
| half price | media tarifa | maydyah tahreefah |
| with surcharge for Talgo/Ter | con suplemento para el Talgo/Ter | kon sooplaymayntoa pahrah ayl tahlgoa/tehr |

## Reservation  *Reserva*

| | | |
|---|---|---|
| I want to book a ... | Quiero reservar ... | kyayroa rayssayrbahr |
| seat by the window | un asiento al lado de la ventana | oon ahssyayntoa ahl lahdhoa day lah bayntahnah |
| smoking/ non-smoking | fumadores/ no fumadores | foomahdhorayss/ noa foomahdhorayss |

Excursiones

| berth | una litera | oonah leetayrah |
| upper | superior | soopayryor |
| middle | media | maydhyah |
| lower | inferior | eenfayryor |
| berth in the sleeping car | una litera en el coche cama | oonah leetayrah ayn ayl koachay kahmah |
| How much does it cost? | ¿Cuánto cuesta? | kwahntoa kwaystah |

## All aboard  ¡Al tren!

| Is this the right platform for the train to Paris? | ¿Es éste el andén del tren para París? | ayss aystay ayl ahndayn dayl trayn pahrah pahreess |
| Is this the train to Madrid? | ¿Es éste el tren para Madrid? | ayss aystay ayl trayn pahrah mahdreedh |
| Excuse me. May I get by? | Perdóneme. ¿Puedo pasar? | pehrdoanaymay. pwaydhoa pahssahr |
| Is this seat taken? | ¿Está occupado este asiento? | aystah oakoopahdhoa aystay ahssyayntoa |
| Do you mind if I smoke? | ¿Le importa si fumo? | lay eempoartah see foomoa |

| FUMADORES | NO FUMADORES |
| SMOKER | NONSMOKER |

| I think that's my seat. | Creo que ése es mi asiento. | krayoa kay ayssay ayss mee ahssyayntoa |
| Would you let me know before we get to Valencia? | ¿Me avisaría antes de llegar a Valencia? | may ahbheessahreeah ahntayss day lyaygahr ah bahlaynthyah |
| What station is this? | ¿Qué estación es ésta? | kay aystahthyon ayss aystah |
| How long does the train stop here? | ¿Cuánto tiempo para el tren aquí? | kwahntoa tyaympoa pahrah ayl trayn ahkee |
| When do we get to Barcelona? | ¿Cuándo llegamos a Barcelona? | kwahndoa lyaygahmoass ah bahrthayloanah |

## Sleeping *Durmiendo*

| | | |
|---|---|---|
| Are there any free compartments in the sleeping-car? | ¿Hay un departamento libre en el coche cama? | igh oon daypahrtah-maynto leebray ayn ayl koachay kahmah |
| Where's the sleeping-car? | ¿Dónde está el coche cama? | doanday aystah ayl koachay kahmah |
| Where's my berth? | ¿Dónde está mi litera? | doanday aystah mee leetayrah |
| Would you make up our berths? | ¿Nos podrá hacer usted la litera? | noss poadrah ahthayr oostaydh lah leetayrah |
| Would you call me at 7 o'clock? | ¿Me podrá llamar usted a las 7? | may poadrah lyahmahr oostaydh ah lahss 7 |
| Would you bring me some coffee in the morning? | ¿Me podrá traer usted café por la mañana? | may poadrah trahehr oostaydh kahfay por lah mahñahnah |

---

### FACTURACION
### REGISTERING (CHECKING) BAGGAGE

---

### Baggage and porters *Equipaje y mozos*

| | | |
|---|---|---|
| Where's the left-luggage office (baggage check)? | ¿Dónde está la oficina de equipaje? | doanday aystah lah oafee-theenah day aykeepahkhay |
| Where are the luggage lockers? | ¿Dónde está la consigna automática? | doanday aystah la kon-seegnah owtoamahteekah |
| I'd like to leave my luggage, please. | Quisiera dejar mi equipaje, por favor. | keessyayrah daykhahr mee aykeepahkhay por fahbhor |
| I'd like to register (check) my luggage, please. | Quisiera facturar mi equipaje, por favor. | keessyayrah fahktoorahr mee aykeepahkhay por fahbhor |
| Where are the luggage trolleys (carts)? | ¿Dónde están los carritos de equipaje? | doanday aystahn loss kahrreetoss day aykee-pahkhay |
| Porter! | ¡Mozo! | moathoa |
| Can you help me with my luggage? | ¿Puede usted ayudarme con mi equipaje? | pwaydhay oostaydh ahyoodhahrmay kon mee aykeepahkhay |

PORTERS, see also page 18

## Coach (long-distance bus) *Autocar*

Travel by coach is good if you want to visit out-of-the-way places. There's no cross-country bus line. Most buses only serve towns and villages within a region or province, or they link the provincial capital with Madrid if there's no rail service.

*Note:* Most of the phrases on the previous pages can be used or adapted for bus travel.

## Bus *Autobús*

In most buses, you pay as you enter. In some rural buses, you may find the driver also acting as the conductor. In major cities it may be worthwhile to get a pass or a booklet of tickets.

| | | |
|---|---|---|
| I'd like a pass/ booklets of tickets. | **Quisiera un pase/ taco de billetes.** | keessyayrah oon pahssay/ tahkoa day beelyaytayss |
| Where can I get a bus to the beach? | **¿Dónde puedo tomar un autobús para la playa?** | doanday pwaydhoa toamahr oon owtoabhooss pahrah lah plahyah |
| Which bus do I take for the university? | **¿Qué autobús debo tomar para la Universidad?** | kay owtoabhooss daybhoa toamahr pahrah lah ooneebhehrseedhahdh |
| Where's the ...? | **¿Dónde está ...?** | doanday aystah |
| bus stop | **la parada de autobuses** | lah pahrahdhah day owtoabhoossayss |
| terminus | **la terminal** | lah tehrmeenahl |
| When is the ... bus to the Prado? | **¿A qué hora sale el ... autobús para El Prado?** | ah kay oarah sahlay ayl ... owtoabhooss pahrah ayl prahdhoa |
| first/last/next | **primer/último/ próximo** | preemayr/oolteemoa/ prokseemoa |
| How often do the buses to the town centre run? | **¿Cada cuánto pasan los autobuses para el centro?** | kahdhah kwahntoa pahssahn loss owtoa- bhoossayss pahrah ayl thayntroa |
| How much is the fare to ...? | **¿Cuánto es la tarifa para ...?** | kwahntoa ayss lah tahreefah pahrah |

| | | |
|---|---|---|
| How many bus stops are there to ...? | ¿Cuántas paradas de autobús hay hasta ...? | kwahntahss pahrahdhahss day owtoabhooss igh ahstah |
| Do I have to change buses? | ¿Tengo que cambiar de autobús? | tayngoa kay kahmbyahr day owtoabhooss |
| How long does the journey (trip) take? | ¿Cuánto dura el viaje? | kwahntoa doorah ayl byahkhay |
| Will you tell me when to get off? | ¿Me diría usted cuándo tengo que apearme? | may deereeah oostaydh kwahndoa tayngoa kay ahpayahrmay |
| I want to get off at the cathedral. | Quiero apearme en la Catedral. | kyayroa ahpayahrmay ayn lah kahtaydrahl |
| Please let me off at the next stop. | Por favor, pare en la próxima parada. | por fahbhor pahray ayn lah prokseemah pahrahdhah |

---

**PARADA DE AUTOBUS** REGULAR BUS STOP
**SOLO PARA A PETICION** STOPS ON REQUEST

---

### Underground (subway) *Estación de metro*

Madrid and Barcelona have extensive underground (subway) networks. The fare is the same irrespective of the distance. The underground is open from 5 a.m. to 11 p.m.

| | | |
|---|---|---|
| Where's the nearest underground station? | ¿Dónde está la estación de metro más cercana? | doanday aystah lah aystahthyon day maytroa mahss thehrkahnah |
| Does this train go to ...? | ¿Va este tren a ...? | bah aystay trayn ah |
| Where do I change for ...? | ¿Dónde tengo que hacer transbordo para ...? | doanday tayngoa kay ahthayr trahnsbordao pahrah |
| Which line do I take? | ¿Qué línea tengo que coger? | kay leenayah tayngoa kay koakhayr |
| Is the next station ...? | ¿Es ... la próxima estación? | ayss ... lah prokseemah aystahthyon |

## Boat service    *Barcos*

| | | |
|---|---|---|
| When does the next/ last boat for ... leave? | ¿Cuándo sale el próximo/último barco para ...? | kwahndoa sahlay ayl prokseemoa/oolteemoa bahrkoa pahrah |
| Where's the embarkation point? | ¿Dónde está el lugar de embarco? | doanday aystah ayl loogahr day aymbahrkoa |
| How long does the crossing take? | ¿Cuánto dura la travesía? | kwahntoa doorah lah trahbhaysseeah |
| At which ports do we stop? | ¿En qué puertos nos detenemos? | ayn kay pwayrtoass noass daytaynaymoass |
| I'd like to take a cruise. | Quisiera tomar un crucero. | keessyayrah toamahr oon kroothayroa |
| boat | el barco | ayl bahrkoa |
| cabin | el camarote | ayl kahmahroatay |
|   single/double | sencillo/doble | sayntheelyoa/doablay |
| cruise | el crucero | ayl kroothayroa |
| deck | la cubierta | lah koobhyayrtah |
| ferry | el transbordador | ayl trahnsboardahdhoar |
| hovercraft | el aerodeslizador | ayl ahayroadhaysleethahdhoar |
| hydrofoil | el hidroplano | ayl eedroaplahnoa |
| life belt/boat | el cinturón/bote salvavidas | ayl theentooron/boatay sahlbahbheedhahss |
| port | el puerto | ayl pwayrtoa |
| ship | la embarcación | lah aymbahrkahthyon |

## Other means of transport    *Otros medios de transporte*

| | | |
|---|---|---|
| bicycle | la bicicleta | lah beetheeklaytah |
| cable car | el funicular | ayl fooneekoolahr |
| car | el coche | ayl koachay |
| helicopter | el helicóptero | ayl ayleekoptayroa |
| moped | el velomotor | ayl bayloamoatoar |
| motorbike | la motocicleta | lah moatoatheeklaytah |
| scooter | el escúter | ayl ayskootayr |

## Or perhaps you prefer:

| | | |
|---|---|---|
| to hitchhike | hacer auto-stop | ahthayr owtoa-stop |
| to ride | montar a caballo | moantahr ah kahbhahlyoa |
| to walk | caminar | kahmeenahr |

## Car *El coche*

Spain's expanding motorway (expressway) network is excellently engineered, but rather expensive tolls are charged. Main roads are adequate to very good. Unclassified country roads can be in a poor driving condition. Wearing of the seat belt *(el cinturón de seguridad)* is compulsory.

### Filling station *Gasolinera*

| | | |
|---|---|---|
| Give me ... litres of petrol (gasoline). | Déme ... litros de gasolina. | daymay ... leetroass day gahssoaleenah |
| Full tank, please. | Llénelo, por favor. | lyaynayloa por fahbhor |
| super (premium)/ normal/unleaded petrol/diesel | super/normal/ gasolina sin plomo/diesel | soopayr/normahl/ gahssoaleenah seen ploamoa/deesayl |
| Please check the ... | Controle ... | kontrolay |
| battery | la batería | lah bahtayreeah |
| brake fluid | el líquido de frenos | ayl leekeedhoa day fraynoass |
| oil/water | el aceite/el agua | ayl ahthaytay/ayl ahgwah |
| Would you check the tyre pressure, please? | ¿Puede controlar la presión de los neumáticos, por favor? | pwaydhay kontrolahr lah prayssyon day loass nayoomahteekoass por fahbhor |
| 1.6 front, 1.8 rear. | 1,6 delanteras, 1,8 traseras. | 1 koamah 6 daylahntayrahss 1 koamah 8 trahssayrahss |
| Please check the spare tyre, too. | Mire la rueda de repuesto también, por favor. | meeray lah rwaydhah day raypwaystoa tahmbyayn por fahbhor |
| Can you mend this puncture (fix this flat)? | ¿Puede arreglar este pinchazo? | pwaydhay ahrrayglahr aystay peenchahthoa |
| Would you please change the ...? | ¿Puede cambiar ..., por favor? | pwaydhay kahmbyahr ... por fahbhor |
| bulb | la bombilla | lah boambeelyah |
| fan belt | la correa del ventilador | lah korrayah dayl bayntee-lahdhor |
| spark(ing) plug | la bujía | lah bookheeah |
| tyre | el neumático | ayl nayoomahteekoa |
| wipers | los limpiaparabrisas | loass leempyahpahrahbreessahss |

CAR HIRE, see page 20/CONVERSION CHARTS, see page 158

| Would you clean the windscreen (windshield)? | ¿Quiere limpiar el parabrisas? | kyayray leempyahr ayl pahrahbreessahss |
| Do you have a road map of this district? | ¿Tiene un mapa de carreteras de esta comarca? | tyaynay oon mahpah day kahrraytayrahss day aystah koamahrkah |

## Asking the way—Street directions   *Preguntas – Direcciones*

| Can you tell me the way to ...? | ¿Me puede decir cómo se va a ...? | may pwaydhay daytheer koamoa say bah ah |
| How do I get to ...? | ¿Cómo se va a ...? | koamoa say bah ah |
| Where does this street lead to? | ¿Adónde lleva esta calle? | ahdhoanday lyaybhah aystah kahlyay |
| Is the road good? | ¿Está la carretera en buen estado? | aystah la kahrraytayrah ayn bwayn aystahdhoa |
| Is there a motorway (expressway)? | ¿Hay una autopista? | igh oonah owtoapeesstah |
| Is there a road with little traffic? | ¿Hay una carretera con poco tráfico? | igh oonah kahrraytayrah kon poakoa trahfeekoa |
| How long does it take by car/on foot? | ¿Cuánto se tarda en coche/a pie? | kwahntoa say tahrdah ayn koachay/ah pyay |
| Are we on the right road for ...? | ¿Es ésta la carretera hacia ...? | ayss aystah lah kahrraytayrah ahthyah |
| How far is the next village? | ¿Qué distancia hay hasta el próximo pueblo? | kay deestahnthyah igh ahstah ayl proakseemoa pwaybloa |
| How far is it to ... from here? | ¿Qué distancia hay desde aquí hasta ...? | kay deestahnthyah igh daysday ahkee ahstah |
| Can you tell me where ... is? | ¿Puede decirme dónde está ...? | pwaydhay daytheermay doanday aystah |
| How do I get to this address? | ¿Cómo puedo llegar a esta dirección? | koamoa pwaydhoa lyaygahr ah aystah deeraykthyon |
| Can I drive to the centre of town? | ¿Puedo conducir hasta el centro de la ciudad? | pwaydhoa kondootheer ahstah ayl thayntroa day lah thyoodhahdh |
| Can you show me on the map where I am? | ¿Puede enseñarme en el mapa dónde estoy? | pwaydhay aynsaynñahrmay ayn ayl mahpah doanday aystoy |

| | |
|---|---|
| **Se ha equivocado usted de carretera.** | You're on the wrong road. |
| **Siga todo derecho.** | Go straight ahead. |
| **norte/sur/este/oeste** | north/south/east/west |
| **Es hacia allí ...** | It's down there ... |
| **a la izquierda/derecha enfrente/atrás ... junto a/después de ...** | on the left/right opposite/behind ... next to/after ... |
| **Tome la carretera para ...** | Take the road for ... |
| **Tiene que regresar hasta ...** | You have to go back to ... |
| **Vaya al primer/segundo cruce.** | Go to the first/second crossroads (intersection). |
| **Doble a la izquierda en el semáforo.** | Turn left at the traffic lights. |
| **Doble a la derecha en la próxima esquina.** | Turn right at the next corner. |

## Parking   *Aparcamiento*

| | | |
|---|---|---|
| Where can I park? | **¿Dónde puedo aparcar?** | doanday pwaydhoa ahpahrkahr |
| Is there a car park nearby? | **¿Hay un estaciona-miento cerca de aquí?** | igh oon aystahthyonah-myayntoa thayrkah day ahkee |
| How long can I park here? | **¿Cuánto tiempo puedo aparcar aquí?** | kwahntoa tyaympoa pwaydhoa ahpahrkahr ahkee |
| What's the charge per hour? | **¿Cuánto cuesta por hora?** | kwahntoa kwaystah por oarah |
| Do you have some change for the parking meter? | **¿Tiene suelto para el parquímetro?** | tyaynay swayltoa pahrah ayl pahrkeemehtroa |
| Where can I get a parking disc? | **¿Dónde puedo con-seguir un disco de aparcamiento?** | doanday pwaydhoa konsaygeer oon deeskoa day ahpahrkahmyayntoa |

## Breakdown *Averías*

| | | |
|---|---|---|
| Where's the nearest garage? | ¿Dónde está el garaje más cercano? | doanday aystah ayl gahrahkhay mahss thehrkahnoa |
| What's the telephone number of the nearest garage? | ¿Cuál es el número de teléfono del garaje más cercano? | kwahl ayss ayl noomayroa day taylayfoanoa dayl gahrahkhay mahss thehrkahnoa |
| My car won't start. | Mi coche no quiere arrancar. | mee koachay noa kyayray ahrrahnkahr |
| The battery is dead. | La batería está descargada. | lah bahtayreeah aystah dayskahrgahdhah |
| I've run out of petrol (gasoline). | Se ha terminado la gasolina. | say ah tayrmeenahdhoa lah gahssoaleenah |
| I have a flat tyre. | Tengo un pinchazo. | tayngoa oon peenchahthoa |
| The engine is overheating. | El motor está demasiado caliente. | ayl moator aystah daymahssyahdhoa kahlyayntay |
| There is something wrong with the ... | Hay algo estropeado en ... | igh ahlgoa aystroapayahdhoa ayn |
| brakes | los frenos | loass fraynoass |
| carburetor | el carburador | ayl kahrboorahdhoar |
| exhaust pipe | el tubo de escape | ayl tooboa day ayskahpay |
| radiator | el radiador | ayl rahdhyahdhoar |
| wheel | la rueda | lah rwaydhah |
| I've had a breakdown at ... | Tengo un coche estropeado en ... | tayngoa oon koachay aystroapayahdhoa ayn |
| Can you send a mechanic? | ¿Puede usted mandar un mecánico? | pwaydhay oostaydh mahndahr oon maykahneekoa |
| Can you send a breakdown van (tow-truck)? | ¿Puede usted mandar un coche grúa? | pwaydhay oostaydh mahndahr oon koachay grooah |
| How long will you be? | ¿Cuánto tardarán? | kwahntoa tahrdahrahn |

## Accident—Police *Accidentes – Policía*

| | | |
|---|---|---|
| Please call the police. | Llamen a la policía, por favor. | lyahmayn ah lah poaleetheeah por fahbhor |
| There's been an accident. | Ha habido un accidente. | ah ahbheedhoa oon ahktheedhayntay |

| It's about 2 km. from ... | Está a unos 2 kilómetros de ... | aystah ah oonoass 2 keeloamaytroass day |
| There are people injured. | Hay gente herida. | igh khayntay ayreedhah |
| Call a doctor/an ambulance. | Llamen a un doctor/una ambulancia. | lyahmayn ah oon doaktor/oonah ahmboolahnthyah |
| Here's my driving licence. | Aquí está mi permiso de conducir. | ahkee aystah mee payrmeessoa day kondootheer |
| What's your name and address? | ¿Cuál es su nombre y dirección? | kwahl ayss soo nombray ee deeraykthyon |
| What's your insurance company? | ¿Cuál es su compañía de seguros? | kwahl ayss soo kompahñeeah day saygooroass |

## Road signs  *Señales de circulación*

| | |
|---|---|
| ADUANA | Customs |
| ¡ALTO! | Stop |
| ATENCION | Caution |
| AUTOPISTA (DE PEAJE) | Motorway/Turnpike (with toll) |
| CALZADA DETERIORADA | Bad road surface |
| CARRETERA CORTADA | No through road |
| CEDA EL PASO | Give way (yield) |
| CRUCE PELIGROSO | Dangerous crossroads |
| CUIDADO | Caution |
| CURVA PELIGROSA | Dangerous bend (curve) |
| DESPACIO | Drive slowly |
| DESVIACION | Diversion (detour) |
| DIRECCION UNICA | One-way street |
| ENCENDER LAS LUCES | Switch on headlights |
| ESCUELA | School |
| ESTACIONAMIENTO PROHIBIDO | No parking |
| ESTACIONAMIENTO REGLAMENTADO | Limited parking zone |
| FUERTE DECLIVE | Steep incline |
| OBRAS | Road works (men working) |
| PASO A NIVEL | Level (railroad) crossing |
| PASO PROHIBIDO | No entry |
| PEATONES | Pedestrians |
| PELIGRO | Danger |
| PROHIBIDO ADELANTAR | No overtaking (passing) |
| PUESTO DE SOCORRO | First-aid |
| SALIDA DE FABRICA | Factory exit |

# Sightseeing

| | | |
|---|---|---|
| Where's the tourist office/information centre? | ¿Dónde está la oficina de turismo/ la información? | doanday aystáh lah oafee-theenah day tooreesmoa/ lah eenformahthyon |
| What are the main points of interest? | ¿Cuáles son los principales puntos de interés? | kwahlayss son loss preentheepahlayss poon-toass day eentayrayss |
| We're here for only a few hours/a day. | Estamos aquí sólo unas pocas horas/ un día. | aystahmoass ahkee soaloa oonahss poakahss oarahss/ oon deeah |
| Can you recommend a ...? | ¿Puede usted recomendarme ...? | pwaydhay oostaydh raykoamayndahrmay |
| sightseeing tour | un recorrido turís-tico | oon rehkorreedhoa tooreesteekoa |
| popular excursion | una excursión popular | oonah aykskoorsyon poapoolahr |
| What's the point of departure? | ¿Cuál es el lugar de salida? | kwahl ayss ayl loogahr day sahleedhah |
| Will the coach pick us up at the hotel? | ¿Nos recogerá el autocar en el hotel? | noss rehkoakhayrah ayl owtoakahr ayn ayl oatehl |
| How much does the tour cost? | ¿Cuánto cuesta el recorrido? | kwahntoa kwaystah ayl rehkorreedhoa |
| What time does the tour start? | ¿A qué hora em-pieza el recorrido? | ah kay oarah aympyaythah ayl rehkorreedhoa |
| Is lunch included? | ¿Está incluido el almuerzo? | aystah eenklooeedhoa ayl ahlmwayrthoa |
| What time do we get back? | ¿A qué hora volvemos? | ah kay oarah bolbaymoass |
| Do we have free time in ...? | ¿Tenemos tiempo libre en ...? | taynaymoass tyaympoa leebray ayn |
| Is there an English-speaking guide? | ¿Hay algún guía que hable inglés? | igh ahlgoon geeah kay ahblay eenglayss |
| I'd like to hire a private guide for ... | Quisiera un guía particular para ... | keassyayrah oon geeah pahrteekoolahr pahrah |
| half a day | medio día | maydhyoa deeah |
| a full day | todo el día | toadoa ayl deeah |

TIME OF THE DAY, see page 153

Visitas turísticas

**Where is ...?**   ¿Dónde está ...?

| Where is/are the ...? | ¿Dónde está/están ...? | doanday aystah/aystahn |
|---|---|---|
| abbey | la abadía | lah ahbhadheeah |
| art gallery | la galería de arte | lah gahlayreeah day ahrtay |
| artist's quarter | el barrio de los artistas | ayl bahrreeoa day loss ahrteestahss |
| botanical gardens | el jardín botánico | ayl khahrdeen boatahneekoa |
| bullring | la plaza de toros | lah plahthah day toroass |
| castle | el castillo | ayl kahsteelyoa |
| cathedral | la catedral | lah kahtaydrahl |
| caves | las cuevas | lahss kwaybhahss |
| cemetery | el cementerio | ayl thaymayntayryoa |
| chapel | la capilla | lah kahpeelyah |
| church | la iglesia | lah eeglayssyah |
| city centre | el centro de la ciudad | ayl thayntroa day lah thyoodhahdh |
| concert hall | la sala de conciertos | lah sahlah day konthyehrtoass |
| convent | el convento | ayl konbayntoa |
| convention hall | el palacio de convenciones | ayl pahlahthyoa day konbaynthyonayss |
| court house | el palacio de justicia | ayl pahlahthyoa day khoosteethyah |
| downtown area | el centro de la ciudad | ayl thayntroa day lah thyoodhahdh |
| exhibition | la exhibición | lah ehkseebheethyon |
| factory | la fábrica | lah fahbreekah |
| fair | la feria | lah fayryah |
| flea market | el mercado de cosas viejas | ayl mehrkahdhoa day kossahss byaykhahss |
| fortress | la fortaleza/el alcázar | lah fortahlaythah/ayl ahlkahthahr |
| fountain | la fuente | lah fwayntay |
| gardens | los jardines públicos | loss khahrdeenayss poobleekoss |
| harbour | el puerto | ayl pwayrtoa |
| library | la biblioteca | lah beeblyoataykah |
| market | el mercado | ayl mehrkahdhoa |
| monastery | el monasterio | ayl moanahstayryoa |
| monument | el monumento | ayl moanoomayntoa |
| museum | el museo | ayl moossayoa |
| old town | la ciudad vieja | lah thyoodhahdh byaykhah |
| palace | el palacio | ayl pahlahthyoa |
| park | el parque | ayl pahrkay |

ASKING THE WAY, see page 76

| parliament building | el edificio de las Cortes | ayl aydheefeethyoa day lahss kortayss |
| royal palace | el palacio real | ayl pahlahthyoa rayahl |
| ruins | las ruinas | lahss rweenahss |
| shopping area | la zona de tiendas | lah thoanah day tyayndahss |
| square | la plaza | lah plahthah |
| stadium | el estadio | ayl aystahdhyoa |
| statue | la estatua | lah aystahtwah |
| stock exchange | la bolsa | lah bolsah |
| tomb | la tumba | lah toombah |
| tower | la torre | lah torray |
| town hall | el ayuntamiento | ayl ahyoontahmyayntoa |
| town walls | las murallas | lahss moorahlyahss |
| university | la universidad | lah ooneebhehrseedhahdh |
| zoo | el zoológico | ayl thoalokheekoa |

## Admission   *Entrada*

| Is ... open on Sundays? | ¿Está ... abierto los domingos? | aystah ... ahbhyayrtoa loss doameengoass |
| When does it open/ close? | ¿A qué hora abren/ cierran? | ah kay oarah ahbrayn/ thyayrrahn |
| How much is the entrance fee? | ¿Cuánto vale la entrada? | kwahntoa bahlay lah ayntrahdhah |
| Is there any reduction for (the) ...? | ¿Hay algún descuento para ...? | igh ahlgoon dayskwayntoa pahrah |
| disabled | incapacitados | eenkahpahtheetahdoass |
| groups | grupos | groopoass |
| pensioners | jubilados | khoobheelahdhoass |
| students | estudiantes | aystoodhyahntayss |
| Have you a guide-book (in English)? | ¿Tiene usted una guía (en inglés)? | tyaynay oostaydh oonah geeah (ayn eenglayss) |
| Can I buy a catalogue? | ¿Puedo comprar un catálogo? | pwaydhoa komprahr oon kahtahloagoa |
| Is it all right to take pictures? | ¿Se pueden tomar fotografías? | say pwaydhayn toamahr foatoagrahfeeahss |

---

| **ENTRADA LIBRE** | ADMISSION FREE |
| **PROHIBIDO TOMAR FOTOGRAFIAS** | NO CAMERAS ALLOWED |

**Who—What—When?**   *¿Quién – Qué – Cuándo?*

| | | |
|---|---|---|
| What's that building? | **¿Qué es ese edificio?** | kay ayss **ayssay** aydheefee**thyoa** |
| Who was the ...? | **¿Quién fue ...?** | kyayn fweh |
| architect | **el arquitecto** | ayl ahrkee**tehk**toa |
| artist | **el artista** | ayl ahr**tees**tah |
| painter | **el pintor** | ayl peen**tor** |
| sculptor | **el escultor** | ayl ayskool**tor** |
| Who painted that picture? | **¿Quién pintó ese cuadro?** | kyayn peen**toa** assay **kwah**droa |
| When did he live? | **¿En qué época vivió?** | ayn kay **ay**poakah bee**bhyoa** |
| When was it built? | **¿Cuándo se construyó?** | **kwahn**doa say konstroo**yoa** |
| Where's the house where ... lived? | **¿Dónde está la casa en que vivió ...?** | **doan**day ay**stah** lah **kah**ssah ayn kay bee**bhyoa** |
| We're interested in ... | **Nos interesa(n) ...** | noss eentay**rays**sah(n) |
| antiques | **las antigüedades** | lahss ahnteegwee-**dhah**dhayss |
| archaeology | **la arqueología** | lah ahrkayoalo**kheea**h |
| art | **el arte** | ayl **ahr**tay |
| botany | **la botánica** | lah boatah**nee**kah |
| ceramics | **la cerámica** | lah thay**rah**meekah |
| coins | **las monedas** | lahss moa**nay**dhahss |
| fine arts | **las bellas artes** | lahss **bayl**yahss **ahr**tayss |
| furniture | **los muebles** | loss **mway**blayss |
| geology | **la geología** | lah khayoalo**khee**ah |
| handicrafts | **la artesanía** | lah ahrtayssah**nee**ah |
| history | **la historia** | lah ee**stoa**ryah |
| medicine | **la medicina** | lah maydee**thee**nah |
| music | **la música** | lah **moos**seekah |
| natural history | **la historia natural** | lah ee**stoa**ryah nahtoo**rahl** |
| ornithology | **la ornitología** | lah oarneetoaloa**khee**ah |
| painting | **la pintura** | lah peen**too**rah |
| pottery | **la alfarería** | lah ahlfahray**ree**ah |
| religion | **la religión** | lah raylee**khyon** |
| sculpture | **la escultura** | lah ayskool**too**rah |
| zoology | **la zoología** | lah thoaloa**khee**ah |
| Where's the ... department? | **¿Dónde está el departamento de ...?** | **doan**day ay**stah** ayl daypahrtah**mayn**toa day |

| It's ... | Es ... | ayss |
|---|---|---|
| amazing | asombroso* | ahssoambroassoa |
| awful | horrible | orreeblay |
| beautiful | hermoso | ayrmoassoa |
| gloomy | lúgubre | loogoobray |
| impressive | impresionante | eemprayssyoanahntay |
| interesting | interesante | eentayrayssahntay |
| magnificent | magnífico | mahgneefeekoa |
| overwhelming | abrumador | ahbroomahdhor |
| strange | extraño | aykstrahñoa |
| superb | soberbio | soabhehrbyoa |
| terrible | terrible | tehrreeblay |
| terrifying | aterrador | ahtehrrahdhor |
| tremendous | tremendo | traymayndoa |
| ugly | feo | fehoa |

## Churches—Religious services  *Iglesias – Servicios religiosos*

Predominantly Roman Catholic, Spain is rich in cathedrals and churches worth visiting. Most are open to the public except, of course, during mass. If you're interested in taking pictures, you should obtain permission first. Shorts and backless dresses are definitely out when visiting churches.

| Is there a/an ... near here? | ¿Hay una ... cerca de aquí? | igh oonah ... therkah day ahkee |
|---|---|---|
| Catholic/Protestant church | iglesia católica/ protestante | eeglayssyah kahtoaleekah/ proataystahntay |
| synagogue | sinagoga | seenahgoagah |
| mosque | mezquita | maythkeetah |
| At what time is ...? | ¿A qué hora es ...? | ah kay oarah ayss |
| mass | la misa | lah meessah |
| the service | el servicio | ayl sehrbeethyoa |
| Where can I find a ... who speaks English? | ¿Dónde puedo encontrar un ... que hable inglés? | doanday pwaydhoa aynkontrahr oon ... kay ahblay eenglayss |
| priest/minister/ rabbi | sacerdote/ministro/ rabino | sahthehrdoatay/mee- neestroa/rahbheenoa |
| I'd like to visit the church. | Quisiera visitar la iglesia. | keessyayrah beesseetahr lah eeglayssyah |

* For feminine and plural forms, see grammar section page 159 (adjectives).

## Countryside *En el campo*

| | | |
|---|---|---|
| How high is that mountain? | ¿Qué altura tiene esa montaña? | kay ahltoorah tyaynay ayssah moantahñah |
| How far is it to ...? | ¿Qué distancia hay hasta ...? | kay deestahnthyah igh ahstah |
| Can we walk? | ¿Podemos ir a pie? | poadaymoass eer ah pyay |
| Is there a scenic route to ...? | ¿Hay una carretera panorámica a ...? | igh oonah kahrraytayrah pahnorahmeekah ah |
| How do we get back to ...? | ¿Cómo regresamos a ...? | koamoa raygrayssahmoass ah |
| What's the name of that ...? | ¿Cómo se llama ...? | koamoa say lyahmah |
| animal/bird/ flower/tree | ese animal/pájaro/ esa flor/ese árbol | ayssay ahneemahl/ pahkhahroa/ayssah floar/ ayssay ahrboal |

## Landmarks *Puntos de referencia*

| | | |
|---|---|---|
| bridge | el puente | ayl pwayntay |
| building | el edificio | ayl aydheefeethyoa |
| church | la iglesia | lah eeglayssyah |
| cliff | el acantilado | ayl ahkahnteelahdhoa |
| farm | la granja | lah grahnkhah |
| field | el campo | ayl kahmpoa |
| footpath | el sendero | ayl sayndayroa |
| forest | el bosque | ayl boaskay |
| fortress | la fortaleza | lah fortahlaythah |
| garden | el jardín | ayl khahrdeen |
| hill | la colina | lah koaleenah |
| house | la casa | lah kahssah |
| hut | la cabaña | lah kahbhahñah |
| lake | el lago | ayl lah  oa |
| meadow | el prado | ayl prahdhoa |
| river | el río | ayl reeoa |
| road | la carretera | lah kahrraytayrah |
| sea | el mar | ayl mahr |
| valley | el valle | ayl bahlyay |
| village | el pueblo | ayl pwaybloa |
| vineyard | el viñedo | ayl beeñaydhoa |
| wall | el muro | ayl mooroa |
| waterfall | la cascada | lah kahskahdhah |
| windmill | el molino de viento | ayl moaleenoa day byayntoa |

ASKING THE WAY, see page 76

# Relaxing

### Cinema (Movies) — Theatre    *Cine – Teatro*

Most films are dubbed in Spanish. The first showing usually starts around 2 p.m. in cities, but at 4 elsewhere. Sometimes there are only two showings in the evening—at 7 and 10.30 or 11 p.m.; for these advance booking is advisable. Curtain time at the theatre is at 7 and 10.30 or 11 p.m. There are daily performances but a few theatres close one day a week.

You can find out what's playing from the newspapers and billboards or from magazines like "This Week in …".

| | | |
|---|---|---|
| What's on at the cinema tonight? | ¿Qué ponen en el cine esta noche? | kay poanehn ayn ayl theenay aystah noachay |
| What's playing at the … theatre? | ¿Qué ponen en el teatro …? | kay poanehn ayn ayl tayahtroa |
| Can you recommend a …? | ¿Puede recomendarme …? | pwaydhay rehkoamayndahrmay |
| comedy | una comedia | oonah koamaydhyah |
| drama | un drama | oon drahmah |
| film | una película | oonah payleekoolah |
| musical | una comedia musical | oonah koamaydhyah moosseekahl |
| revue | una revista | oonah rehbheestah |
| thriller | una película de suspense | oonah payleekoolah day soospaynsay |
| western | una película del Oeste | oonah payleekoolah dayl oaaystay |
| What time does the first evening performance begin? | ¿A qué hora empieza la primera función de noche? | ah kay oarah aympyaythah lah preemayrah foonthyon day noachay |
| Are there any seats for …? | ¿Quedan localidades para …? | kaydhahn loakahleedhahdhayss pahrah |
| How much are the seats? | ¿Cuánto valen las localidades? | kwahntoa bahlayn lahss loakahleedhahdhayss |
| I want to reserve 2 seats for the show on Friday evening. | Quiero reservar 2 localidades para la función del viernes por la noche. | kyayroa rayssayrbahr 2 loakahleedhahdhayss pahrah lah foonthyon dayl byayrnayss por lah noachay |

DAYS, see page 151

| Can I have a seat for the matinée on Tuesday? | ¿Me puede dar una localidad para la sesión de tarde del martes? | may pwaydhay dahr oonah loakahleedhahdh pahrah lah sayssyon day tahrday dayl mahrtayss |
| I want a seat in the stalls (orchestra). | Quiero una localidad de platea. | kyayroa oonah loakahleedhahdh day plahtayah |
| Not too far back. | No muy atrás. | noa mwee ahtrahss |
| Somewhere in the middle. | En algún lugar en el medio. | ayn ahlgoon loogar ayn ayl maydhyoa |
| How much are the seats in the circle (mezzanine)? | ¿Cuánto valen las localidades de anfiteatro? | kwahntoa bahlayn lahss loakahleedhahdhayss day ahnfeetayahtroa |
| May I please have a programme? | ¿Me da un programa, por favor? | may dah oon proagrahmah por fahbhor |

---

| Lo siento, las localidades están agotadas. | I'm sorry, we're sold out. |
| Sólo quedan algunos asientos en el anfiteatro. | There are only a few seats left in the circle (mezzanine). |
| ¿Puedo ver su entrada? | May I see your ticket? |
| Este es su sitio. | This is your seat. |

---

## Opera—Ballet—Concert   *Opera – Ballet – Concierto*

| Where's the opera house? | ¿Dónde está el Teatro de la Opera? | doanday aystah ayl tayahtroa day lah oapayrah |
| Where's the concert hall? | ¿Dónde está la Sala de Conciertos? | doanday aystah lah sahlah day konthyayrtoass |
| Can you recommend a ...? | ¿Puede recomendarme ...? | pwaydhay raykoamayndahrmay |
| ballet | un ballet | oon bahlayt |
| concert | un concierto | oon konthyayrtoa |
| opera | una ópera | oonah oapayrah |
| operetta | una opereta | oonah oapayraytah |
| What's on at the opera tonight? | ¿Qué ópera ponen esta noche? | kay oapayrah poanehn aystah noachay |

| Who's singing/ dancing? | ¿Quién canta/baila? | kyayn **kahn**tah/**bigh**lah |
| What time does the programme start? | ¿A qué hora empieza el programa? | ah kay **o**arah aym**pyay**thah ayl proa**grah**mah |
| Which orchestra is playing? | ¿Qué orquesta toca? | kay oar**kay**stah **to**akah |
| What are they playing? | ¿Qué tocan? | kay **to**akahn |
| Who's the conductor? | ¿Quién es el director? | kyayn ayss ayl dee**reh**ktor |

### Nightclubs  *Centros nocturnos*

Nightclubs—with dinner, dancing and a floor show—are found only in major cities and popular resorts. But you'll certainly want to experience the informal atmosphere of a *bodega* or *taberna*. Some of them are found in candlelit cellars or in bars where a tiny space has been set aside for entertainment. While sipping a sherry or Spanish brandy, you might watch fiery flamenco dancing or listen to melancholy guitar music.

| Can you recommend a good nightclub? | ¿Puede recomendarme un buen centro nocturno? | **pway**dhay raykoamayn-**dahr**may oon bwayn **thayn**troa noak**toor**noa |
| Is there a floor show? | ¿Hay atracciones? | igh ahtrahk**thyo**nayss |
| What time does the floor show start? | ¿A qué hora empiezan las atracciones? | ah kay **o**arah aym**pyay**-thahn lahss ahtrahk**thyo**-nayss |
| Is evening attire necessary? | ¿Se necesita traje de noche? | say naythays**see**tah **trah**khay day **no**achay |

### Disco  *Discoteca*

| Where can we go dancing? | ¿Dónde podemos ir a bailar? | **doan**day poa**dhay**moass eer ah **bigh**lahr |
| Is there a discotheque in town? | ¿Hay alguna discoteca en la ciudad? | igh ahl**goo**nah deeskoa**tay**-kah ayn lah thyoo**dhahdh** |
| May I have this dance? | ¿Me permite este baile? | may payr**mee**tay **ay**stay **bigh**lay |

### Bullfight  *La corrida*

The *corrida* (literally "running of the bulls") will either fascinate you or appal you. To a Spaniard, a bullfight is not a choice of life and death for the bull. It is simply an opportunity for it to die heroically.

In some ways the spectacle resembles a ballet. There are colourful moments when the procession *(paseo)* arrives. The entry of the bull into the arena is a moment of high suspense. The movements of cape and bullfighter are graceful and precise.

The *matador* and his team of assistants goad the bull so as to assess its reactions to the cape. A *picador* weakens the bull by piercing its neck muscles with a lance.

A *banderillero* then confronts the animal. At great peril, he thrusts three sets of barbed sticks between its shoulder blades. Throughout each stage of the performance, the Spanish crowd will be watching critically for the finer points—weighing the fearlessness of bull and man, and the *matador's* skill as he executes a series of dangerous passes, leading up to the final climax of the kill.

You may well find the whole performance cruel. Should death be a public spectacle? Disturbing, too, is the treatment of the *picador's* horse. Although protected by padding, he catches the repeated fury of the bull's charge and horns. The horse takes this in silence, incidentally, because his vocal cords have been cut.

You'll be asked whether you want a seat in the sun or shade *(sol o sombra).* Be sure to specify *sombra,* for the Spanish sun is hot. Rent a cushion for the hard concrete stands.

| | | |
|---|---|---|
| I'd like to see a bullfight. | **Quisiera ver una corrida.** | keessyayrah behr oonah korreedhah |
| I want a seat in the shade/in the sun. | **Quisiera una localidad de sombra/de sol.** | keessyayrah oonah loakah-leedhahdh day soambrah/day sol |
| I'd like to rent a cushion. | **Quisiera alquilar una almohadilla.** | keessyayrah ahlkeelahr oonah ahlmoaahdheelyah |

## Sports *Deportes*

Football (soccer) and *pelota* are as popular in Spain as bull-fighting. *Pelota* is similar to handball but instead of a glove, the players wear a curved wicker basket *(cesta)*. The ball *(pelota)* is hard and covered with goatskin. It can be played off the back and side walls as well as the front. Caught in the *cesta,* and hurled at the wall with great force, it bounces with extraordinary speed. Usually played in the late afternoon or evening, *pelota* is well worth watching. In Latin America, the game is known as *jai alai* (the Basque word for the sport).

In spring and fall, there's good horse racing in Madrid, San Sebastián and Sevilla. Besides, facilities abound to go fishing—even deep-sea fishing—hunting, golfing, swimming, sailing, windsurfing or play tennis.

Though one wouldn't think of going to Spain to ski, you can don your ski togs from December to April in the Catalonian Pyrenees, near Madrid and in the Sierra Nevada near Granada.

| | | |
|---|---|---|
| Is there a football (soccer) match anywhere today? | ¿Hay algún partido de fútbol hoy? | igh ahlgoon pahrteedhoa day footbol oy |
| Who's playing? | ¿Quiénes juegan? | kyaynayss khwaygahn |
| Can you get me 2 tickets? | ¿Puede conseguirme 2 entradas? | pwaydhay konsaygeermay 2 ayntrahdhahss |

| | | |
|---|---|---|
| basketball | el baloncesto | ayl bahloanthaystoa |
| boxing | el boxeo | ayl boaksayoa |
| cycling | el ciclismo | ayl theekleesmoa |
| dog racing | las carreras de galgos | lahs kahrrayrahss day gahlgoass |
| horse riding | la equitación | lah aykeetahthyon |
| skiing | el esquí | ayl ayskee |
| swimming | la natación | lah nahtahthyon |
| volleyball | el balonvolea | ayl bahloanboalayah |

| | | |
|---|---|---|
| I'd like to see a pelota match. | Quisiera ver un partido de pelota. | keessyayrah behr oon pahrteedhoa day payloatah |
| Where's the nearest golf course? | ¿Dónde está el campo de golf más cercano? | doanday aystah ayl kahmpoa day goalf mahss thehrkahnoa |
| Can we hire (rent) clubs? | ¿Podemos alquilar los palos? | poadhaymoass ahlkeelahr loss pahloass |
| Where are the tennis courts? | ¿Dónde están las pistas de tenis? | doanday aystahn lahss peestahss day tayneess |
| Can I hire rackets? | ¿Puedo alquilar raquetas? | pwaydhoa ahlkeelahr rahkaytahss |
| What's the charge per ...? | ¿Cuánto cuesta por ...? | kwahntoa kwaystah por |
| day/round/hour | día/juego/hora | deeah/khwaygoa/oarah |
| Where's the nearest race course (track)? | ¿Dónde está la pista de carreras más cercana? | doanday aystah lah peestah day kahrrayrahss mahss thehrkahnah |
| What's the admission charge? | ¿Cuánto vale la entrada? | kwahntoa bahlay lah ayntrahdhah |
| Is there a swimming pool here? | ¿Hay una piscina aquí? | igh oonah peestheenah ahkee |
| Is it open-air/indoors? | ¿Está al aire libre/ Es cubierta? | aystah ahl ighray lēebray/ ayss koobhyayrtah |
| Can one swim in the lake/river? | ¿Se puede nadar en el lago/río? | say pwaydhay nahdhahr ayn ayl lahgoa/reeoa |
| Is there a sandy beach? | ¿Hay una playa de arena? | igh oonah plahyah day ahraynah |
| Is there any good fishing/hunting around here? | ¿Hay un buen lugar para pescar/cazar en los alrededores? | igh oon bwayn loogahr pahrah payskahr/kahthahr ayn loass ahlraydhaydhoa- rayss |
| Do I need a permit? | ¿Se requiere per- miso? | say raykyayray payrmee- ssoa |
| Where can I get one? | ¿Dónde puedo con- seguir uno? | doanday pwaydhoa konsay- geer oonoa |
| What are the skiing conditions like at ...? | ¿Cómo están las condiciones para esquiar en ...? | koamoa aystahn lahss kondeethyonayss pahrah ayskyahr ayn |
| Are there ski lifts? | ¿Hay telesquís? | igh taylayskeess |

## On the beach   *En la playa*

| Is it safe for swimming? | ¿Se puede nadar sin peligro? | say pwaydhay nahdhahr seen pehleegroa |
|---|---|---|
| Is there a lifeguard? | ¿Hay vigilante? | igh beekheelahntay |
| There are some big waves. | Hay algunas olas muy grandes. | igh ahlgoonahss oalahss mwee grahndayss |
| Are there any dangerous currents? | ¿Hay alguna corriente peligrosa? | igh ahlgoonah korryayntay pehleegroassah |
| Is it safe for children? | ¿Es seguro para los niños? | ayss sehgooroa pahrah loos neeñoass |
| What time is high/ low tide? | ¿A qué hora es la marea alta/baja? | ah kay oarah ayss lah mahrehah ahltah/bahkhah |
| What's the temperature of the water? | ¿Cuál es la temperatura del agua? | kwahl ayss lah taympayrahtoorah dayl ahgwah |
| I want to hire a/an/ some ... | Quiero alquilar ... | kyayroa ahlkeelahr |
| air mattress (raft) | un colchón neumático | oon koalchon nayoomahteekoa |
| bathing hut (cabana) | una cabina | oonah kahbheenah |
| deck-chair | una silla de lona | oonah seelyah day loanah |
| skin-diving equipment | un equipo para natación submarina | oon aykeepoa pahrah nah-tahthyon soobmahreenah |
| sunshade (umbrella) | una sombrilla | oonah soambreelyah |
| surfboard | una plancha de deslizamiento | oonah plahnchah day daysleethahmyayntoa |
| water-skis | unos esquís acuáticos | oonoass ayskeess ahkwahteekoass |
| Where can I rent a ...? | ¿Dónde puedo alquilar ...? | doanday pwaydhoa ahlkeelahr |
| canoe | una canoa | oonah kahnoaah |
| motorboat | una motora | oonah moatoarah |
| rowing-boat | una barca | oonah bahrkah |
| sailing-boat | un velero | oon baylehroa |
| What's the charge per hour? | ¿Cuánto cobran por hora? | kwahntoa koabrahn por oarah |

---

**PLAYA PARTICULAR**    PRIVATE BEACH

**PROHIBIDO BAÑARSE**    NO SWIMMING

---

# Making friends

## Introductions  *Presentaciones*

| | | |
|---|---|---|
| How do you do? (Pleased to meet you.) | Encantado(a)* de conocerle. | aynkahntahdhoa(ah) day koanoathayrlay |
| How are you? | ¿Cómo está usted? | koamoa aystah oostaydh |
| Fine, thanks. And you? | Bien, gracias. ¿Y usted? | byayn grahthyahss. ee oostaydh |
| May I introduce ... | Quiero presentarle a ... | kyayroa prayssayntahrlay ah |
| My name's ... | Me llamo ... | may lyahmoa |
| What's your name? | ¿Cómo se llama? | koamoa say lyahmah |
| Glad to know you. | Tanto gusto. | tahntoa goostoa |

## Follow-up  *Continuación ...*

| | | |
|---|---|---|
| How long have you been here? | ¿Cuánto tiempo lleva usted aquí? | kwahntoa tyaympoa lyaybhah oostaydh ahkee |
| We've been here a week. | Llevamos aquí una semana. | lyaybhahmoass ahkee oonah saymahnah |
| Is this your first visit? | ¿Es la primera vez que viene? | ayss lah preemayrah behth kay byaynay |
| No, we came here last year. | No, vinimos el año pasado. | noa beeneemoass ayl ahñoa pahssahdhoa |
| Are you enjoying your stay? | ¿Está disfrutando de su estancia? | aystah deesfrootahndoa day soo aystahnthyah |
| Yes, I like ... very much. | Sí, me gusta mucho ... | see may goostah moochoa |
| Where do you come from? | ¿De dónde es usted? | day doanday ayss oostaydh |
| I'm from ... | Soy de ... | soy day |
| Where are you staying? | ¿Dónde se hospeda? | doanday say ospehdhah |

*A woman would say *encantada*

COUNTRIES, see page 146

| | | |
|---|---|---|
| Are you on your own? | ¿Ha venido usted solo/sola? | ah bayneedhoa oostaydh soaloa/soalah |
| I'm with my ... | Estoy con ... | aystoy kon |
| husband | mi marido | mee mahreedhoa |
| wife | mi mujer | mee mookhehr |
| family | mi familia | mee fahmeelyah |
| parents | mis padres | meess pahdrayss |
| boyfriend | mi amigo | mee ahmeegoa |
| girlfriend | mi amiga | mee ahmeegah |

| | | |
|---|---|---|
| father/mother | el padre/la madre | ayl pahdray/lah mahdray |
| son/daughter | el hijo/la hija | ayl eekhoa/lah eekhah |
| brother/sister | el hermano/ la hermana | ayl ayrmahnoa/ lah ayrmahnah |
| uncle/aunt | el tío/la tía | ayl teeoa/lah teeah |
| nephew/niece | el sobrino/la sobrina | ayl soabreenoa/ lah soabreenah |
| cousin | el primo/la prima | ayl preemoa/lah preemah |

| | | |
|---|---|---|
| Are you married/ single? | ¿Está casado(a)/ soltero(a)*? | aystah kahssahdhoa(ah) soaltayroa(ah) |
| Do you have children? | ¿Tiene niños? | tyaynay neeñoass |
| What's your occupation? | ¿Cuál es su ocupación? | kwahl ays soo oakoopahthyon |
| I'm a student. | Soy estudiante. | soy aystoodhyahntay |
| I'm here on a business trip. | Estoy aquí en viaje de negocios. | aystoy ahkee ayn byah-khay day naygoathyoass |
| We hope to see you again soon. | Esperamos verle pronto por aquí. | ayspayrahmoass bayrlay proantoa por ahkee |
| See you later/See you tomorrow. | Hasta luego/Hasta mañana. | ahstah lwaygoa/ahstah mahñahnah |

## The weather  *El tiempo*

| | | |
|---|---|---|
| What a lovely day! | ¡Qué día tan bueno! | kay deeah tahn bwaynoa |
| What awful weather! | ¡Qué tiempo más malo! | kay tyaympoa mahss mahloa |

---

* If addressing a woman *casada/soltera*

| Is it usually as cold/ warm as this? | ¿Hace normalmente este frío/calor? | ahthay noarmahlmayntay aystay freeoa/kahlor |
| Do you think it'll ... tomorrow? | ¿Cree usted que ... mañana? | krayeh oostaydh kay ... mahñahnah |
| rain/snow clear up/be sunny be windy/cloudy | lloverá/nevará hará mejor/hará sol hará viento/estará nublado | lyoabhayrah/naybhahrah ahrah mehkhor/ahrah sol ahrah byayntoa/aystahrah nooblahdhoa |

### Invitations  *Invitaciones*

| Would you like to have dinner with us on ...? | ¿Quiere acompañarnos a cenar en ...? | kyayray ahkoampahñahrnoass ah thaynahr ayn |
| May I invite you for lunch? | ¿Puedo invitarlo/la a almorzar? | pwaydhoa eenbeetahrloa/lah ah ahlmoarthahr |
| Can you come over for a drink this evening? | ¿Puede usted venir a tomar una copa esta noche? | pwaydhay oostaydh bayneer ah toamahr oonah koapah aystah noachay |
| That's very kind of you. | Es usted muy amable. | ayss oostaydh mwee ahmahblay |
| What time shall we come? | ¿A qué hora vamos? | ah kay oarah bahmoass |
| May I bring a friend? | ¿Puedo llevar a un amigo/una amiga? | pwaydhoa lyaybhar ah oon ahmeegoa/oonah ahmeegah |
| I'm afraid we've got to leave now. | Me temo que debemos marcharnos ahora. | may taymoa kay daybhaymoass mahrchahrnoass ahoarah |
| Next time you must come to visit us. | Otro día tienen que venir ustedes a vernos. | oatroa deeah tyaynayn kay bayneer oostaydhayss ah bayrnoass |
| Thanks for the evening. It was great. | Muchas gracias por la velada. Ha sido estupenda. | moochahss grahthyahss por lah baylahdhah. ah seedhoa aystoopayndah |

### Dating  *Citas*

| Would you like a cigarette? | ¿Quiere usted un cigarrillo? | kyayray oostaydh oon theegahrreelyoa |
| Do you have a light, please? | ¿Tiene usted lumbre, por favor? | tyaynay oostaydh loombray por fahbhor |

DAYS, see page 151

| Can I get you a drink? | ¿Quiere usted beber algo? | kyayray oostaydh baybhayr ahlgoa |
| Are you waiting for someone? | ¿Está usted esperando a alguien? | aystah oostaydh ayspayrahndoa ah ahlgyayn |
| Do you mind if I sit down here? | ¿Le importa si me siento aquí? | lay eempoartah see may syayntoa ahkee |
| Are you free this evening? | ¿Está usted libre esta tarde? | aystah oostaydh leebray aystah tahrday |
| Would you like to go out with me tonight? | ¿Quisiera usted salir conmigo esta noche? | keessyayrah oostaydh sahleer konmeegoa aystah noachay |
| Would you like to go dancing? | ¿Quisiera usted ir a bailar? | keessyayrah oostaydh eer ah bighlahr |
| Shall we go to the cinema (movies)? | ¿Quiere que vayamos al cine? | kyayray kay bahyahmoass ahl theenay |
| Would you like to go for a drive? | ¿Quiere usted dar un paseo en coche? | kyayray oostaydh dahr oon pahssayoa ayn koachay |
| Where shall we meet? | ¿Dónde nos encontramos? | doanday noss aynkontrahmoass |
| What's your address/ telephone number? | ¿Cuál es su dirección/ número de teléfono? | kwahl ayss soo deeraykthyon/noomayroa day taylayfoanoa |
| I'll call for you at 8 o'clock. | Iré a recogerla a las 8. | eeray ah rehkohkhayrlah ah lahss 8 |
| May I take you home? | ¿Puedo acompañarla hasta su casa? | pwaydhoa ahkoampahñahrlah ahstah soo kahssah |
| Can I see you again tomorrow? | ¿Puedo verla mañana? | pwaydhoa bayrlah mahñahnah |

## ... and you might answer:

| I'd love to, thank you. | **Me encantaría, gracias.** | may aynkahntahreeah grahthyahss |
| I've enjoyed myself. | **Lo he pasado muy bien.** | loa ay pahssahdhoa mwee byayn |
| Thank you, but I'am busy. | **Gracias, pero estoy ocupado(a).** | grathyahss payroa aystoy oakoopahdhoa(ah) |
| No, thank you, I'd rather not. | **No gracias, mejor no.** | noa grathyahss maykhoar noa |

# Shopping guide

This shopping guide is designed to help you find what you want with ease, accuracy and speed. It features:

1. A list of all major shops, stores and services (p. 98)

2. Some general expressions required when shopping to allow you to be specific and selective (p. 100)

3. Full details of the shops and services most likely to concern you, grouped under the headings below.

|  |  | Page |
|---|---|---|
| **Bookshop/ Stationer's** | books, magazines, newspapers, stationery | 104 |
| **Camping equipment** | all items required for camping | 106 |
| **Chemist's (drugstore)** | medicine, first-aid, cosmetics, toilet articles | 108 |
| **Clothing** | shoes, clothes, accessories | 112 |
| **Electrical appliances** | radios, cassette-recorders, shavers | 119 |
| **Grocery** | some general expressions, weights, measures and packaging | 120 |
| **Jeweller's/ Watchmaker's** | jewellery, watches, watch repairs | 121 |
| **Optician** | glasses, lenses, binoculars | 123 |
| **Photography** | cameras, films, developing accessories | 124 |
| **Tobacconist's** | smoker's supplies | 126 |
| **Miscellaneous** | souvenirs, records, cassettes, toys | 127 |

LAUNDRY, see page 29/HAIRDRESSER'S, see page 30

**Shops and services**   *Comercios y servicios*

Shopping hours: 9.30 a.m. to 1.30 p.m. and 4 to 8 p.m.
Monday to Friday, 9.30 a.m. to 2 p.m. on Saturdays; department stores are generally open from 10 a.m. to 8 p.m. without a break, Monday to Saturday.

| Where's the nearest ...? | ¿Dónde está ... más cercano/cercana? | doanday aystah ... mahss thayrkahnoa/thayrkahnah |
|---|---|---|
| antique shop | la tienda de antigüedades | lah **tyayn**dah day ahnteegwaydhahdhayss |
| art gallery | la galería de arte | lah gahlayreeah day **ahr**tay |
| baker's | la panadería | lah pahnahdhayreeah |
| bank | el banco | ayl **bahn**koa |
| barber's | la barbería | lah bahrbayreeah |
| beauty salon | el salón de belleza | ayl sahlon day baylyaythah |
| bookshop | la librería | lah leebrayreeah |
| butcher's | la carnicería | lah kahrneethayreeah |
| cake shop | la pastelería | lah pahstaylayreeah |
| camera shop | la tienda de fotografía | lah **tyayn**dah day foatoagrahfeeah |
| candy store | la bombonería | lah boamboanayreeah |
| chemist's | la farmacia | lah fahr**mah**thyah |
| confectioner's | la confitería | lah konfeethayreeah |
| dairy | la lechería | lah laychayreeah |
| delicatessen | la mantequería | lah mahntaykayreeah |
| dentist | el dentista | ayl dayn**tees**tah |
| department store | los grandes almacenes | loss **grahn**dayss ahlmah**thay**nayss |
| doctor | el médico | ayl **may**deekoa |
| drugstore | la farmacia | lah fahr**mah**thyah |
| dry cleaner's | la tintorería | lah teentoarayreeah |
| electrician | el electricista | ayl aylayktree**thees**tah |
| fishmonger's | la pescadería | lah payskahdhayreeah |
| flower shop | la florería | lah floarayreeah |
| fruit stand | la frutería | lah frootayreeah |
| furrier's | la peletería | lah paylaytayreeah |
| greengrocer's | la verdulería | lah bayrdoolayreeah |
| grocery | la tienda de comestibles | lah **tyayn**dah day koamaysteeblayss |
| hairdresser's (ladies) | la peluquería | lah paylookayreeah |
| hardware store | la ferretería | lah fehrraytayreeah |
| health food shop | la tienda de alimentos dietéticos | lah **tyayn**dah day ahleemayntoass dyaytayteekoass |
| hospital | el hospital | ayl oaspeetahl |
| ironmonger's | la ferretería | lah fehrraytayreeah |

| jeweller's | la joyería | lah khoyayreeah |
| launderette | la launderama | lah lahoondayrahmah |
| laundry | la lavandería | lah lahbhahndayreeah |
| leather goods store | la tienda de artí- culos de cuero | lah tyayndah day ahrtee- kooloass day kwayroa |
| library | la biblioteca | lah beeblyotaykah |
| market | el mercado | ayl mehrkahdhoa |
| newsstand | el quiosco de periódicos | ayl kyoskoa day payryodheekoass |
| optician | el óptico | ayl opteekoa |
| pastry shop | la pastelería | lah pahstaylayreeah |
| photographer | el fotógrafo | ayl foatoagrahfoa |
| police station | la comisaría | lah koameessahreeah |
| post office | la oficina de correos | lah oafeetheenah day korrehoass |
| shirt-maker's | la camisería | lah kahmeessehreeah |
| shoemaker's (repairs) | el zapatero | ayl thahpahtayroa |
| shoe shop | la zapatería | lah thahpahtayreeah |
| shopping centre | el centro comercial | ayl thayntroa koamayrthyahl |
| souvenir shop | la tienda de objetos de regalo | lay tyayndah day oabkhay- toass day raygahloa |
| sporting goods shop | la tienda de artícu- los de deportes | lah tyayndah day ahrtee- kooloass day dayportayss |
| stationer's | la papelería | lah pahpaylayreeah |
| supermarket | el supermercado | ayl soopayrmayrkahdhoa |
| sweet shop | la bombonería | lah boamboanayreeah |
| tailor's | el sastre | ayl sahstray |
| telephone office | la oficina de teléfonos | lah oafeetheenah day taylayfoanoass |
| tobacconist's | el estanco/los tabacos | ayl ehstahnkoa/loss tahbhahkoass |
| toy shop | la juguetería | lah khoogaytayreeah |
| travel agency | la agencia de viajes | lah ahkhaynthyah day byahkhayss |
| vegetable store | la verdulería | lah bayrdoolayreeah |
| veterinarian | el veterinario | ayl baytayreenahryoa |
| watchmaker's | la relojería | lah rehlokhayreeah |
| wine merchant's | la tienda de vinos/ la bodega | lah tyayndah day bee- noass/lah boadhaygah |

| **ENTRADA** | ENTRANCE |
| **SALIDA** | EXIT |
| **SALIDA DE EMERGENCIA** | EMERGENCY EXIT |

### Where? *¿Dónde?*

| Where's a good ...? | ¿Dónde hay un buen/una buena ...? | doanday igh oon bwayn/ oonah bwaynah |
| Where can I find a ...? | ¿Dónde puedo encontrar un/una ...? | doanday pwaydhoa aynkoantrahr oon/oonah |
| Where do they sell ...? | ¿Dónde venden ...? | doanday bayndayn |
| Where's the main shopping area? | ¿Dónde está la zona de tiendas más importante? | doanday aystah lah thoanah day tyayndahss mahss eempoartahntay |
| Is it far from here? | ¿Está muy lejos de aquí? | aystah mwee lehkhoass day ahkee |
| How do I get there? | ¿Cómo puedo llegar allí? | koamoa pwaydhoa lyaygahr ahlyee |

### Service *Servicio*

| Can you help me? | ¿Puede usted atenderme? | pwaydhay oostaydh ahtayndayrmay |
| I'm just looking. | Estoy sólo mirando. | aystoy soaloa meerahndoa |
| I want ... | Quiero ... | kyayroa |
| Do you have any ...? | ¿Tiene usted ...? | tyaynay oostaydh |
| Where is the ... department? | ¿Dónde está el departamento de ...? | doanday aystah ayl daypahrtahmayntoa day |
| Where's the lift (elevator)/escalator? | ¿Dónde está el ascensor/la escalera mecánica? | doanday aystah ayl ahsthaynsoar/lah ayskahlayrah maykahneekah |
| Where do I pay? | ¿Dónde pago? | doanday pahgoa |

### That one *Ese*

| Can you show me ...? | ¿Puede usted enseñarme ...? | pwaydhay oostaydh aynsaynyahrmay |
| that/those | ése/ésos | ayssay/ayssoass |
| the one in the window/in the display case | el del escaparate/ de la vitrina | ayl dayl ehskahpahrahtay/ day lah beetreenah |
| It's over there. | Está allí. | aystah ahlyee |

## Preference  *Preferencias*

| Can you show me some more? | ¿Puede usted enseñarme algo más? | pwaydhay oostaydh aynsayñahrmay ahlgoa mahss |
| Haven't you anything …? | ¿No tiene usted algo …? | noa tyaynay oostaydh ahlgoa |
| cheaper/better | más barato/mejor | mahss bahrahtoa/mehkhor |
| larger/smaller | más grande/más pequeño | mahss grahnday/mahss paykayñoa |
| more/less colourful | más/menos colorido | mahss/maynoass koaloareedhoa |

| big | grande* | grahnday |
| cheap | barato | bahrahtoa |
| dark | oscuro | oskooroa |
| good | bueno | bwaynoa |
| heavy | pesado | payssahdhoa |
| large | grande | grahnday |
| light (weight) | ligero | leekhayroa |
| light (colour) | claro | klahroa |
| rectangular | rectangular | rehktahngoolahr |
| round | redondo | raydhondoa |
| small | pequeño | paykayñoa |
| square | cuadrado | kwahdrahdhoa |

## How much?  *¿Cuánto cuesta?*

| How much is this? | ¿Cuánto cuesta esto? | kwahntoa kwaystah aystoa |
| I don't understand. | No entiendo. | noa ayntyayndoa |
| Please write it down. | Escríbamelo, por favor. | ayskreebhahmayloa por fahbhor |
| I don't want anything too expensive. | No quiero algo muy caro. | noa kayroa ahlgoa mwee kahroa |
| I don't want to spend more than … | No quiero gastar más de … | noa kyayroa gahstahr mahss day … |

REBAJAS    SALE

*For feminine and plural forms, see grammar section page 159 (adjectives).

COLOURS, see page 113

### Decision   *Decisión*

| It's not quite what I want. | No es realmente lo que quiero. | noa ayss rehahlmayntay loa kay kyayroa |
| No, I don't like it. | No, no me gusta. | noa noa may goostah |
| I'll take it. | Me lo llevo. | may loa lyaybhoa |

### Anything else?   *¿Algo más?*

| No, thanks, that's all. | No gracias, eso es todo. | noa grahthyahss ayssoa ayss toadhoa |
| Yes, I want ... | Sí, quiero ... | see kyayroa |

### Ordering   *Encargar*

| Can you order it for me? | ¿Puede usted encargarlo para mí? | pwaydhay oostaydh aynkahrgahrloa pahrah mee |
| How long will it take? | ¿Cuánto tardará? | kwahntoa tahrdahrah |

### Delivery   *Enviar*

| Deliver it to the ... Hotel. | Envíelo al hotel ... | aynbeeayloa ahl oatehl |
| Please send it to this address. | Por favor, mándelo a estas señas. | por fahbhor mahndayloa ah aystahss sayñahss |
| Do I have to pay the sales tax? | ¿Tengo que pagar el impuesto? | tayngoa kay pahgahr ayl eempwaysstoa |
| Will I have any difficulty with the customs? | ¿Tendré alguna dificultad con la aduana? | tayndray ahlgoonah deefeekooltahdh kon lah ahdwahnah |

### Paying   *Pagar*

| How much is it? | ¿Cuánto es? | kwahntoa ayss |
| Can I pay by traveller's cheque? | ¿Puedo pagar con cheque de viajero? | pwaydhoa pahgahr kon chaykay day byahkhayroa |
| Do you accept dollars/ pounds/credit cards? | ¿Acepta usted dólares/libras/ tarjetas de crédito? | ahthayptah oostaydh doalahrayss/leebrahss/tahrkhaytahss day kraydheetoa |

| | | |
|---|---|---|
| Haven't you made a mistake in the bill? | **¿No se ha equivocado usted en la cuenta?** | noa say ah aykeebhoa-kahdhoa oostaydh ayn lah **kwayn**tah |
| Will you please wrap it? | **¿Me hace el favor de envolverlo?** | may **ahth**ay ayl fahbhor day aynboalbehrloa |
| May I have a bag, please? | **¿Puede darme una bolsa, por favor?** | **pway**day **dahr**may oonah **boal**sah por fahbhor |

## Dissatisfied  *Descontento*

| | | |
|---|---|---|
| Can you please exchange this? | **¿Podría usted cambiarme esto, por favor?** | poa**dree**ah oostaydh kahm**byahr**may aystoa por fahbhor |
| I want to return this. | **Quiero devolver esto.** | **kyay**roa daybhol**behr** aystoa |
| I'd like a refund. Here's the receipt. | **Quisiera que me devolviesen el dinero. Aquí está el recibo.** | kees**syay**rah kay may daybhol**byays**sayn ayl **deen**ayroa. ah**kee** aystah ayl ray**thee**bhoa |

---

| | |
|---|---|
| **¿En qué puedo ayudarle?** | Can I help you? |
| **¿Qué desea?** | What would you like? |
| **¿Qué ... desea?** | What ... would you like? |
| **color/forma calidad/cantidad** | colour/shape quality/quantity |
| **Lo siento, no lo tenemos.** | I'm sorry, we haven't any. |
| **Se nos ha agotado.** | We're out of stock. |
| **¿Quiere que se lo encarguemos?** | Shall we order it for you? |
| **¿Lo llevará consigo o se lo enviamos?** | Will you take it with you or shall we send it? |
| **¿Algo más?** | Anything else? |
| **Son ... pesetas, por favor.** | That's ... pesetas, please. |
| **La caja está allí.** | The cashier's over there. |

Guía de compras

**Bookshop—Stationer's** *Librería – Papelería*

In Spain, bookshops and stationer's are usually separate shops, though the latter will often sell paperbacks. Newspapers and magazines are sold at newsstands.

| | | |
|---|---|---|
| Where's the nearest ...? | ¿Dónde está ... más cercano/cercana? | doanday aystah ... mahss thehrkahnoa/thehrkahnah |
| bookshop | la librería | lah leebrayreeah |
| stationer's | la papelería | lah pahpaylayreeah |
| newsstand | el quiosco de periódicos | ayl kyoskoa day payryo-dheekoass |
| Where can I buy an English newspaper? | ¿Dónde puedo comprar un periódico inglés? | doanday pwaydhoa komprahr oon payryo-dheekoa eenglayss |
| Where's the guide-book section? | ¿Dónde está la sec-ción de libros-guía? | doanday aystah lah sayk-thyon day leebroass geeah |
| Where do you keep the English/second-hand books? | ¿Dónde están los libros ingleses/de segunda mano? | doanday aystahn loss leebroass eenglayssayss/day saygoondoa mahnoa |
| Where can I make photocopies? | ¿Dónde puedo hacer fotocopias? | doanday pwaydhoa ahthayr foatoakoapyahss |
| I want to buy a/an/some ... | Quiero ... | kyayroa |
| address book | un librito de direcciones | oon leebreetoa day deerehkthyonayss |
| ball-point pen | un bolígrafo | oon boaleegrahfoa |
| book | un libro | oon leebroa |
| calendar | un calendario | oon kahlayndahryoa |
| carbon paper | papel carbón | pahpehl kahrbon |
| cellophane tape | cinta adhesiva | theentah ahdaysseebhah |
| crayons | unos lápices de color | oonoas lahpeethayss day koaloar |
| dictionary Spanish-English | un diccionario Español-Inglés | oon deekthyoanahryoa ayspahñoal-eenglayss |
| drawing paper | papel de dibujo | pahpehl day deebhookhoa |
| drawing pins | chinchetas | cheenchaytahs |
| envelopes | unos sobres | oonoas soabrayss |
| eraser | una goma de borrar | oonah goamah day borrahr |
| exercise book | un cuaderno | oon kwahdhernoa |
| felt-tip pen | un rotulador | oon roatoolahdhoar |
| file | una carpeta | oonah kahrpaytah |
| fountain pen | una pluma estilo-gráfica | oonah ploomah aysteeloa-grahfeekah |

| glue | cola de pegar | koalah day paygahr |
| grammar book | un libro de gramática | con leebroa day grah-mahteekah |
| guidebook | una guía | oonah geeah |
| ink | tinta | teentah |
| black/red/blue | negra/roja/azul | naygrah/roakhah/ahthool |
| (adhesive) labels | unas etiquetas (adhesivas) | oonahss ayteekaytahss (ahdaysseebhahss) |
| magazine | una revista | oonah raybheestah |
| map | un mapa | oon mahpah |
| of the town | de la ciudad | day lay thyoodhahdh |
| road map of ... | de carreteras de ... | day kahrraytayrahss day |
| newspaper | un periódico | oon payryodheekoa |
| American/English | americano/inglés | ahmayreekahnoa/eenglayss |
| notebook | un cuaderno | oon kwahdhehrnoa |
| note paper | papel de cartas | pahpehl day kahrtahss |
| paperback | una rústica | oonah roosteekah |
| paper napkins | unas servilletas de papel | oonahss sayrbeelyaytahss day pahpehl |
| paintbox | una caja de pinturas | oonah kahkhah day peentoorahss |
| paste | engrudo | ayngroodhoa |
| pen | una pluma | oonah ploomah |
| pencil | un lápiz | oon lahpeeth |
| pencil sharpener | un sacapuntas | oon sahkahpoontahss |
| playing cards | unas naipes | oonahss nighpayss |
| pocket calculator | una calculadora de bolsillo | oonah kahlkoolahdhoarah day boalseelyoa |
| post cards | unas tarjetas postales | oonahss tahrkhaytahss poastahlayss |
| refill (for a pen) | un recambio (para pluma) | oon raykahmbyoa (pahrah ploomah) |
| rubber | una goma de borrar | oonah goamah day boarrahr |
| ruler | una regla | oonah rehglah |
| sketching block | un bloc de dibujo | oon bloak day deebhookhoa |
| staples | unas grapas | oonahss grahpahss |
| string | una cuerda | oonah kwayrdah |
| thumbtacks | chinchetas | cheenchaytahss |
| tissue paper | papel de seda | pahpehl day saydhah |
| tracing paper | papel transparente | pahpehl trahnspahrayntay |
| typewriter ribbon | una cinta para máquina | oonah theentah pahrah mahkeenah |
| typing paper | papel de máquina | pahpehl day mahkeenah |
| wrapping paper | papel de envolver | pahpehl day aynboalbehr |
| writing pad | un bloc de papel | oon bloak day pahpehl |

## Camping equipment   *Equipo de camping*

| I'd like a/an/some ... | Quisiera ... | keessyayrah |
|---|---|---|
| bottle-opener | **un abridor de botellas** | oon ahbreedhor day boataylyahss |
| bucket | **un cubo** | oon koobhoa |
| butane gas | **gas butano** | gahss bootahnoa |
| campbed | **una cama de campaña** | oonah kahmah day kahmpahñah |
| can opener | **un abrelatas** | oon ahbraylahtahss |
| candles | **unas velas** | oonahss baylahss |
| chair | **una silla** | oonah seelyah |
| folding chair | **silla plegable** | seelyah playgahblay |
| charcoal | **carbón** | kahrbon |
| clothes pegs | **unas perchas** | oonahss payrchahss |
| compass | **una brújula** | oonah brookhoolah |
| cool box | **una nevera portátil** | oonah naybhayrah poar-tahteel |
| corkscrew | **un sacacorchos** | oon sahkahkoarchoass |
| crockery | **una vajilla** | oonah bahkheelyah |
| cutlery | **unos cubiertos** | oonoass koobhyayrtoass |
| deckchair | **una silla de lona** | oonah seelyah day loanah |
| dishwashing detergent | **detergente para la vajilla** | daytayrkhayntay pahrah lah bahkheelyah |
| first-aid kit | **un botiquín** | oon boateekeen |
| fishing tackle | **un aparejo de pesca** | oon ahpahrehkhoa day payskah |
| flashlight | **una linterna** | oonah leentehrnah |
| food box | **una fiambrera** | oonah fyahmbrayrah |
| frying pan | **una sartén** | oonah sahrtayn |
| groundsheet | **una alfombra (de hule)** | oonah ahlfoambrah (day oolay) |
| hammer | **un martillo** | oon mahrteelyoa |
| ice pack | **un elemento congelable** | oon aylaymayntoa koan-khaylahblay |
| kerosene | **petróleo** | paytroalehoa |
| lamp | **una lámpara** | oonah lahmpahrah |
| matches | **unas cerillas** | oonahss thayreelyahss |
| mattress | **un colchón** | oon koalchon |
| methylated spirits | **alcohol de quemar** | ahlkoaol day kaymahr |
| mosquito net | **una red para mosquitos** | oonah raydh pahrah moaskeetoass |
| paraffin | **petróleo** | paytroalehoa |
| penknife | **un cortaplumas** | oon koartahploomahss |
| picnic basket | **una bolsa para merienda** | oonah boalsah pahrah mayryayndah |

| plastic bags | unas bolsas de plástico | oonahss boalsahss day plahsteekoa |
| rope | una cuerda | oonah kwayrdah |
| rucksack | una mochila | oonah moacheelah |
| saucepan | un cazo | oon kahthoa |
| scissors | unas tijeras | oonahss teekhayrahss |
| screwdriver | un destornillador | oon daystoarneelyahdhor |
| sleeping bag | un saco de dormir | oon sahkoa day doarmeer |
| stew pot | una cacerola | oonah kahthayroalah |
| table | una mesa | oonah mayssah |
| folding table | mesa plegable | mayssah playgahblay |
| tent | una tienda de campaña | oonah tyayndah day kahmpahñah |
| tent peg | una estaca | oonah ehstahkah |
| tent pole | un mástil | oon mahsteel |
| tinfoil | papel de estaño | pahpehl day aystahñoa |
| tin opener | un abrelatas | oon ahbraylahtahss |
| tool kit | una caja de herramientas | oonah kahkhah day ehrrahmyayntahss |
| torch | una linterna | oonah leentehrnah |
| vacuum flask | un termo | oon tayrmoa |
| washing powder | jabón en polvo | khahbhoan ayn poalboa |
| washing-up liquid | detergente para la vajilla | daytayrkhayntay pahrah lah bahkheelyah |
| water flask | una cantimplora | oonah kahnteemploarah |
| wood alcohol | alcohol de quemar | ahlkoaol day kaymahr |

## Crockery  *Vajilla*

| cups | unas tazas | oonahss tahthahss |
| mugs | unas tazas altas sin plato | oonahss tahthahss ahl-tahss seen plahtoa |
| plates | unos platos | oonoass plahtoass |
| saucers | unos platillos | oonoass plahteelyoass |

## Cutlery  *Cubiertos*

| forks | unos tenedores | oonoass taynaydhoarayss |
| knives | unos cuchillos | oonoass koocheelyoass |
| spoons | unas cucharas | oonahss koochahrahss |
| teaspoons | unas cucharillas | oonahss koochahreelyahss |
| (made of) plastic | (de) plástico | (day) plahsteekoa |
| (made of) stain-less steel | (de) acero inoxidable | (day) ahthayroa eenoakseedhahblay |

**Chemist's (drugstore)**   *Farmacia*

A Spanish chemist's normally doesn't stock the range of items that you'll find in England or in the U.S. For example, he doesn't sell photographic equipment or books. And for perfume, make-up, •tc., you must go to a *perfumería* (payrfoomay**ree**ah).

This section has been divided into two parts:

1. Pharmaceutical—medicine, first-aid, etc.
2. Toiletry—toilet articles, cosmetics

| | | |
|---|---|---|
| Where's the nearest (all-night) chemist's? | ¿Dónde está la farmacia (de guardia) más cercana? | doanday aystah lah fahrmahthyah (day gwahrdyah) mahss thehrkahnah |
| What time does the chemist's open/close? | ¿A qué hora abren/cierran la farmacia? | ah kay oarah ahbrayn/thyerrahn lah fahrmahthyah |

**1 — Pharmaceutical**   *Productos farmacéuticos*

| | | |
|---|---|---|
| I want something for ... | Quiero algo para ... | kyayroa ahlgoa pahrah |
| a cold/a cough | un resfriado/una tos | oon raysfryahdhoa/oonah toss |
| hay fever | la fiebre del heno | lah fyehbray dayl aynoa |
| a hangover | la resaca | lah rayssahkah |
| insect bites | las picaduras de insecto | lahss peekahdhoorahss day eensayktoa |
| sunburn  • | las quemaduras del sol | lahss kaymahdhoorahss dayl sol |
| travel sickness | el mareo | ayl mahrehoa |
| an upset stomach | las molestias de estómago | lahss moalaystyahss day aystoamahgoa |
| How many do I take? | ¿Cuántos(as) debo tomar? | kwahntoass(ahss) daybhoa toamahr |
| Can you make up this prescription for me? | ¿Puede usted prepararme esta receta? | pwaydhay oostaydh praypahrahrmay aystah raythaytah |
| Shall I wait? | ¿Espero? | ayspayroa |
| Can I get it without a prescription? | ¿Puede dármelo sin receta? | pwaydhay dahrmayloa seen raythaytah |

DOCTOR, see page 137

| Can I have a/an/ some ...? | ¿Puede darme ...? | pwaydhay dahrmay |
|---|---|---|
| antiseptic cream | una crema anti- séptica | oonah kraymah ahntee- ssaypteekah |
| aspirins | unas aspirinas | oonahss ahspeereenahss |
| bandage | una venda | oonah bayndah |
| elastic bandage | vendas elásticas | bayndahss aylahsteekahss |
| Band Aids | esparadrapo | ehspahrahdrahpoa |
| contraceptives | unos anticoncep- tivos | oonoass ahnteekoanthayp- teebhoass |
| corn plasters | unos callicidas | oonoass kahlyeethee- dhahss |
| cotton wool (ab- sorbent cotton) | algodón | ahlgoadon |
| cough drops | unas gotas para la tos | oonahss goatahss pahrah lah toss |
| disinfectant | un desinfectante | oon daysseenfehktahntay |
| ear drops | gotas para los oídos | goatahss pahrah loss oaeedhoass |
| Elastoplast | esparadrapo | ehspahrahdrahpoa |
| eye drops | unas gotas para los ojos | oonahss goatahss pahrah loss okhoass |
| gauze | gasa | gahssah |
| insect repellent/ spray | un repelente/spray para insectos | oon raypaylayntay/aysprehy pahrah eensehktoass |
| iodine | yodo | yoadhoa |
| laxative | un laxante | oon lahksahntay |
| mouthwash | unos gargarismos | oonoass gahrgahreesmoass |
| sanitary towels (napkins) | unos paños higiénicos | oonoass pahñoass eekhyayneekoass |
| sleeping pills | un somnífero | oon soamneefayroa |
| suppositories | unos supositorios | oonoass soopoasseetoaryoass |
| surgical dressing | unas hilas | oonahss eelahss |
| ... tablets | unas tabletas para ... | oonahs tahblaytahss pahrah |
| tampons | unos tampones higiénicos | oonoass tahmpoanayss eekhyayneekoass |
| thermometer | un termómetro | oon tayrmoamaytroa |
| throat lozenges | unas pastillas para la garganta | oonahss pahsteelyahss pahrah lah gahrgahntah |
| tranquillizer | un sedante | oon saydhahntay |

---

¡VENENO!              POISON!
SOLO PARA USO EXTERNO    FOR EXTERNAL USE ONLY

## 2—Toiletry   *Artículos de tocador*

| I'd like a/an/some ... | **Quisiera ...** | keessyayrah |
|---|---|---|
| acne cream | **una crema para el acné** | oonah kraymah pahrah ayl ahknay |
| after-shave lotion | **una loción para después del afeitado** | oonah loathyon pahrah dayspwayss dayl ahfaytahdhoa |
| astringent | **un astringente** | oon ahstreenkhayntay |
| bath salts | **sales de baño** | sahlayss day bahñoa |
| cologne | **agua de colonia** | ahgwah day koaloanyah |
| cream | **una crema** | oonah kraymah |
| cleansing cream | **limpiadora** | leempyahdhoarah |
| cold cream | **nutritiva** | nootreeteebhah |
| foundation cream | **maquillaje** | mahkeelyahkhay |
| moisturizing cream | **hidratante** | eedrahtahntay |
| night cream | **de noche** | day noachay |
| cuticle remover | **un quitacutículas** | oon keetahkooteekoolahss |
| deodorant | **un desodorante** | oon dayssoadhoarahntay |
| emery boards | **unas limas de papel** | oonahss leemahss day pahpehl |
| eye liner | **un perfilador de ojos** | oon pehrfeelahdhor day okhoss |
| eye pencil | **un lápiz de ojos** | oon lahpeeth day okhoss |
| eye shadow | **una sombra de ojos** | oonah soambrah day okhoss |
| face powder | **polvos de la cara** | poalboass day lah kahrah |
| foot cream | **una crema para los pies** | oonah kraymah pahrah loss pyayss |
| hand cream/lotion | **una crema/loción para las manos** | oonah kraymah/loathyon pahrah lahss mahnoass |
| lipsalve | **cacao para los labios** | kahkahoa pahrah loss lahbhyoass |
| lipstick | **un lápiz de labios** | oon lahpeeth day lahbhyoass |
| make-up remover pads | **unas toallitas de maquillage** | oonahss toaahlyeetahss day mahkeelyahkhay |
| mascara | **pintura de pestañas** | peentoorah day pehstahñahss |
| nail clippers | **alicates de uñas** | ahleekahtayss day ooñahss |
| nail file | **una lima de uñas** | oonah leemah day ooñahss |
| nail polish | **un esmalte de uñas** | oon ehsmahltay day ooñahss |
| nail polish remover | **acetona quita-esmalte de uñas** | ahthaytoanah keetahehsmahltay day ooñahss |
| nail scissors | **tijeras de uñas** | teekhayrahss day ooñahss |
| perfume | **perfume** | pehrfoomay |

| powder | polvos | poalboass |
| razor | una máquina (navaja) de afeitar | oonah mahkeenah (nah-bhahkhah) day ahfaytahr |
| razor blades | unas hojas de afeitar | oonahss oakhahss day ahfaytahr |
| rouge (blusher) | colorete | koaloaraytay |
| safety pins | unos imperdibles | oonoass eempehrdeeblayss |
| shaving cream | crema de afeitar | kraymah day afaytahr |
| soap | jabón | khahbhon |
| sponge | una esponja | oonah ehsponkhah |
| sun-tan cream | una crema solar | oonah kraymah soalahr |
| talcum powder | polvos de talco | poalboass day tahlkoa |
| tissues | unos pañuelos de papel | oonoass pahñwayloass day pahpehl |
| toilet paper | papel higiénico | pahpehl eekhyayneekoa |
| toothbrush | un cepillo de dientes | oon thaypeelyoa day dyayntayss |
| toothpaste | pasta de dientes | pahstah day dyayntayss |
| tweezers | unas pinzas | oonahss peenthahss |

## For your hair *Para su cabello*

| colour shampoo | un champú colorante | oon champoo koaloarahntay |
| comb | un peine | oon paynay |
| dye | una tintura | oonah teentoorah |
| hairbrush | un cepillo para el pelo | oon thaypeelyoa pahrah ayl pehloa |
| hairgrips (bobby pins) | unas horquillas de pinza | oonahss orkeelyahss day peenthah |
| hair lotion | un loción capilar | oonah loathyon kahpeelahr |
| hair spray | una laca para el pelo | oonah lahkah pahrah ayl payloa |
| hairpins | unas horquillas | oonahss oarkeelyahss |
| rollers | unos rulos | oonoass rooloass |
| setting lotion | un fijador | oon feekhahdhoar |
| (dry) shampoo for dry/greasy (oily) hair | un champú (seco) para cabellos secos/grasos | oon chahmpoo (saykoa) pahrah kahbhaylyoass saykoass/grahssoass |
| tint | un tinte | oon teentay |

## For the baby *Para el bebé*

| baby food | alimento para bebé | ahleemayntoa pahrah baybhay |
| bib | un babero | oon bahbhayroa |
| dummy (pacifier) | un chupete | oon choopaytay |
| feeding bottle | un biberón | oon beebhayroan |
| nappies (diapers) | pañales | pahñahlayss |
| teat (nipple) | una tetina | oonah tayteenah |

### Clothing   *Prendas de vestir*

If you want to buy something specific, prepare yourself in advance. Look at the list of clothing on page 117. Get some idea of the colour, material and size you want. They're all listed on the next few pages.

| | | |
|---|---|---|
| I'd like ... | **Quisiera ...** | keessyayrah |
| I want ... for a 10 year-old boy/girl. | **Quiero ... para un niño/una niña de 10 años.** | kyayroa ... pahrah oon neeñoa/oonah neeñah day 10 ahñoass |
| I want something like this. | **Quiero algo como esto.** | kyayroa ahlgoa koamoa aystoa |
| I like the one in the window. | **Me gusta el que está en el escaparate.** | may goostah ayl kay aystah ayn ayl eskahpah-rahtay |
| How much is that per metre? | **¿Cuánto cuesta el metro?** | kwahntoa kwaystah ayl maytroa |

| | | | |
|---|---|---|---|
| 1 centimetre (cm.) | = 0.39 in. | 1 inch | = 2.54 cm. |
| 1 metre (m.) | = 39.37 in. | 1 foot | = 30.5 cm. |
| 10 metres (m.) | = 32.81 ft. | 1 yard | = 0.91 m. |

### Colour   *Color*

| | | |
|---|---|---|
| I want something in ... | **Quiero algo en ...** | kyayroa ahlgoa ayn |
| I want a darker/lighter shade. | **Quiero un tono más oscuro/claro.** | kyayroa oon toanoa mahss oaskooroa/klahroa |
| I want something to match this. | **Quiero algo que haga juego con esto.** | kyayroa ahlgoa kay ahgah khwaygoa kon aystoa |
| I don't like the colour. | **No me gusta el color.** | noa may goostah ayl koaloar |

**liso**
(leesoa)

**rayas**
(rahyahss)

**lunares**
(loonahrayss)

**cuadros**
(kwahdroass)

**estampado**
(ehstahmpahdhoa)

| beige | beige* | "behzh" |
| black | negro | nehgroa |
| blue | azul | ahthool |
| brown | marrón | mahrron |
| cream | crema | kraymah |
| golden | dorado | doarahdhoa |
| green | verde | behrday |
| grey | gris | greess |
| mauve | malva | mahlbah |
| orange | naranja | nahrahnkhah |
| pink | rosa | rossah |
| purple | purpúreo | poorpoorehoa |
| red | rojo | roakhoa |
| scarlet | escarlata | ayskahrlahtah |
| silver | plateado | plahtayahdhoa |
| turquoise | turquesa | toorkayssah |
| white | blanco | blahnkoa |
| yellow | amarillo | ahmahreelyoa |
| light ... | ... claro | klahroa |
| dark ... | ... oscuro | oaskooroa |

## Material  *Tejidos*

| Do you have anything in ...? | ¿Tiene usted algo en ...? | tyaynay oostaydh ahlgoa ayn |
| I want a cotton blouse. | Quisiera una blusa de algodón. | keessyayrah oonah bloosah day ahlgoadon |
| Is that handmade/ made here? | ¿Está hecho a mano/ aquí? | aystah aychoa ah mahnoa/ahkee |
| Is it ...? | ¿Es ...? | ayss |
| pure cotton/wool | puro algodón/ pura lana | pooroa ahlgoadhon/poorah lahnah |
| colour fast | color fijo | koaloar feekhoa |
| machine/hand washable | lavable en máquina/ a mano | lahbhahblay ayn mahkeenah/ah mahnoa |
| Can it be dry-cleaned? | ¿Puede limpiarse en seco? | pwaydhay leempyahrsay ayn saykoa |
| Will it shrink? | ¿Encogerá? | aynkoakhayrah |

---

* For feminine and plural forms, see grammar section page 159 (adjectives).

| I want something thinner. | **Quiero algo más tenue.** | kyayroa ahlgoa mahss taynooay |
| Do you have any better quality? | **¿Tiene usted una calidad mejor?** | tyaynah oostaydh oonah kahleedhadh mehkhor |
| What's it made of? | **¿De qué está hecho?** | day kay aystah aychoa |

| cambric | **batista** | bahteestah |
| camel hair | **pelo de camello** | pehloa day kahmaylyoa |
| chiffon | **gasa** | gahssah |
| corduroy | **pana** | pahnah |
| cotton | **algodón** | ahlgoadon |
| crepe | **crepé** | kraypay |
| denim | **algodón asargado** | ahlgoadon ahssahrgahdhoa |
| felt | **fieltro** | fyayltroa |
| flannel | **franela** | frahnaylah |
| gabardine | **gabardina** | gahbahrdeenah |
| lace | **encaje** | aynkahkhay |
| leather | **cuero** | kwayroa |
| linen | **hilo** | eeloa |
| pique | **piqué** | peekay |
| poplin | **popelín** | poapayleen |
| satin | **raso** | rahssoa |
| serge | **estameña** | aystahmayñah |
| silk | **seda** | saydhah |
| suede | **ante** | ahntay |
| taffeta | **tafetán** | tahfaytahn |
| terrycloth | **tela de toalla** | taylah day toaahlyah |
| tulle | **tul** | tool |
| tweed | **cheviot** | chaybhyoat |
| velvet | **terciopelo** | tehrthyoapehloa |
| wool | **lana** | lahnah |
| worsted | **estambre** | aystahmbray |
| artificial | **artificial** | ahrteefeethyahl |
| synthetic | **sintético** | seentayteekoa |

## Size *Talla*

| My size is 38. | **Mi talla es la 38.** | mee tahlyah ayss lah 38 |
| Could you measure me? | **¿Puede usted medirme?** | pwaydhay oostaydh maydheermay |
| I don't know Spanish sizes. | **No conozco las tallas españolas.** | noa koanoathkoa lahss tahlyahss ayspahñolahss |

**This is your size**   *Esta es su talla*

Sizes can vary somewhat from country to country and from one manufacturer to another, so be sure to try on shoes and clothing before you buy.

**Women**   *Señoras*

| Dresses/Suits | | | | | |
|---|---|---|---|---|---|
| American | 8 | 10 | 12 | 14 | 16 | 18 |
| British | 10 | 12 | 14 | 16 | 18 | 20 |
| Continental | 36 | 38 | 40 | 42 | 44 | 46 |

| Stockings | | | | | | Shoes | | | |
|---|---|---|---|---|---|---|---|---|---|
| American | | | | | | 6 | 7 | 8 | 9 |
| British | 8 | 8½ | 9 | 9½ | 10 | 10½ | 4½ | 5½ | 6½ | 7½ |
| Continental | 0 | 1. | 2 | 3 | 4 | 5 | 37 | 39 | 40 | 41 |

**Men**   *Caballeros*

| Suits/Overcoats | | | | | | Shirts | | | |
|---|---|---|---|---|---|---|---|---|---|
| American | | | | | | | 15 | 16 | 17 | 18 |
| British | 36 | 38 | 40 | 42 | 44 | 46 | | | | |
| Continental | 46 | 48 | 50 | 52 | 54 | 56 | 38 | 41 | 43 | 45 |

| Shoes | | | | | | | | | |
|---|---|---|---|---|---|---|---|---|---|
| American | | | | | | | 9 | 9½ | 10 | 11 |
| British | 5 | 6 | 7 | 8 | 8½ | | | | | |
| Continental | 38 | 39 | 41 | 42 | 43 | 43 | 44 | 44 | 45 |

**A good fit?**   *Una buena caída*

| | | |
|---|---|---|
| Can I try it on? | **¿Puedo probármelo?** | pwaydhoa probhahrmayloa |
| Where's the fitting room? | **¿Dónde está el probador?** | doanday aystah ayl probhahdhor |
| Is there a mirror? | **¿Tiene usted un espejo?** | tyaynay oostaydh oon ayspaykhoa |
| It fits very well. | **Me queda muy bien.** | may kaydhah mwee byayn |

NUMBERS, see page 147

| It doesn't fit. | No me queda bien. | noa may kaydhah byayn |
| It's too ... | Es demasiado ... | ayss daymahssyahdhoa |
| short/long | corto/largo | koartoa/lahrgoa |
| tight/loose | ajustado/ancho | ahkhoostahdoa/ahnchoa |
| How long will it take to alter? | ¿Cuánto tardarán en arreglarlo? | kwahntoa tahrdahrahn ayn ahrrayglahrloa |

## Shoes  Zapatos

| I'd like a pair of ... | Quisiera un par de ... | keessyayrah oon pahr day |
| (rain) boots | botas (par la lluvia) | boatahss pahrah lah lyoobhyah |
| plimsolls (sneakers) | zapatos de lona | thahpahtoass day loanah |
| sandals | sandalias | sahndahlyahss |
| shoes | zapatos | thahpahtoass |
| flat/with a heel | planos/con tacón | plahnoass/kon tahkon |
| leather/suede | de cuero/de ante | day kwayroa/day ahntay |
| slippers | zapatillas | tahpahteelyahss |
| These are too ... | Estos son demasiado ... | aystoass son daymahssyahdhoa |
| narrow/wide | estrechos/anchos | aystraychoass/ahnchoass |
| large/small | grandes/pequeños | grahndayss/paykayñoass |
| Do you have a smaller/larger size? | ¿Tiene una talla más pequeña/grande? | tyaynay oonah tahlyah mahss/paykayñah/grahnday |
| Do you have the same in brown/black? | ¿Tiene usted lo mismo en marrón/negro? | tyaynay oostaydh loa meessmoa ayn mahrron/nehgroa |
| I need some shoe polish/shoelaces. | Necesito crema/cordones para zapatos. | naythaysseetoa kraymah/koardoanayss pahrah thahpahtoass |

Shoes worn out? Here's the key to getting them fixed again:

| Can you repair these shoes? | ¿Puede usted reparar estos zapatos? | pwaydhay oostaydh raypahrahr aystoass thahpahtoass |
| I want new soles and heels. | Quiero nuevas suelas y tacones. | kyayroa nwaybhahss swaylahss ee tahkoanayss |
| When will they be ready? | ¿Cuándo estarán listos? | kwahndoa aystahrahn leestoass |

COLOURS, see page 113

## Clothes and accessories   *Ropa y accessorios*

| I'd like a/an/some ... | Quisiera ... | keessyayrah |
|---|---|---|
| bathing cap | un gorro de baño | oon gorroa day bahñoa |
| bathing suit | un traje de baño | oon trahkhay day bahñoa |
| bathrobe | un albornoz | oon ahlboarnoth |
| blazer | un blázer | oon blahther |
| blouse | una blusa | oonah bloossah |
| bow tie | una corbata de lazo | oonah korbahtah day lahthoa |
| bra | un sostén | oon soastayn |
| braces | unos tirantes | oonoass teerahntayss |
| briefs | unos calzoncillos | oonoass kahlthontheelyoass |
| cap | una gorra | oonah gorrah |
| cardigan | una chaqueta de punto | oonah chakaytah day poontoa |
| coat (woman's) | un abrigo | oon ahbreegoa |
| coat (man's) | un gabán | oon gahbhahn |
| dinner jacket | un smoking | oon smoakeeng |
| dress | un vestido | oon baysteedhoa |
| dressing gown | una bata | oonah bahtah |
| evening dress (woman's) | un traje de noche | oon trahkhay day noachay |
| garter belt | un portaligas | oon poartahleegahss |
| garters | unas ligas | oonahss leegahss |
| girdle | una faja | oonah fahkhah |
| gloves | unos guantes | oonoass gwahntayss |
| handbag | un bolso de mano | oon boalsoa day mahnoa |
| handkerchief | un pañuelo | oon pahñwayloa |
| hat | un sombrero | oon soambrayroa |
| jacket | una chaqueta | oonah chakaytah |
| jeans | unos tejanos | oonoass tehkhahnoass |
| jersey | un jersey | oon khayrsay |
| nightdress | un camisón | oon kahmeesson |
| panties | unas bragas | oonahss brahgahss |
| pants (Am.) | unos pantalones | oonoass pahntahloanayss |
| panty girdle | una faja braga | oonah fahkhah brahgah |
| panty hose | unos leotardos | oonoass layoatahrdoass |
| pullover | un pullover | oon pooloabhehr |
| roll-neck (turtle-neck)/round-neck/V-neck | cuello vuelto/ redondo/en forma de V | kwaylyoa bwehltoa/ raydoandoa/ayn foarmah day bayeh |
| with long/short sleeves | con mangas largas/ cortas | kon mahngahss lahrgahss/ koartahss |
| without sleeves | sin mangas | seen mahngahss |

| | | |
|---|---|---|
| pyjamas | un pijama | oon peekhahmah |
| raincoat | un impermeable | oon eempehrmayahblay |
| scarf | una bufanda | oonah boofahndah |
| shirt | una camisa | oonah kahmeessah |
| shorts | unos pantalones cortos | oonoass pahntahloanayss koartoass |
| skirt | una falda | oonah fahldah |
| slip | una combinación | oonah koambeenahthyon |
| socks | unos calcetines | oonoass kahlthayteenayss. |
| stockings | unas medias | oonahss maydhyahss |
| suit (man's) | un traje | oon trahkhay |
| suit (woman's) | un vestido | oon baysteedhoa |
| suspenders | unos tirantes | oonoass teerahntayss |
| sweater | un suéter | oon swaytehr |
| sweatshirt | un suéter de tela de punto | oon swaytehr day taylah day poontoa |
| swimming trunks | un bañador | oon bañahdoar |
| swimsuit | un traje de baño | oon trahkhay day bahñoa |
| T-shirt | una camiseta | oonah kahmeessaytah |
| tie | una corbata | oonah korbahtah |
| tights | unos leotardos | oonoass layoatahrdoass |
| tracksuit | un chandal de entrenamiento | oon chahndahl day ehntraynahmyayntoa |
| trousers | unos pantalones | oonoass pahntahloanayss |
| tuxedo | un smoking | oon smoakeeng |
| twin set | un conjunto de lana | oon koankhoontoa day lahnah |
| umbrella | un paraguas | oon pahrahgwahss |
| underpants | unos calzoncillos | oonoass kahlthontheelyoass |
| undershirt | una camiseta | oonah kahmeessaytah |
| vest (Am.) | un chaleco | oon chahlaykoa |
| vest (Br.) | una camiseta | oonah kahmeessaytah |
| waistcoat | un chaleco | oon chahlaykoa |

| | | |
|---|---|---|
| belt | un cinturón | oon theentooron |
| buckle | una hebilla | oonah aybheelyah |
| button | un botón | oon boaton |
| collar | un cuello | oon kwaylyoa |
| elastic | un elástico | oon aylahsteekoa |
| pocket | un bolsillo | oon boalseelyoa |
| press stud (snap fastener) | un broche de presión | oon broachay day prayssyon |
| zip (zipper) | una cremallera | oonah kraymahlyayrah |

**Electrical appliances**  *Aparatos eléctricos*

Today 220-volt A.C. 50 cycles is becoming standard, but older installations of 125 volts can still be found. So check the voltage before you plug your appliance in. Don't forget to take along a plug adaptor: two-pin (prong) continental plugs are used in Spain.

| | | |
|---|---|---|
| What's the voltage? | **¿Cuál es el voltaje?** | kwahl ayss ayl boaltahkhay |
| This is broken. Can you repair it? | **Esto está roto.** **¿Puede usted arreglarlo?** | aystoa aystah roatoa. pwaydhay oostaydh ahrrayglahrloa |
| I'd like (to hire) a video cassette/ video recorder. | **Quisiera (alquilar) una video-cassette/ video-grabadora.** | keessyayrah (ahlkeelahr) oonah beedhayoa-kahssayttay/beedhayoa-grahbhahdhoarah |
| Can you show me how it works? | **¿Puede mostrarme cómo funciona?** | pwaydhay moastrahrmay koamoa foonthyonah |
| I'd like a/an/some ... | **Quisiera ...** | keessyayrah |
| adaptor | **un adaptador** | oon ahdhahptahdhor |
| amplifier | **un amplificador** | oon ahmpleefeekahdhor |
| battery | **una pila** | oonah peelah |
| bulb | **una bombilla** | oonah boambeelyah |
| electric toothbrush | **un cepillo de dientes eléctrico** | oon thaypeelyoa day dyayntayss aylayktreekoa |
| hair dryer | **un secador de pelo** | oon saykahdhor day pehloa |
| headphones | **un casco con auriculares** | oon kahskoa kon owreekoolahrayss |
| (travelling) iron | **una plancha (de viaje)** | oonah plahnchah day byahkhay |
| lamp | **una lámpara** | oonah lahmpahrah |
| plug | **una clavija de enchufe** | oonah klahbheekhah day aynchoofay |
| portable ... | **... portátil** | ... portahteel |
| radio | **una radio** | oonah rahdhyoa |
| car radio | **una radio para coche** | oonah rahdhyoa pahrah koachay |
| record player | **un tocadiscos** | oon toakahdheeskoass |
| shaver | **una máquina de afeitar eléctrica** | oonah mahkeenah day ahfaytahr aylayktreekah |
| speakers | **unos altavoces** | oonoass ahltahbhoathayss |
| (cassette) tape recorder | **un magnetófono (cassette)** | oon mahgnaytofoanoa (kahssayttay) |
| transformer | **un transformador** | oon trahnsformahdhor |

## Grocery   *Tienda de comestibles*

| I want some bread, please. | Quiero pan, por favor. | kyayroa pahn por fabhor |
|---|---|---|
| What sort of cheese do you have? | ¿Qué clases de queso tiene? | kay klahssayss day kayssoa tyaynay |
| A piece of ... | Un trozo ... | oon troathoa |
| that one | de ése | day ayssay |
| the one on the shelf | del que está en el estante | dayl kay aystah ayn ayl aystahntay |
| I'd like one of these and two of those. | Quisiera uno de éstos y dos de ésos. | keessyayrah oonoa day aystoass ee oonoa day ayssoass |
| May I help myself? | ¿Puedo servirme yo mismo? | pwaydhoa sehrbeermay yoa meesmoa |
| I'd like ... | Quisiera ... | keessyayrah |
| a kilo of apples | un kilo de manzanas | oon keeloa day mahnthahnahss |
| half a kilo of tomatoes | medio kilo de tomates | maydhyoa keeloa day toamahtayss |
| 100 g of butter | 100 gr. de mantequilla | 100 grahmoass day mahntaykeelyah |
| a litre of milk | un litro de leche | oon leetroa day laychay |
| 4 slices of ham | 4 rebanadas de jamón | 4 raybhahnahdhahss day khahmon |
| a packet of tea | un paquete de té | oon pahkaytay day tay |
| a jar of honey | un tarro de miel | oon tahrroa day myehl |
| a tin (can) of pears | una lata de peras | oonah lahtah day pehrahss |
| a tube of mustard | un tubo de mostaza | oon toobhoa day moastahthah |

---

1 kilogram or kilo (kg.) = 1000 grams (g.)

| 100 g. = 3.5 oz. | ½ kg. = 1.1 lbs. |
|---|---|
| 200 g. = 7.0 oz. | 1 kg. = 2.2 lbs. |

1 oz. =   28.35 g.
1 lb. = 453.60 g.

---

1 litre (l.) = 0.88 imp. quarts = 1.06 U.S. quarts

| 1 imp. quart = 1.14 l. | 1 U.S. quart = 0.95 l. |
|---|---|
| 1 imp. gallon = 4.55 l. | 1 U.S. gallon = 3.8  l. |

FOOD, see also page 63

# Jeweller's—Watchmaker's *Joyería – Relojería*

| I'd like a small present for ... | Quisiera un rega-lito para ... | keesyayrah oon raygah-leetoa pahrah |
|---|---|---|
| Is this real silver? | ¿Es esto de plata auténtica? | ayss aystoa day plahtah owtaynteekah |
| Do you have any-thing in gold? | ¿Tiene usted algo de oro? | tyaynay oostaydh ahlgoa day oaroa |
| How many carats is this? | ¿De cuántos quilates es esto? | day kwahntoass keelah-tayss ayss aystoa |
| Can you repair this watch? | ¿Puede arreglar este reloj? | pwaydhay ahrrayglahr aystay rehlokh |
| I'd like a/an/some ... | Quisiera ... | keessyayrah |
| alarm clock | un despertador | oon dayspayrtahdhor |
| bangle | una esclava | oonah aysklahbhah |
| battery | una pila | oonah peelah |
| bracelet | una pulsera | oonah poolsayrah |
| charm bracelet | pulsera de fetiches | poolsayrah day fayteechayss |
| brooch | un broche | oon brochay |
| chain | una cadena | oonah kahdhaynah |
| charm | un amuleto | oon ahmoolaytoa |
| cigarette case | una pitillera | oonah peeteelyayrah |
| cigarette lighter | un encendedor | oon aynthayndaydhor |
| clip | un clip | oon kleep |
| clock | un reloj | oon rehlokh |
| cross | una cruz | oonah krooth |
| cuff links | unos gemelos | oonoass khaymayloass |
| cutlery | unos cubiertos | oonoass koobhyehrtoass |
| earrings | unos pendientes | oonoass payndyayntayss |
| jewel box | un joyero | oon khoyayroa |
| mechanical pencil | un lapicero | oon lahpeethayroa |
| necklace | un collar | oon koalyahr |
| pendant | un medallón | oon maydhahlyon |
| pin | un alfiler | oon ahlfeelehr |
| pocket watch | un reloj de bolsillo | oon rehlokh day boalseelyoa |
| powder compact | una polvera | oonah poalbayrah |
| propelling pencil | un lapicero | oon lahpeethayroa |
| ring | una sortija | oonah sorteekhah |
| engagement ring | sortija de pedida | sorteekhah day paydheedhah |
| signet ring | sortija de sello | sorteekhah day saylyoa |
| wedding ring | un anillo de boda | oon ahneelyoa day boadhah |

| rosary | un rosario de cuentas | oon roassahryoa day kwayntahss |
| silverware | unos objetos de plata | oonoass obkhaytoass day plahtah |
| tie clip | un sujetador de corbata | oon sookhaytahdhor day korbahtah |
| tie pin | un alfiler de corbata | oon ahlfeelehr day korbahtah |
| watch (wristwatch) | un reloj (de pulsera) | oon rehlokh (day poolsayrah) |
| automatic | automático | aotoamahteekoa |
| with a second hand | con segundero manecilla | kon saygoondayroa mahnaytheelyah |
| with quartz movement | con mecanismo de cuarzo | kon maykahneesmoa day kwahrthoa |
| watchstrap (watchband) | una correa de reloj | oonah korrehah day rehlokh |

| amber | ámbar | ahmbahr |
| amethyst | amatista | ahmahteestah |
| copper | cobre | koabray |
| coral | coral | korahl |
| crystal | cristal | kreestahl |
| cut glass | cristal tallado | kreestahl tahlyahdhoa |
| diamond | diamante | dyahmahntay |
| emerald | esmeralda | aysmayrahldah |
| enamel | esmalte | aysmahltay |
| gold | oro | oaroa |
| gold plate | lámina de oro | lahmeenah day oaroa |
| ivory | marfil | mahrfeel |
| jade | jade | khahdheh |
| onyx | ónix | oneekss |
| pearl | perla | pehrlah |
| pewter | peltre | pehltray |
| platinum | platino | plahteenoa |
| ruby | rubí | roobhee |
| sapphire | zafiro | thahfeeroa |
| silver | plata | plahtah |
| silver plate | plata chapada | plahtah chahpahdhah |
| stainless steel | acero inoxidable | ahthayroa eenokseedhahblay |
| topaz | topacio | topahthyoa |
| turquoise | turquesa | toorkayssah |

## Optician *El óptico*

| Where can I find an optician? | ¿Dónde puedo encontrar un óptico? | doanday pwaydhoa aynkoantrahr oon oapteekoa |
|---|---|---|
| I've broken my glasses. | Se me han roto las gafas. | say may ahn roatoa lahss gahfahss |
| Can you repair them for me? | ¿Me las puede usted arreglar? | may lahss pwaydhay oostaydh ahrrayglahr |
| When will they be ready? | ¿Cuándo estarán listas? | kwahndhoa aystahrahn leestahss |
| Can you change the lenses? | ¿Puede cambiar los lentes? | pwaydhay kahmbyahr loss layntayss |
| I want tinted lenses. | Quiero cristales ahumados. | kyayroa kreestahlayss owmahdhoass |
| I'd like to have my eyes checked. | Quisiera que me controlara los ojos. | keessyayrah kay may koantroalahrah loass oakhoass |
| I'm short-sighted/ long-sighted. | Soy miope/présbite. | soy myoapay/praysbeetay |
| I want some contact lenses. | Quiero lentes de contacto. | kyayroa layntayss day kontahktoa |
| I've lost a contact lens. | He perdido un lente de contacto. | ay payrdheedhoa oon layntay day koantahktoa |
| I have hard/soft lenses. | Tengo lentes duros/ suaves. | tayngoa layntays dooroas/ swahbhayss |
| Do you have some solution for contact lenses? | ¿Tiene una solución para lentes de contacto? | tyaynay oonah soaloothyon pahrah layntayss day koantahktoa |
| May I look in a mirror? | ¿Puedo verme en un espejo? | pwaydhoa bayrmay ayn oon ayspaykhoa |
| I'd like a spectacle case. | Quisiera un estuche para gafas. | keessyayrah oon aystoo- chay pahrah gahfahss |
| I'd like to buy a pair of binoculars. | Quisiera comprar unos binoculares. | keessyayrah komprahr oonoass beenoakoolah- rayss |
| I'd like to buy a pair of sunglasses. | Quisiera comprar unas gafas de sol. | keessyayrah komprahr oonahss gahfass day sol |
| How much do I owe you? | ¿Cuánto le debo? | kwahntoa lay daybhoa |

NUMBERS, see page 147

## Photography   *Fotografía*

| I want a camera. | **Quisiera una cámara.** | keessyayrah oonah kahmahrah |
|---|---|---|
| automatic/in-expensive/simple | **automática/ barata/sencilla** | owtoamahteekah/ bahrahtah/sayntheelyah |
| Show me a cine (movie) camera, please. | **Enséñeme una cámara de filmar, por favor.** | aynsaynyaymay oonah kahmahrah day feelmahr por fahbhor |
| I'd like to have some passport photos taken. | **Quisiera que me haga unas fotos para pasaporte.** | keessyayrah kay may ahgah oonahss foatoass pahrah pahssahpoartay |

## Film   *Rollos/Películas*

| I'd like a film for this camera. | **Quisiera un rollo para esta cámara.** | keessyayrah oon roalyoa pahrah aystah kahmahrah |
|---|---|---|
| black and white | **en blanco y negro** | ayn blahnkoa ee naygroa |
| colour | **en color** | ayn koaloar |
| colour negative | **negativo de color** | naygahteebhoa day koaloar |
| colour slide | **diapositivas** | dyahposseteebhahss |
| cartridge | **un cartucho** | oon kahrtoochoa |
| disc film | **un disco-película** | oon deeskoa payleekoolah |
| roll film | **un carrete/rollo** | oon kahrraytay/roalyoa |
| cine (movie) film | **una película** | oonah payleekoolah |
| super eight | **super ocho** | soopehr oachoa |
| video tape | **una cinta video** | oonah theentah beedhayoa |
| 24/36 exposures | **24/36 exposiciones** | baynteekwahtroa/trayntah ee sayss aykspoasseethyonayss |
| this ASA/DIN number | **este número de ASA/DIN** | aystay noomayroa day ahssah/deen |
| this size | **de este tamaño** | day aystay tahmahñoa |
| artificial light/ daylight type | **para luz artificial/ del dia** | pahrah looth ahrteefee-thyahl/dayl deeah |
| fast (high-speed) | **rápido** | rahpeedhoa |
| fine grain | **de grano fino** | day grahnoa feenoa |

## Processing   \ *Revelado*

| How much do you charge for develop-ing/printing? | **¿Qué cobra por el revelado/la impresión?** | kay koabrah por ayl raybhaylahdhoa/lah eemprayssyon |
|---|---|---|

NUMBERS, see page 147

| I want ... prints of each negative. | Quiero ... copias de cada negativo. | kyayroa ... koapyahss day kahdhah naygahteebhoa |
| with a mat/glossy finish | con acabado mate/ de brillo | kon ahkahbhahdhoa mahtay/day breelyoa |
| Will you please enlarge this? | ¿Haría usted una ampliación de ésta, por favor? | ahreeah oostaydh oonah ahmplyahthyon day aystah por fahbhor |
| When will the photos be ready? | ¿Cuándo estarán listas las fotos? | kwahndoa aystahrahn lees-tahss lahss foatoas |

## Accessories and repairs  *Accesorios y reparaciones*

| I want a/an ... | Quisiera ... | keessyayrah |
| battery | una pila | oonah peelah |
| cable release | un cable del dispa-rador | oon kahblay dayl dees-pahrahdhoar |
| camera case | una funda | oonah foondah |
| (electronic) flash | un flash (electrónico) | oon flash (aylayktroa-neekoa) |
| filter | un filtro | oon feeltroa |
| for black and white | para blanco y negro | pahrah blahnkoa ee naygroa |
| for colour | para color | pahrah koaloar |
| lens | un objetivo | oon obkhayteebhoa |
| telephoto lens | de acercamiento | day ahthayrkahmyayntoa |
| wide-angle lens | gran angular | grahn ahngoolahr |
| lens cap | un capuchón para el objetivo | oon kapoochon pahrah ayl obkhayteebhoa |
| This camera doesn't work. Can you repair it? | Esta cámara está estropeada. ¿Puede usted repararla? | aystah kahmahrah aystah aystroapehahdhah. pwaydhay oostaydh raypahrahrlah |
| The film is jammed. | La película está atrancada. | lah payleekoolah aystah ahtrahnkahdhah |
| There's something wrong with the ... | Hay algo que va mal en ... | igh ahlgoa kay bah mahl ayn |
| exposure counter | la escala de expo-sición | lah ayskahlah day aykspoasseethyon |
| film winder | el enrollador | ayl aynroalyahdhor |
| light meter | el exposímetro | ayl aykspoasseemehtroa |
| rangefinder | el telémetro | ayl taylaymaytroa |
| shutter | el obturador | ayl obtoorahdhor |

## Tobacconist's   *Tabacos*

Most Spanish cigarettes are made of strong, black tobacco.
Nearly all major foreign brands are available in Spain at two
to three times the price of local cigarettes.

| | | |
|---|---|---|
| A packet/carton of cigarettes, please. | Una cajetilla/un cartón de cigarrillos, por favor. | oonah kahkhayteelyah/oon kahrton day theegahr-reelyoass por fahbhor |
| I'd like a box of ... | Quisiera una caja de ... | keessyayrah oonah kahkhah day |
| May I have a/an/some ..., please? | ¿Puede darme ..., por favor? | pwayday dahrmay por fahbhor |
| candy | unos caramelos | oonoass kahrahmayloass |
| chewing gum | un chicle | oon cheeklay |
| chocolate | un chocolate | oon choakoalahtay |
| cigarettes | unos cigarrillos | oonoass theegahrreelyoass |
|   American |   americanos |   ahmayreekahnoass |
|   English |   ingleses |   eenglayssayss |
|   menthol |   mentolados |   mayntoalahdhoass |
|   mild/strong |   suaves/fuertes |   swahbhayss/fwehrtayss |
| cigarette lighter | un encendedor | oon aynthayndaydhor |
| cigarette paper | papel para cigarrillos | pahpehl pahrah theegahrreelyoass |
| cigars | unos puros | oonoass pooroass |
| flints | unas piedras de mechero | oonahss pyaydrahss day maychayroa |
| lighter fluid/gas | gasolina/gas para encendedor | gahssoaleenah/gahss pahrah aynthayndaydhor |
| matches | unas cerillas | oonahss thayreelyahss |
| pipe | una pipa | oonah peepah |
| pipe cleaners | unas limpiapipas | oonahss leempyahpeepahss |
| pipe tobacco | tabaco para pipa | tahbhahkoa pahrah peepah |
| pipe tool | utensilios para pipa | ootaynseelyoass pahrah peepah |
| post cards | unas tarjetas postales | oonahss tahrkhaytahss poastahlayss |
| snuff | rapé | rahpay |
| stamps | unos sellos | oonoass saylyoass |
| sweets | unos caramelos | oonoass kahrahmayloass |
| wick | una mecha | oonah maychah |

| | | |
|---|---|---|
| filter tipped | con filtro | kon feeltroa |
| without filter | sin filtro | seen feeltroa |

**Miscellaneous** *Diversos*

**Souvenirs** *Recuerdos*

Spain's souvenir industry churns out everything from personalized bull-fighting posters to plastic castanets. Kitsch aside, you will also find a selection of fine hand-crafted articles: shawls, embroidered linen, lace-work, painted fans, hand-woven shopping baskets, wicker-work and carved wood.

You may come across special outlets for handicrafts *(artesanía)*, some of them government sponsored.

| | | |
|---|---|---|
| bullfight poster | el cartel de toros | ayl kahrtayl day toaroass |
| bullfighter's cap | la montera | lah moantayrah |
| castanets | las castañuelas | lahss kahstahñwaylahss |
| copperware | objetos de cobre | oabkhaytoass day koabray |
| doll | la muñeca | lah mooñaykah |
| earrings | los pendientes | loss payndyayntayss |
| earthenware | la loza de barro | lah loathah day bahrroa |
| embossed leather | el cuero repujado | ayl kwayroa raypookhah-dhoa |
| embroidery | el bordado | ayl boardahdhoa (day |
| fan | el abanico | ayl ahbhahneekoa |
| guitar | la guitarra | lah geetahrrah |
| jewellery | las joyas | lahss khoyahss |
| lace | los encajes | loss aynkahkhayss |
| mantilla | la mantilla | lah mahnteelyah |
| pitcher | el botijo | ayl boateekhoa |
| poncho | el poncho | ayl ponchoa |
| rosary | el rosario | ayl roassahryoa |
| tambourine | la pandereta | lah pahndayraytah |
| wineskin | la bota | lah boatah |
| woodcarving | la talla en madera | lah tahlyah ayn mahdhayrah |

**Records — Cassettes** *Discos – Cassettes*

| | | |
|---|---|---|
| I'd like a ... | Quisiera ... | keessyayrah |
| cassette | una cassette | oonah kahssayttay |
| compact disc | un disco compacto | oon deeskoa koampahktoa |
| record | un disco | oon deeskoa |
| video cassette | una video-cassette | oonah beedhayoa-kah-ssayttay |

| Can I listen to this record? | ¿Puedo escuchar este disco? | pwaydhoa aysskoochahr aystay deeskoa |
|---|---|---|

| L.P. (33 rmp) | 33 revoluciones | trayntah ee trayss raybhoaloothyonayss |
| E.P. (45 rmp) | maxi 45 | maxi kwahrayntah ee theenkoa |
| single | 45 revoluciones | kwahrayntah ee theenkoa raybhoaloothyonayss |

| chamber music | música de cámara | moosseekah day kahmahrah |
|---|---|---|
| classical music | música clásica | moosseekah klahsseekah |
| folk music | música folklórica | moosseekah folkloareekah |
| instrumental music | música instrumental | moosseekah eenstroomayntahl |
| light music | música ligera | moosseekah leekhayrah |
| orchestral music | música de orquesta | moosseekah day orkaystah |
| pop music | música pop | moosseekah pop |

## Toys  *Juguetes*

| I'd like a toy for a boy/a 5-year-old-girl. | Quisiera un juguete para un niño/una niña de 5 años. | keessyayrah oon khoogaytay pahrah oon neeñoa/oonah neeñah day 5 ahñoass |
|---|---|---|
| I'd like a/an/some ... | Quisiera ... | keessyayrah |
| beach ball | una pelota de playa | oonah payloatah day plahyah |
| bucket and spade (pail and shovel) | un cubo y una pala | oon koobhoa ee oonah pahlah |
| building blocks | unos cubos de construcción | oonoass koobhoass day koanstrookthyon |
| card game | un juego de cartas | oon khwaygoa day kahrtahss |
| chess set | un ajedrez | oon ahkhaydrayth |
| dice | unos dados | oonoass dadhoass |
| electronic game | un juego electrónico | oon khwaygoa aylayktroaneekoa |
| flippers | unas aletas para nadar | oonahss ahlaytahss pahrah nahdhahr |
| roller skates | unos patines de ruedas | oonoass pahteenayss day rwaydhahss |
| snorkel | unos espantasuegras | oonoass ayspahntahswaygrahss |

# Your money: bank's — currency

The normal banking hours in Spain are from 9 a.m. to 2 p.m. Monday to Friday (Saturday 9 a.m. to 1 p.m.). Outside normal banking hours, many travel agencies, major hotels and other businesses displaying a *cambio* sign will change foreign currency into pesetas. Always take your passport with you for identification when you go to change money.

### Credit cards    *Tarjetas de crédito*

All the internationally recognized credit cards are accepted by hotels, restaurants and businesses in Spain.

### Traveller's cheques    *Cheques de viajero*

In tourist areas, shops and all banks, hotels and travel agencies accept traveller's cheques, though you are likely to get a better rate of exchange at a national or regional bank. You'll have no problem settling bills or paying for purchases with Eurocheques.

### Monetary unit    *La unidad monetaria*

The basic unit of currency is the *peseta* (pay**ssay**tah), abbreviated *pta*. There are coins of 1, 2, 5, 10, 25, 50, 100 and 200 pesetas and banknotes of 100, 200 (rare), 500, 1,000, 2,000 and 5,000 pesetas.

| | | |
|---|---|---|
| Where's the nearest bank? | ¿Dónde está el banco más cercano? | doanday aystah ayl bahn-koa mahss thehrkahnoa |
| Where's the nearest currency exchange office? | ¿Dónde está la oficina de cambio más cercana? | doanday aystah lah oafeetheenah day kahm-byoa mahss thehrkahnah |
| What time does the bank open/close? | ¿A qué hora abren/cierran el banco? | ah kay oarah ahbrayn/thyayrrahn ayl bahnkoa |
| Where can I cash a traveller's cheque (check)? | ¿Dónde puedo cobrar un cheque de viajero? | doanday pwaydhoa koa-brahr oon chaykay day byahkhayroa |

## At the bank   *En el banco*

| | | |
|---|---|---|
| I want to change some dollars/ pounds. | **Quiero cambiar unos dólares/unas libras esterlinas.** | kyayroa kahmbyahr oonoass doalahrayss/ oonahss leebrahss aystayr-leenahss |
| I want to cash a traveller's cheque. | **Quiero cobrar un cheque de viajero.** | kyayroa koabrahr oon chaykay day byahkhayroa |
| Here's my passport. | **Aquí está mi pasaporte.** | ahkee aystah mee passahportay |
| What's the exchange rate? | **¿A cómo está el cambio?** | ah koamoa aystah ayl kahmbyoa |
| How much of commission do you charge? | **¿Qué comisión cargan?** | kay koameessyon kahrgahn |
| Can you cash a personal cheque? | **¿Puede hacer efectivo un cheque personal?** | pwaydhay ahthayr ayfaykteebhoa oon chaykay pehrsoanahl |
| How long will it take to clear? | **¿Cuánto tardará en tramitarlo?** | kwahntoa tahrdahrah ayn trahmeetahrloa |
| Can you telex my bank in London? | **¿Puede mandar un télex a mi banco en Londres?** | pwaydhay mahndahr oon taylayks ah mee bahnkoa ayn londrayss |
| I have a/an/some ... | **Tengo ...** | tayngoa |
| credit card | **una tarjeta de crédito** | oonah tahrkhaytah day kraydeetoa |
| Eurocheques | **unos eurocheques** | oonoass ayooroachaykayss |
| introduction from ... | **un formulario de presentación de ...** | oon foarmoolahryoa day prayssayntahthyon day |
| letter of credit | **una carta de crédito** | oonah kahrtah day kraydeetoa |
| I'm expecting some money from Chicago. Has it arrived yet? | **Espero una transferencia de Chicago. ¿Ha llegado ya?** | ayspayroa oonah trahnsfayraynthyah day cheekahgoa ah lyaygahdhoa yah |
| Please give me ... notes (bills) and some small change. | **Por favor, déme ... billetes y algo en moneda.** | por fahbhor daymay ... beelyaytayss ee ahlgoa ayn moanaydhah |
| Give me ... large notes and the rest in small notes. | **Déme ... en los billetes de más valor que tenga y el resto en billetes de menor valor.** | daymay ... ayn loss beelyaytayss day mahss bahlor kay tayngah ee ayl raystoa ayn beelyaytayss day maynor bahlor |

NUMBERS, see page 146

### Depositing *Depósitos*

| | | |
|---|---|---|
| I want to credit this to my account. | **Quiero acreditar esto a mi cuenta.** | kyayroa ahkraydheet**ahr** aystoa ah mee kwayntah |
| I want to credit this to Mr ... 's account. | **Quiero acreditar esto a la cuenta del Señor ...** | kyayroa ahkraydheet**ahr** aystoa ah lah **kwayn**tah dayl sayñor |
| I want to open an account/withdraw ... pesetas. | **Quiero abrir una cuenta/retirar ... pesetas.** | kyayroa ah**breer** oonah **kwayn**tah/rayteer**ahr** ... payssaytahss |

### Business terms *Expresiones de negocios*

| | | |
|---|---|---|
| My name is ... | **Me llamo ...** | may **lyah**moa |
| Here's my card. | **Aquí está mi tarjeta.** | ahkee aystah mee tahr**khay**tah |
| I have an appointment with ... | **Tengo una cita con ...** | **tayn**goa oonah **thee**tah kon |
| Can you give me an estimate of the cost? | **¿Puede darme una estimación del precio?** | **pway**dhay **dahr**may oonah aysteemahth**yon** dayl **pray**thyoa |
| What's the rate of inflation? | **¿Cuál es la tasa de inflación?** | kwahl ayss lah **tah**ssah day eenflath**yon** |
| Can you provide me with an interpreter/ a secretary? | **¿Puede conseguirme un intérprete/una secretaria?** | **pway**dhay konsaygeer**may** oon eentayr**pray**tay/ oonah saykraytah**ryah** |

| | | |
|---|---|---|
| amount | **la suma** | lah **soo**mah |
| balance | **el balance** | ayl bah**lahn**thay |
| capital | **el capital** | ayl kahpee**tahl** |
| cheque book | **la chequera** | lah chay**kay**rah |
| interest | **el interés** | ayl eentay**rayss** |
| investment | **la inversión** | lah eenbayr**syon** |
| invoice | **la factura** | lah fahk**too**rah |
| loss | **la pérdida** | lah **payr**deedhah |
| mortgage | **la hipoteca** | lah eepoa**tay**kah |
| payment | **el pago** | ayl **pah**goa |
| profit | **la ganancia** | lah gahn**ahn**thyah |
| purchase | **la compra** | lah **koam**prah |
| sale | **la venta** | lah **bayn**tah |
| transfer | **la transferencia** | lah trahnsfayray**nthyah** |
| value | **el valor** | ayl bah**loar** |

# At the post office

Post offices are for mail and telegrams only; normally you can't make telephone calls from them. Hours vary slightly from town to town, but routine postal business is generally transacted from 9 a.m. to 1 or 1.30 p.m. and 4 to 6 or 7 p.m., Monday to Saturday except for Saturday afternoons.

Stamps are also on sale at tobacconists' *(tabacos)* and often at hotels. Letter boxes (mailboxes) are yellow with a red insignia.

| | | |
|---|---|---|
| Where's the nearest post office? | ¿Dónde está la oficina de correos más cercana? | doanday aystah lah oafee-theenah day korrehoass mahss thehrkahnah |
| What time does the post office open/close? | ¿A qué hora abren/cierran correos? | ah kay oarah ahbrayn/thyayrrahn korrehoass |
| Which window do I go to for stamps? | ¿A qué ventanilla debo ir para comprar sellos? | ah kay bayntahneelyah daybhoa eer pahrah koamprahr saylyoass |
| At which counter can I cash an international money order? | ¿En qué mostrador puedo hacer efectivo un giro postal internacional? | ayn kay moastrahdhor pwaydhoa ahthayr ayfayk-teebhoa oon kheeroa pos-tahl eentehrnahthyonahl |
| I want some stamps, please. | Quiero unos sellos, por favor. | kyayroa oonoass saylyoass por fahbhor |
| A stamp for this letter/postcard, please. | Un sello para esta carta/tarjeta, por favor. | oon saylyoa pahrah aystah kahrtah/tahrkhaytah por fahbhor |
| What's the postage for a letter/postcard to London? | ¿Cuál es el franqueo para una carta/tarjeta para Londres? | kwahl ayss ayl frahnkayoa pahrah oonah kahrtah/tahrkhaytah pahrah londrayss |
| Do all letters go airmail? | ¿Van todas las cartas por correo aéreo? | bahn toadhahss lahss kahrtahss por korrehoa ahayrehoa |
| I want to send this parcel. | Quiero mandar este paquete. | kyayroa mahndahr aystay pahkaytay |

| | | |
|---|---|---|
| Do I need to fill in a customs declaration? | ¿Es necesario que cumplimente una declaración para la aduana? | ayss naythayssahryoa kay koompleemayntay oonah dayklahrahthyon pahrah lah ahdwahnah |
| Where's the letter box (mailbox)? | ¿Dónde está el buzón? | doanday aystah ayl boothon |
| I want to send this ... | Quiero mandar esto ... | kyayroa mahndahr aystoa |
| airmail | por correo aéreo | por korrehoa ahayrehoa |
| express (special delivery) | urgente | oorkhayntay |
| registered mail | por correo certificado | por korrehoa thayrteefee-kahdhoa |
| Where's the poste restante (general delivery)? | ¿Dónde está la Lista de Correos? | doanday aystah lah leestah day korrehoass |
| Is there any mail for me? My name is ... | ¿Hay correo para mí? Me llamo ... | igh korrehoa pahrah mee. may lyahmoa |

| | |
|---|---|
| **SELLOS** | STAMPS |
| **PAQUETES** | PARCELS |
| **GIROS POSTALES** | MONEY ORDERS |

**Telegrams**  *Telegramas*

In Spain telegrams are dispatched by the post office.

| | | |
|---|---|---|
| I want to send a telegram/telex. | Quiero mandar un telegrama/télex. | kyayroa mahndahr oon taylaygrahmah/taylayks |
| May I please have a form? | ¿Me da un impreso, por favor? | may dah oon eemprayssoa por fahbhor |
| How much is it per word? | ¿Cuánto cuesta por palabra? | kwahntoa kwaystah por pahlahbrah |
| How long will a cable to Boston take? | ¿Cuánto tardará un telegrama a Boston? | kwahntoa tahrdahrah oon taylaygrahmah ah boston |
| I'd like to reverse the charges. | Quisiera que fuera por cobro revertido. | keessyayrah kay fwayrah por koabroa raybhayrteedhoa |

### Telephoning   *Teléfonos*

Local and international calls can be made from call boxes (phone booths). Area codes for different countries are displayed in booths. In main towns, long-distance calls can also be placed from telephone offices (usually distinct from post offices).

| | | |
|---|---|---|
| Where's the telephone? | ¿Dónde está el teléfono? | doanday aystah ayl taylayfoanoa |
| Where's the nearest call box (phone booth)? | ¿Dónde está la cabina de teléfonos más cercana? | doanday aystah lah kahbheenah day taylayfoanoass mahss thehrkahnah |
| May I use your phone? | ¿Puedo usar su teléfono? | pwaydho oossahr soo taylayfoanoa |
| Do you have a telephone directory for Valladolid? | ¿Tiene usted una guía de teléfonos de Valladolid? | tyaynay oostaydh oonah geeah day taylayfoanoass day bahlyahdhoaleedh |
| Can you help me get this number? | ¿Me puede usted obtener este número? | may pwaydhay oostaydh obtehnnayr aystay noomayroa |
| Can I dial direct? | ¿Puedo marcar directamente? | pwaydhoa mahrkahr deerayktahmayntay |
| What's the dialing (area) code for ...? | ¿Cuál es el indicativo para ...? | kwahl ayss ayl eendeekahteebhoa pahrah |
| How do I get the (international) operator? | ¿Cómo puedo conseguir la telefonista (internacional)? | koamoa pwaydhoa konsaygeer lah taylayfoaneestah (eentayrnahthyoanahl) |

### Operator   *La telefonista*

| | | |
|---|---|---|
| Do you speak English? | ¿Habla usted inglés? | ahblah oostaydh eenglayss |
| Good morning, I want Madrid 123 45 67. | Buenos días, quiero hablar con Madrid, número 123 45 67. | bwaynoass deeahss kyayroa ahblahr kon mahdreedh noomayroa 123 45 67 |
| I want to place a personal (person-to-person) call. | Quiero una llamada personal. | kyayroa oonah lyahmahdhah pehrsoanahl |

| | | |
|---|---|---|
| I want to reverse the charges. | **Quiero que sea con cobro revertido.** | kyayroa kay sehah kon koabroa raybhayrteedhoa |
| Will you tell me the cost of the call afterwards? | **¿Puede decirme el coste de la llamada después?** | pwaydhay daytheermay ayl koastay day lah lyah-mahdhah dayspwayss |

### Telephone alphabet

| | | | | | |
|---|---|---|---|---|---|
| A | **Antonio** | antoanyoa | N | **Navarra** | nahbhahrrah |
| B | **Barcelona** | bahrthehloanah | Ñ | **Ñoño** | ñoañoa |
| C | **Carmen** | kahrmayn | O | **Oviedo** | oabhyaydhoa |
| CH | **Chocolate** | choakoalahtay | P | **París** | pahreess |
| D | **Dolores** | doaloarayss | Q | **Querido** | kayreedhoa |
| E | **Enrique** | aynreekay | R | **Ramón** | rahmon |
| F | **Francia** | frahnthyah | S | **Sábado** | sahbhahdhoa |
| G | **Gerona** | khehroanah | T | **Tarragona** | tahrrahgoanah |
| H | **Historia** | eestoaryah | U | **Ulises** | ooleessayss |
| I | **Inés** | eenayss | V | **Valencia** | bahlaynthyah |
| J | **José** | khoassay | W | **Washington** | wahsheenton |
| K | **Kilo** | keeloa | X | **Xiquena** | kseekaynah |
| L | **Lorenzo** | loaraynthoa | Y | **Yegua** | yehgwah |
| LL | **Llobregat** | lyoabraygaht | Z | **Zaragoza** | thahrahgothah |
| M | **Madrid** | mahdreedh | | | |

### Speaking  *Hablando*

| | | |
|---|---|---|
| Hello. This is ... speaking. | **Oiga. Aquí habla con ...** | oygah. ahkee ahblah kon |
| I want to speak to ... | **Quiero hablar con ...** | kyayroa ahblahr kon |
| I want extension ... | **Quisiera la extensión ...?** | keessyayrah lah aykstayn-ssyon |
| Is this ...? | **¿Es ...?** | ayss |
| Speak louder/more slowly, please. | **Hable más fuerte/ más despacio, por favor.** | ahblay mahss fwayrtay/ mahss dayspahthyoa por fabhor |

### Bad luck  *Mala suerte*

| | | |
|---|---|---|
| Would you please try again later? | **¿Querría intentarlo de nuevo más tarde?** | kehrreeah eentayntahrloa day nwaybhoa mahss tahrday |

| English | Spanish | Pronunciation |
|---|---|---|
| Operator, you gave me the wrong number. | **Señorita, me ha dado el número equivocado.** | sayñoar**ee**tah may ah **dah**dhoa ayl **noo**mayroa aykeebhoa**kah**dhoa |
| Operator, we were cut off. | **Señorita, se nos ha cortado la línea.** | sayñoar**ee**tah say noas ah koar**tah**dhoa lah **lee**nayah |

## Not there  *Está ausente*

| English | Spanish | Pronunciation |
|---|---|---|
| When will he/she be back? | **¿Cuándo estará de vuelta?** | k**wah**ndoa aystah**rah** day **bway**ltah |
| Will you tell him/her I called? My name is ... | **Dígale que lo/la he llamado. Mi nombre es ...** | **dee**gahlay kay loa/lah ay lyah**mah**dhoa. mee **noam**bray ayss |
| Would you ask him/her to call me? | **¿Querría pedirle que me llame?** | kehrr**ee**ah peh**dheer**lay kay may **lyah**may |
| Would you please take a message? | **¿Por favor, quiere tomar un recado?** | por fah**bhor** k**yay**ray toa**mahr** oon ray**kah**dhoa |

## Charges  *Tarifas*

| English | Spanish | Pronunciation |
|---|---|---|
| What was the cost of that call? | **¿Cuál ha sido el coste de esa llamada?** | k**wahl** ah **see**dhoa ayl **koas**tay day **ays**sah lyah**mah**dhah |
| I want to pay for the call. | **Quiero pagar la llamada.** | k**yay**roa pah**gahr** lah lyah**mah**dhah |

|  |  |
|---|---|
| **Hay una llamada para usted.** | There's a telephone call for you. |
| **¿A qué número llama?** | What number are you calling? |
| **Comunica.** | The line's engaged. |
| **No contestan.** | There's no answer. |
| **Tiene el número equivocado.** | You've got the wrong number. |
| **No está ahora.** | He's/She's out at the moment. |
| **Un momento.** | Just a moment. |
| **Espere, por favor.** | Hold on, please. |

# Doctor

To be at ease, make sure your health insurance policy covers any illness or accident while on holiday. If not, ask your insurance representative, automobile association or travel agent for details of special health insurance.

## General *Locuciones básicas*

| | | |
|---|---|---|
| Can you get me a doctor? | ¿Puede llamar a un médico? | pwaydhay lyahmahr ah oon mehdheekoa |
| Is there a doctor here? | ¿Hay un médico aquí? | igh oon mehdheekoa ahkee |
| I need a doctor— quickly. | Necesito un médico —rápidamente. | naythayseetoa oon meh- dheekoa rahpeedhahmayntay |
| Where can I find a doctor who speaks English? | ¿Dónde puedo encontrar un médico que hable inglés? | doanday pwaydhoa aynkon- trahr oon mehdheekoa kay ahblay eenglayss |
| Where's the surgery (doctor's office)? | ¿Dónde es la con- sulta? | doanday ayss lah koan- sooltah |
| What are the surgery (office) hours? | ¿Cuáles son las horas de consulta? | kwahlayss son lahss oarahss day koansooltah |
| Could the doctor come to see me here? | ¿Podría venir el mé- dico a reconocerme? | poadreeah bayneer ayl meh- deekoa ah raykoanoathayrmay |
| What time can the doctor come? | ¿A qué hora puede venir el doctor? | ah kay oarah pwaydhay bayneer ayl doaktoar |
| Can you recommend a/an...? | ¿Me puede recomen- dar a un...? | may pwaydhay raykoamayn- dahr ah oon |
| general practitioner | generalista | khaynayrahleestah |
| children's doctor | pediatra | paydhyahtrah |
| eye specialist | oculista | oakooleestah |
| gynaecologist | ginecólogo | kheenaykoaloagoa |
| Can I have an appointment...? | ¿Me puede dar una cita...? | may pwaydhay dahr oonah theetah |
| right now | inmediatamente | eenmaydhyahtahmayntay |
| tomorrow | mañana | mahñahnah |
| as soon as possible | tan pronto como sea posible | tahn proantoa koamoa sayah poasseeblay |

CHEMIST'S, see page 108

## Parts of the body *Partes del cuerpo*

| arm | el brazo | ayl **brah**thoa |
| artery | la arteria | lah ahr**tayr**yah |
| back | la espalda | lah ays**pahl**dah |
| bladder | la vesícula | lah bays**see**koolah |
| bone | el hueso | ayl **ways**soa |
| bowels | los intestinos | loass eentay**stee**noass |
| breast | el seno | ayl **say**noa |
| chest | el pecho | ayl **pay**choa |
| ear | la oreja | lah oa**rayk**hah |
| eye | el ojo | ayl **oak**hoa |
| face | la cara | lah **kah**rah |
| finger | el dedo | ayl **dayd**hoa |
| foot | el pie | ayl pyay |
| gland | la glándula | lah **glahn**doolah |
| hand | la mano | lah **mah**noa |
| head | la cabeza | lah kahb**hay**thah |
| heart | el corazón | ayl koarah**thon** |
| jaw | la mandíbula | lah mahn**dee**bhoolah |
| joint | la articulación | lah ahrteekoolah**thyon** |
| kidney | el riñón | ayl ree**ñon** |
| knee | la rodilla | lah roa**dheel**yah |
| leg | la pierna | lah **pyehr**nah |
| lip | el labio | ayl **lah**bhyoa |
| liver | el hígado | ayl **ee**gahdhoa |
| lung | el pulmón | ayl pool**mon** |
| mouth | la boca | lah **boa**kah |
| muscle | el músculo | ayl **moos**kooloa |
| neck | el cuello | ayl **kway**lyoa |
| nerve | el nervio | ayl **nehr**byoa |
| nervous system | el sistema nervioso | ayl see**stay**mah |
| | | nehr**byoa**assoa |
| nose | la nariz | lah nah**reeth** |
| rib | la costilla | lah koa**steel**yah |
| shoulder | la espalda | lah ays**pahl**dah |
| skin | la piel | lah pyayl |
| spine | la espina dorsal | lah ays**pee**nah doar**sahl** |
| stomach | el estómago | ayl ay**stoa**mahgoa |
| tendon | el tendón | ayl tayn**don** |
| thigh | el muslo | ayl **moos**loa |
| throat | la garganta | lah gahr**gahn**tah |
| thumb | el pulgar | ayl pool**gahr** |
| toe | el dedo del pie | ayl **dayd**hoa dayl pyay |
| tongue | la lengua | lah **layng**wah |
| tonsils | las amígdalas | lahss ah**meeg**dahlahss |
| vein | la vena | lah **bay**nah |

## Accident—Injury    *Accidente – Herida*

| There has been an accident. | **Ha habido un accidente.** | ah ahbheedhoa oon aktheedayntay |
| My child has had a fall. | **Se ha caído el niño/la niña.** | say ah kaheedhoa ayl neeñoa/lah neeñah |
| He/She has hurt his/her head. | **Se ha dado un golpe en la cabeza.** | say ah dahdhoa oon goalpay ayn lah kahbhaythah |
| He's/She's unconscious. | **Está inconsciente.** | aystah eenkoansthyayntay |
| He's/She's bleeding heavily. | **Está sangrando mucho.** | aystah sahngrahndoa moochoa |
| He's/She's (seriously) injured. | **Tiene una herida (muy seria).** | tyaynay oonah ayreedhah (mwee sayrryah) |
| His/Her arm is broken. | **Su brazo está roto.** | soo brahthoa aystah roatoa |
| His/Her ankle is swollen. | **Su tobillo está hinchado.** | soo toabheelyoa aystah eenchahdhoa |
| I've cut myself. | **Me he cortado.** | may ay koartahdhoa |
| I've pulled a muscle. | **Tengo un músculo distendido.** | tayngoa oon mooskooloa deestayndeedhoa |
| I've got something in my eye. | **Me ha entrado algo en el ojo.** | may ah ayntrahdhoa ahlgoa ayn ayl oakhoa |
| I've got a/an ... | **Tengo ...** | tayngoa |
| blister | **una ampolla** | oonah ahmpoalyah |
| boil | **un forúnculo** | oon foaroonkooloa |
| bruise | **un cardenal** | oon kahrdaynahl |
| burn | **una quemadura** | oonah kaymahdhoorah |
| cut | **una cortadura** | oonah koartahdhoorah |
| graze | **un arañazo** | oon ahrahñahthoa |
| insect bite | **una picadura de insecto** | oonah peekahdhoorah day eensehktoa |
| lump | **un chichón** | oon cheechoan |
| rash | **un sarpullido** | oon sahrpoolyeedhoa |
| sting | **una picadura** | oonah peekahdhoorah |
| swelling | **una hinchazón** | oonah eenchahthon |
| wound | **una herida** | oonah ayreedhah |
| Could you have a look at it? | **¿Podría mirarlo?** | poadreeah meerahrloa |
| I can't move my ... It hurts. | **No puedo mover el/la ... Me duele.** | noa pwaydhoa moabher ayl/lah ... may dwaylay |

| | |
|---|---|
| No se mueva. | Don't move. |
| ¿Dónde le duele? | Where does it hurt? |
| ¿Qué clase de dolor es? | What kind of pain is it? |
| apagado/agudo palpitante/constante intermitente | dull/sharp throbbing/constant on and off |
| Está roto/torcido/ dislocado/desgarrado. | It's broken/sprained/ dislocated/torn. |
| Quiero que le hagan una radiografía. | I want you to have an X-ray taken. |
| Lo van a enyesar. | You'll get a plaster. |
| Está infectado. | It's infected. |
| ¿Lo han vacunado contra el tétanos? | Have you been vaccinated against tetanus? |
| Le daré un antiséptico/ un analgésico. | I'll give you an antiseptic/ a painkiller. |
| Quiero que venga a verme dentro de … días. | I'd like you to come back in … days. |

### Illness *Enfermedad*

| | | |
|---|---|---|
| I'm not feeling well. | No me siento bien. | noa may syayntoa byayn |
| I'm ill. | Estoy enfermo(a). | aystoy aynfehrmoa(ah) |
| I feel … | Me siento … | may syayntoa |
| dizzy | mareado(a) | mahrayahdhoa(ah) |
| nauseous | con náuseas | kon nowssayahss |
| shivery | con escalofríos | kon ayskahloafreeoass |
| I've got a fever. | Tengo fiebre. | tayngoa fyehbray |
| My temperature is 38 degrees. | Tengo 38 grados de temperatura. | tayngoa 38 grahdhoass day taympayrahtoorah |
| I've been vomiting. | He tenido vómitos. | ay tayneedhoa boameetoass |
| I'm constipated. | Estoy estreñido(a). | aystoy aystrehñeedhoa(ah) |
| I've got diarrhoea. | Tengo diarrea. | tayngoa dyahrrayah |
| My … hurts. | Me duele … | may dwaylay |

NUMBERS, see page 147

| I've got (a/an) ... | Tengo ... | tayngoa |
|---|---|---|
| asthma | asma | ahsmah |
| backache | dolor de espalda | doalor day ayspahldah |
| cold | un resfriado | oon raysfryahdhoa |
| cough | tos | toass |
| cramps | calambres | kahlahmbrayss |
| earache | dolor de oídos | doalor day oaeedhoass |
| headache | dolor de cabeza | doalor day kahbhaythah |
| indigestion | una indigestión | oonah eendeekhaystyon |
| nosebleed | una hemorragia nasal | oonah aymoarrahkhyah nahssahl |
| palpitations | palpitaciones | pahlpeetahthyonayss |
| rheumatism | reumatismo | rayoomahteesmoa |
| sore throat | anginas | ahnkheenahss |
| stiff neck | tortícolis | torteekoaleess |
| stomach ache | dolor de estómago | doalor day aystoamahgoa |
| sunstroke | una insolación | oonah eensoalahthyon |
| I have difficulties breathing. | Tengo dificultades respiratorias. | tayngoa deefeekooltahdhayss rayspeerahtoaryahss |
| I have a pain in my chest. | Tengo un dolor en el pecho. | tayngoa oon doalor ayn ayl paychoa |
| I had a heart attack ... years ago. | Tuve un ataque al corazón hace ... años. | toobhay oon ahtahkay ahl koarahthon ahthay ... ahñoass |
| My blood pressure is too high/too low. | Mi presión sanguínea es demasiado alta/baja. | mee prayssyon sahngeenayah ayss daymahssyahdhoa ahltah/bahkhah |
| I'm allergic to ... | Soy alérgico(a) a ... | soy ahlehrkheekoa(ah) ah |
| I'm a diabetic. | Soy diabético(a). | soy dyahbhayteekoa(ah) |

## Women's section   *Asuntos de la mujer*

| I have period pains. | Tengo dolores menstruales. | tayngoa doaloarayss maynstrooahlayss |
|---|---|---|
| I have a vaginal infection. | Tengo una infección vaginal. | tayngoa oonah eenfaykthyon bahkheenahl |
| I'm on the pill. | Tomo la píldora. | toamoa lah peeldoarah |
| I haven't had my period for 2 months. | Hace dos meses que no tengo reglas. | ahthay doass mayssayss kay noa tayngoa rayglahss |
| I'm pregnant. | Estoy embarazada. | aystoy aymbahrahthahdhah |

| | |
|---|---|
| ¿Cuánto tiempo hace que se siente así? | How long have you been feeling like this? |
| ¿Es la primera vez que ha tenido esto? | Is this the first time you've had this? |
| Le voy a tomar la presión/ la temperatura. | I'll take your blood pressure/ temperature. |
| Súbase la manga, por favor. | Roll up your sleeve, please. |
| Desvístase (hasta la cintura), por favor. | Please undress (down to the waist). |
| Acuéstese ahí, por favor. | Please lie down over there. |
| Abra la boca. | Open your mouth. |
| Respire profundo. | Breathe deeply. |
| Tosa, por favor. | Cough, please. |
| ¿Dónde le duele? | Where do you feel the pain? |
| Tiene (un/una) ... | You've got (a/an) ... |
| apendicitis | appendicitis |
| cistitis | cystitis |
| enfermedad venérea | venereal disease |
| gastritis | gastritis |
| gripe | flu |
| ictericia | jaundice |
| inflamación de ... | inflammation of ... |
| intoxicación | food poisoning |
| neumonía | pneumonia |
| sarampión | measles |
| Le pondré una inyección. | I'll give you an injection. |
| Necesito una muestra de sangre/heces/orina. | I want a specimen of your blood/stools/urine. |
| Debe quedarse en cama durante ... días. | You must stay in bed for ... days. |
| Quiero que consulte a un especialista. | I want you to see a specialist. |
| Quiero que vaya al hospital para un reconocimiento general. | I want you to go to the hospital for a general check-up. |
| Tendrán que operarlo. | You'll have to have an operation. |

### Prescription—Treatment  *Prescripción – Tratamiento*

| This is my usual medicine. | Esta es la medicina que tomo normalmente. | aystah ayss lah maydheethee-nah kay toamoa noarmahl-mayntay |
| Can you give me a prescription for this? | ¿Puede darme una receta para esto? | pwaydhay dahrmay oonah raythaytah pahrah aystoa |
| Can you prescribe an antidepressant/ some sleeping pills? | ¿Puede recetarme un antidepresivo/ un somnífero? | pwaydhay raythaytahrmay oon ahnteedaypraysseebhoa oon soamneefayroa |
| I'm allergic to antibiotics/penicilline. | Soy alérgico(a) a los antibióticos/ la penicilina. | soy ahlehrkheekoa(ah) ah loass ahnteebhyoateekoass/ lah payneetheeleenah |
| I don't want anything too strong. | No quiero nada demasiado fuerte. | noa kyayroa nahdhah day-mahssyahdhoa fwayrtay |
| How many times a day should I take it? | ¿Cuántas veces al día tengo que tomarlo? | kwahntahss baythayss ahl deeah tayngoa kay toamahrloa |

| ¿Qué tratamiento está siguiendo? | What treatment are you having? |
| ¿Qué medicina está tomando? | What medicine are you taking? |
| ¿Qué dosis utiliza normalmente? | What's your normal dose? |
| En inyección u oral? | Injection or oral? |
| Tome .. cucharillas de esta medicina ... cucharillas de esta medicina ... | Take ... teaspoons of this medicine ... |
| Tome una píldora con un vaso de agua ... | Take one pill with a glass of water ... |
| cada ... horas<br>... veces por día<br>antes/después de cada comida<br>por la mañana/por la noche<br>en caso de dolor<br>durante ... días | every ... hours<br>... times a day<br>before/after each meal<br>in the morning/at night<br>in case of pain<br>for ... days |

## Fee *Honorarios*

| | | |
|---|---|---|
| How much do I owe you? | ¿Cuánto le debo? | kwahntoa lay daybhoa |
| May I have a receipt for my health insurance? | ¿Puede darme un recibo para mi seguro? | pwaydhay dahrmay oon raytheebhoa pahrah mee saygooroa |
| Can I have a medical certificate? | ¿Me puede dar un certificado médico? | may pwaydhay dahr oon thayrteefeekahdhoa maydheekoa |
| Would you fill in this health insurance form, please? | ¿Quiere llenar esta hoja de seguro, por favor? | kyayray lyaynahr aystah oakhah day saygooroa por fahbhor |

## Hospital *Hospital*

| | | |
|---|---|---|
| What are the visiting hours? | ¿Cuáles son las horas de visita? | kwahlayss son lahss oarahss day beeseetah |
| When can I get up? | ¿Cuándo puedo levantarme? | kwahndoa pwaydhoa laybhahntahrmay |
| When will the doctor come? | ¿Cuándo viene el médico? | kwahndoa byaynay ayl maydheekoa |
| I can't eat/sleep. | No puedo comer/dormir. | noa pwaydhoa koamayr/dormeer |
| I'm in pain. | Me duele. | may dwaylay |
| Can I have a pain-killer? | ¿Me puede dar un analgésico? | may pwaydhay dahr oon ahnahlkhaysseekoa |

| | | |
|---|---|---|
| doctor/surgeon | el médico/cirujano | ayl maydheekoa/thee-rookhahnoa |
| nurse | la enfermera | lah aynfayrmayrah |
| patient | el/la paciente | ayl/lah pahthyayntay |
| anaesthetic | el anestésico | ayl ahnaystaysseekoa |
| blood transfusion | la transfusión de sangre | lah trahnsfoossyon day sahngray |
| injection | la inyección | lah eenyaykthyon |
| operation | la operación | lah oapayrahthyon |
| bed | la cama | lah kahmah |
| bedpan | la silleta | lah seelyaytah |
| thermometer | el termómetro | ayl tayrmoamaytroa |

## Dentist   *Dentista*

| | | |
|---|---|---|
| Can you recommend a good dentist? | **¿Puede recomendarme un buen dentista?** | pway**dhay** raykoamayn-**dahr**may oon bwayn daynt**eestah** |
| Can I make an (urgent) appointment to see Dr ...? | **¿Puedo pedir cita (urgente) para ver al Doctor ...?** | pway**dhoa** payd**heer** **thee**tah (oork**hayn**tay) pahrah behr ahl doak**tor** |
| Can't you possibly make it earlier than that? | **¿No sería posible antes?** | noa sayr**eeah** poass**eeblay ahntayss** |
| I have a broken tooth. | **Me he roto un diente.** | may ay **roa**toa oon **dyayn**tay |
| I have a toothache. | **Tengo dolor de muelas.** | **tayn**goa **doalor** day **mway**lahss |
| I have an abscess. | **Tengo un flemón.** | **tayn**goa oon flay**mon** |
| This tooth hurts. | **Me duele este diente.** | may **dway**lay **ays**tay **dyayn**tay |
| at the top | **arriba** | ah**rree**bhah |
| at the bottom | **abajo** | ah**bhah**khoa |
| in the front | **delante** | day**lahn**tay |
| at the back | **detrás** | day**trahss** |
| Can you fix it temporarily? | **¿Puede usted arreglarlo temporalmente?** | pway**dhay** oos**taydh** ahrray**glahr**loa taympoarahl**mayn**tay |
| I don't want it extracted. | **No quiero que me la saque.** | noa **kyay**roa kay may lah **sahk**ay |
| Could you give me an anaesthetic? | **¿Puede ponerme anestesia local?** | pway**dhay** poan**ayr**may ahn**aystays**syah loa**kahl** |
| I've lost a filling. | **He perdido un empaste.** | ay pehr**deed**hoa oon aym**pahs**tay |
| The gum is very sore/bleeding. | **La encía está muy inflamada/sangra.** | lah aynth**eeah** ays**tah** m**wee** eenflah**mahd**hah/**sahng**rah |
| I've broken this denture. | **Se me ha roto la dentadura.** | say may ah **roa**toa lah daynta**hd**hoorah |
| Can you repair this denture? | **¿Puede usted arreglar esta dentadura?** | pway**dhay** oos**taydh** ahrray**glahr** aystah daynta**hd**hoorah |
| When will it be ready? | **¿Cuándo estará lista?** | **kwahn**doa aystah**rah lees**tah |

# Reference section

## Where do you come from?   *¿De dónde viene usted?*

| | | |
|---|---|---|
| Africa | **Africa** | ahfreekah |
| Asia | **Asia** | ahssyah |
| Australia | **Australia** | owstrahlyah |
| Europe | **Europa** | ayooroapah |
| North/South/ Central America | **América del Norte/ del Sur/Central** | ahmayreekah dayl nortay/ dayl soor/thayntrahl |
| Algeria | **Argelia** | ahrkhaylyah |
| Austria | **Austria** | owstryah |
| Belgium | **Bélgica** | baylkheekah |
| Canada | **Canadá** | kahnahdhah |
| China | **China** | cheenah |
| Denmark | **Dinamarca** | deenahmahrka |
| England | **Inglaterra** | eenglahtayrrah |
| Finland | **Finlandia** | feenlahndyah |
| France | **Francia** | frahnthyah |
| Germany | **Alemania** | ahlaymahnyah |
| Gibraltar | **Gibraltar** | kheebrahltahr |
| Great Britain | **Gran Bretaña** | grahn braytahñah |
| Greece | **Grecia** | graythyah |
| India | **India** | eendyah |
| Ireland | **Irlanda** | eerlahndah |
| Israel | **Israel** | eesrahayl |
| Italy | **Italia** | eetahlyah |
| Japan | **Japón** | khahpon |
| Luxembourg | **Luxemburgo** | looksaymboorgoa |
| Morocco | **Marruecos** | mahrrwaykoass |
| Netherlands | **Países Bajos** | paheessayss bahkhoass |
| New Zealand | **Nueva Zelandia** | nwaybhah thaylahndyah |
| Norway | **Noruega** | noarwaygah |
| Portugal | **Portugal** | portoogahl |
| Scotland | **Escocia** | ayskoathyah |
| South Africa | **Africa del Sur** | ahfreekah dayl soor |
| Soviet Union | **Unión Soviética** | oonyon soabhyayteekah |
| Spain | **España** | ayspahñah |
| Sweden | **Suecia** | swaythyah |
| Switzerland | **Suiza** | sweethah |
| Tunisia | **Túnez** | toonayth |
| Turkey | **Turquía** | toorkeeah |
| United States | **Estados Unidos** | aystahdhoass ooneedhoass |
| Wales | **País de Gales** | paheess day gahlayss |
| Yugoslavia | **Yugoslavia** | yogoaslahbhyah |

## Numbers *Números*

| | | |
|---|---|---|
| 0 | cero | thayroa |
| 1 | uno | oonoa |
| 2 | dos | doss |
| 3 | tres | trayss |
| 4 | cuatro | kwahtroa |
| 5 | cinco | theenkoa |
| 6 | seis | sayss |
| 7 | siete | syaytay |
| 8 | ocho | oachoa |
| 9 | nueve | nwaybhay |
| 10 | diez | dyayth |
| 11 | once | onthay |
| 12 | doce | doathay |
| 13 | trece | traythay |
| 14 | catorce | kahtorthay |
| 15 | quince | keenthay |
| 16 | dieciséis | dyaytheessayss |
| 17 | diecisiete | dyaytheessyaytay |
| 18 | dieciocho | dyaytheeoachoa |
| 19 | diecinueve | dyaytheenwaybhay |
| 20 | veinte | bayntay |
| 21 | veintiuno | baynteeoonoa |
| 22 | veintidós | baynteedoss |
| 23 | veintitrés | baynteetrayss |
| 24 | veinticuatro | baynteekwahtroa |
| 25 | veinticinco | baynteetheenkoa |
| 26 | veintiséis | baynteessayss |
| 27 | veintisiete | baynteessyaytay |
| 28 | veintiocho | baynteeoachoa |
| 29 | veintinueve | baynteenwaybhay |
| 30 | treinta | trayntah |
| 31 | treinta y uno | trayntah ee oonoa |
| 32 | treinta y dos | trayntah ee doss |
| 33 | treinta y tres | trayntah ee trayss |
| 40 | cuarenta | kwahrayntah |
| 50 | cincuenta | theenkwayntah |
| 60 | sesenta | sayssayntah |
| 70 | setenta | saytayntah |
| 80 | ochenta | oachayntah |
| 90 | noventa | noabhayntah |
| 100 | cien/ciento* | thyayn/thyayntoa |
| 101 | ciento uno | thyayntoa oonoa |
| 102 | ciento dos | thyayntoa doss |

*cien* is used before nouns and adjectives.

| 110 | ciento diez | thyayntoa dyayth |
|---|---|---|
| 120 | ciento veinte | thyayntoa bayntay |
| 200 | doscientos | dosthyayntoass |
| 300 | trescientos | traysthyayntoass |
| 400 | cuatrocientos | kwahtroathyayntoass |
| 500 | quinientos | keenyayntoass |
| 600 | seiscientos | saysthyayntoass |
| 700 | setecientos | saytaythyayntoass |
| 800 | ochocientos | oachoathyayntoass |
| 900 | novecientos | noabhaythyayntoass |
| 1,000 | mil | meel |
| 1,100 | mil cien | meel thyayn |
| 2,000 | dos mil | dos meel |
| 10,000 | diez mil | dyayth meel |
| 100,000 | cien mil | thyayn meel |
| 1,000,000 | un millón | oon meelyon |

| 1981 | mil novecientos ochenta y uno | meel noabhaythyayntoass oachayntah ee oonoa |
|---|---|---|
| 1992 | mil novecientos noventa y dos | meel noabhaythyayntoass noabhayntah ee doss |
| 2003 | dos mil tres | dos meel trayss |

| first | primero | preemayroa |
|---|---|---|
| second | segundo | saygoondoa |
| third | tercero | tehrthayroa |
| fourth | cuarto | kwahrtoa |
| fifth | quinto | keentoa |
| sixth | sexto | saykstoa |
| seventh | séptimo | saypteemoa |
| eighth | octavo | oaktahbhoa |
| ninth | noveno | noabhaynoa |
| tenth | décimo | daytheemoa |

| once | una vez | oonah behth |
|---|---|---|
| twice | dos veces | doss baythayss |
| three times | tres veces | trayss baythayss |

| a half | una mitad | oonah meetahdh |
|---|---|---|
| half a ... | medio ... | maydhyoa |
| half of ... | la mitad de ... | lah meetahdh day |
| half (adj.) | medio | maydhyoa |
| a quarter | un cuarto | oon kwahrtoa |
| one third | un tercio | oon tehrthyoa |
| a dozen | una docena | oonah dothaynah |
| 3.4% | 3,4 por ciento | trayss koamah cuatro por thyayntoa |

## Year and age   *Año y edad*

| | | |
|---|---|---|
| year | **el año** | ayl ah**ñ**oa |
| leap year | **el año bisiesto** | ayl ah**ñ**oa beessyaystoa |
| decade | **la década** | lah **d**aykahdah |
| century | **el siglo** | ayl seegloa |
| this year | **este año** | ay**s**tay ah**ñ**oa |
| last year | **el año pasado** | ayl ah**ñ**oa pah**s**sahdhoa |
| next year | **el año próximo** | ayl ah**ñ**oa proakseemoa |
| each year | **cada año** | kah**d**hah ah**ñ**oa |
| Which year? | **¿Qué año?** | kay ah**ñ**oa |
| two years ago | **hace dos años** | ah**t**hay doss ah**ñ**oass |
| in one year | **dentro de un año** | **d**ayntroa day oon ah**ñ**oa |
| in the eighties | **en los años ochenta** | ayn loass ah**ñ**oass oa**ch**ayntah |
| from the fifties | **desde los años cincuenta** | **d**aysday loass ah**ñ**oass theen**kw**ayntah |
| the 16th century | **el siglo XVI** | ayl seegloa dyathee**ss**ayss |
| from the 19th century | **desde el siglo XIX** | **d**aysday ayl **s**eegloa dyathee-n**way**bhay |
| in the 20th century | **en el siglo XX** | ayn ayl **s**eegloa **b**ayntay |
| old/young | **viejo/joven** | b**y**ay**kh**oa/**kh**oabhehn |
| old/new | **viejo/nuevo** | b**y**ay**kh**oa/n**way**bhoa |
| recent | **reciente** | ray**th**ya**yn**tay |
| How old are you? | **¿Cuántos años tiene?** | **kw**ah**n**toass ah**ñ**oass t**y**ay**n**ay |
| I'm 30 years old. | **Tengo 30 años.** | **t**ayngoa 30 ah**ñ**oass |
| What's his/her age? | **¿Cuál es su edad?** | **kw**ahl ays soo ay**d**hahdh |
| He/She was born in 1977. | **Nació en 1977.** | nah**th**yoa ayn 1977 |
| Children under 16 are not admitted. | **No se admiten niños menores de 16 años.** | noa say ahd**m**eetayn nee**ñ**oass may**n**oarayss day 16 ah**ñ**oass |

## Seasons   *Estaciones*

| | | |
|---|---|---|
| spring | **la primavera** | lah preemah**bh**ayrah |
| summer | **el verano** | ayl **b**ayrahnoa |
| autumn | **el otoño** | ayl otoa**ñ**oa |
| winter | **el invierno** | ayl eenb**y**ayrnoa |
| in spring | **en primavera** | ayn preemah**bh**ayrah |
| during the summer | **durante el verano** | doorahntay ayl **b**ayrahnoa |
| high season | **alta estación** | **ah**ltah aystah**th**yon |
| low season | **baja estación** | **b**ah**kh**ah aystah**th**yon |

## Months *Meses*

| January | enero* | aynayroa |
|---|---|---|
| February | febrero | fehbrehroa |
| March | marzo | mahrthoa |
| April | abril | ahbreel |
| May | mayo | mahyoa |
| June | junio | khoonyoa |
| July | julio | khoolyoa |
| August | agosto | ahgoastoa |
| September | septiembre | sehptyaymbray |
| October | octubre | oktoobray |
| November | noviembre | noabhyaymbray |
| December | diciembre | deethyaymbray |
| after June | después de junio | dayspwayss day khoonyoa |
| before July | antes de julio | ahntays day khoolyoa |
| during the month of August | durante el mes de agosto | doorahntay ayl mayss day ahgoastoa |
| in September | en septiembre | ayn sehptyaymbray |
| until November | hasta noviembre | ahstah noabhyaymbray |
| since December | desde diciembre | daysday deethyaymbray |
| last month | el mes pasado | ayl mayss pahssahdhoa |
| next month | el mes próximo | ayl mayss prokseemoa |
| the month before | el mes anterior | ayl mayss ahntehryor |
| the month after | el mes siguiente | ayl mayss seegyayntay |
| the beginning of January | a principios de enero | ah preentheepyoass day aynayroa |
| the middle of February | a mediados de febrero | ah maydhyahdhoass day fehbrehroa |
| the end of March | a finales de marzo | ah feenahlayss day mahrthoa |

## Dates *Fechas*

| What's the date today? | ¿En qué fecha estamos? | ayn kay faychah aystahmoass |
|---|---|---|
| When's your birthday? | ¿Cuándo es su cumpleaños? | kwahndoa ayss soo koomplayahñoass |
| July 1 | el primero de julio | ayl preemayroa day khoolyoa |
| March 10 | el diez de marzo | ayl dyayth day mahrthoa |

* The names of months aren't capitalized in Spanish.

### Days  *Días de la semana*

| | | |
|---|---|---|
| What day is it today? | ¿Qué día es hoy? | kay deeah ayss oy |
| Sunday | domingo* | doameengoa |
| Monday | lunes | loonayss |
| Tuesday | martes | mahrtayss |
| Wednesday | miércoles | myayrkoalayss |
| Thursday | jueves | khwaybhayss |
| Friday | viernes | byayrnayss |
| Saturday | sábado | sahbhadhoa |
| in the morning | por la mañana | por lah mahñahnah |
| during the day | durante el día | doorahntay ayl deeah |
| in the afternoon | por la tarde | por lah tahrday |
| in the evening | por la tarde | por lah tahrday |
| at night | por la noche | por lah noachay |
| at dawn | al amanecer | ahl ahmahnaythayr |
| at dusk | al anochecer | ahl ahnoachaythayr |
| yesterday | ayer | ahyehr |
| today | hoy | oy |
| tomorrow | mañana | mahñahnah |
| the day before | el día anterior | ayl deeah ahntehryor |
| the next day | el día siguiente | ayl deeah seegyayntay |
| two days ago | hace dos días | ahthay doss deeahss |
| in three days' time | en tres días | ayn trayss deeahss |
| last week | la semana pasada | lah saymahnah pahssahdhah |
| next week | la semana próxima | lah saymahnah prokseemah |
| in two weeks | por una quincena | por oonah keenthehnah |
| birthday | el cumpleaños | ayl koomplayahñoass |
| day | el día | ayl deeah |
| day off | el día libre | ayl deeah leebray |
| holiday | el día festivo | ayl deeah faysteebhoa |
| holidays | las vacaciones | lahss bahkahthyonayss |
| school holidays | las vacaciones del colegio | lahss bahkahthyonayss dayl koalehkhyoa |
| vacation | las vacaciones | lahss bahkahthyonayss |
| week | la semana | lah saymahnah |
| weekday | el día de la semana | ayl deeah day lah saymahnah |
| weekend | el fin de semana | ayl feen day saymahnah |
| working day | el día laborable | ayl deeah lahbhoarahblay |

---

* The names of days aren't capitalized in Spanish.

## Public holidays   *Días festivos*

These are the main public holidays in Spain when banks, offices and shops are closed. In addition, there are various regional holidays.

| | | |
|---|---|---|
| January 1 | **Año Nuevo** | New Year's Day |
| January 6 | **Epifanía** | Epiphany |
| March 19 | **San José** | St Joseph's Day |
| | **Viernes Santo** | Good Friday |
| | **Lunes de Pascua** | Easter Monday (Catalonia only) |
| May 1 | **Día del Trabajo** | Labour Day |
| | **Corpus Christi** | Corpus Christi Day |
| July 25 | **Santiago Apóstol** | St James's Day |
| August 15 | **Asunción** | Assumption Day |
| October 12 | **Día de la Hispanidad** | Columbus Day |
| November 1 | **Todos los Santos** | All Saints' Day |
| December 6 | **Día de la Constitución Española** | Constitution Day |
| December 8 | **Inmaculada Concepción** | Immaculate Conception Day |
| December 25 | **Navidad** | Christmas Day |

## Greetings   *Saludos*

| | | |
|---|---|---|
| Merry Christmas! | **¡Feliz Navidad!** | fayleeth nahbheedhahdh |
| Happy New Year! | **¡Feliz Año Nuevo!** | fayleeth ahñoa nwaybhoa |
| Happy Easter! | **¡Felices Pascuas!** | fayleethayss pahskwahss |
| Happy birthday! | **¡Feliz cumpleaños!** | fayleeth koomplayahñoass |
| Best wishes! | **¡Mejores deseos!** | maykhoarayss dayssayoass |
| Congratulations! | **¡Enhorabuena!** | aynoarahbwaynah |
| Good luck! | **¡Buena suerte!** | bwaynah swayrtay |
| Have a nice trip! | **¡Buen viaje!** | bwayn byahkhay |
| All the best! | **¡Qué todo salga bien!** | kay toadhoa sahlgah byayn |
| Best regards from/to ... | **Recuerdos de/a ...** | raykwayrdoass day/ah |
| Give my love to ... | **Saludos cariñosos a ...** | sahloodhoass kahreeñoassoass ah |

## What time is it?   *¿Qué hora es?*

| | | |
|---|---|---|
| Excuse me. Can you tell me the time? | **Perdone. ¿Puede decirme la hora?** | payrdoanay. pwaydhay daytheermay lah oarah |
| It's ... | **Es/Son ...** | ayss/son |
| five past one | **la una y cinco** | lah oonah ee theenkoa |
| ten past two | **las dos y diez** | lahss doss ee dyayth |
| a quarter past three | **las tres y cuarto** | lahss trayss ee kwahrtoa |
| twenty past four | **las cuatro y veinte** | lahss kwahtroa ee bayntay |
| twenty-five past five | **las cinco y veinticinco** | lahss theenkoa ee baynteetheenkoa |
| half past six | **las seis y media** | lahss sayss ee maydhyay |
| twenty-five to seven | **las siete menos veinticinco** | lahss saytay maynoass baynteetheenkoa |
| twenty to eight | **las ocho menos veinte** | lahss oachoa maynoass bayntay |
| a quarter to nine | **las nueve menos cuarto** | lahss nwaybhay maynoass kwahrtoa |
| ten to ten | **las diez menos diez** | lahss dyayth maynoass dyayth |
| five to eleven | **las once menos cinco** | lahss onthay maynoass theenkoa |
| twelve o'clock | **las doce** | lahss doathay |
| a.m. | **de la mañana** | de lah mahñahnah |
| p.m. | **de la tarde** | de lah tahrday |
| The train leaves at ... | **El tren sale a ...** | ayl trayn sahlay ah |
| 13.04 (1.04 p.m.) | **las trece y cuatro** | lahss traythay ee kwahtroa |
| 0.45 (0.45 a.m.) | **las cero horas y cuarenta y cinco** | lahss thayroa oarahss ee kwahrayntah ee theenkoa |
| in five minutes | **en cinco minutos** | ayn theenkoa meenootoass |
| in a quarter of an hour | **en un cuarto de hora** | ayn oon kwahrtoa day oarah |
| half an hour ago | **hace media hora** | ahthay maydhyah oarah |
| about two hours | **aproximadamente dos horas** | ahproakseemahdhahmayntay doss oarahss |
| more than ten minutes | **más de diez minutos** | mahss day dyayth meenootoass |
| less than thirty seconds | **menos de treinta segundos** | maynoass day trayntah saygoondoass |
| noon | **mediodía** | maydhyoadheeah |
| midnight | **medianoche** | maydhyahnoachay |
| early | **temprano** | taymprahnoa |
| late | **tarde** | tahrday |
| in time | **a tiempo** | ah tyaympoa |

## Abbreviations *Abreviaturas*

| | | |
|---|---|---|
| A.C. | año de Cristo | A.D. |
| a/c | al cuidado de | c/o |
| a. de J.C. | antes de Jesucristo | B.C. |
| admón. | administración | administration |
| apdo. | apartado de correos | post office box |
| Av., Avda. | Avenida | avenue |
| C., Cía. | Compañía | company |
| C/ | Calle | street |
| cta. | cuenta | account |
| cte. | corriente | of the present month |
| C.V. | caballos de vapor | horsepower |
| D. | Don | courtesy title (gentleman) |
| Da., Dª | Doña | courtesy title (lady) |
| EE.UU. | Estados Unidos | United States |
| f.c. | ferrocarril | railway |
| G.C. | Guardia Civil | police |
| h. | hora | hour |
| hab. | habitantes | population |
| M.I.T. | Ministerio de Información y Turismo | Ministry of Information and Tourism |
| Nª Sª | Nuestra Señora | Our Lady, the Virgin |
| Nº, núm. | número | number |
| p. ej. | por ejemplo | for example |
| P.P. | porte pagado | postage paid |
| pta., ptas. | peseta(s) | peseta(s) |
| P.V.P. | precio de venta al público | retail price |
| R.A.C.E. | Real Automóvil Club de España | Royal Automobile Club of Spain |
| R.C. | Real Club ... | Royal ... Club |
| RENFE | Red Nacional de Ferrocarriles Españoles | Spanish National Railway |
| R.N.E. | Radio Nacional de España | Spanish National Broadcasting Company |
| S., Sta. | San, Santa | Saint |
| S.A. | Sociedad Anónima | Ltd., Inc. |
| Sr. | Señor | Mr. |
| Sra. | Señora | Mrs. |
| Sres., Srs. | Señores | gentlemen |
| Srta. | Señorita | Miss |
| TVE | Televisión Española | Spanish Television |
| Ud., Vd. | Usted | you (singular) |
| Uds., Vds. | Ustedes | you (plural) |
| v.g., v.gr. | verbigracia | viz., namely |

## Signs and notices  *Letreros e indicaciones*

| | |
|---|---|
| Abajo | Down |
| Abierto | Open |
| Arriba | Up |
| Ascensor | Lift (elevator) |
| Averiado | Out of order |
| Caballeros | Gentlemen |
| Caja | Cash desk |
| Caliente | Hot |
| Carretera particular | Private road |
| Cerrado | Closed |
| Cierre la puerta | Close the door |
| Completo | No vacancy |
| Cuidado | Caution |
| Cuidado con el perro | Beware of the dog |
| Empujar | Push |
| Entrada | Entrance |
| Entrada libre | Admission free |
| Entre sin llamar | Enter without knocking |
| Frío | Cold |
| Libre | Vacant |
| No molestar | Do not disturb |
| No obstruya la entrada | Do not block entrance |
| No tocar | Do not touch |
| Ocupado | Occupied |
| Peligro | Danger |
| Peligro de muerte | Danger of death |
| Pintura fresca | Wet paint |
| Privado | Private |
| Prohibido arrojar basuras | No littering |
| Prohibido entrar | No entry |
| Prohibido fumar | No smoking |
| Prohibida la entrada a personas no autorizadas | No trespassing |
| Rebajas | Sale |
| Reservado | Reserved |
| Sala de espera | Waiting room |
| Salida | Exit |
| Salida de emergencia | Emergency exit |
| Se alquila | To let (for rent) |
| Se vende | For sale |
| Sendero para bicicletas | Bicycle path |
| Señoras | Ladies |
| Servicios | Toilets |
| Tirar | Pull |
| Toque el timbre, por favor | Please ring |

## Emergency    *Urgencia*

| | | |
|---|---|---|
| Call the police | **Llama a la policía** | lyahmah ah lah poaleetheeah |
| DANGER | **PELIGRO** | payleegroa |
| FIRE | **FUEGO** | **fway** oa |
| Gas | **Gas** | gahss |
| Get a doctor | **Busque un doctor** | booskay oon doaktor |
| Go away | **Váyase** | bahyahssay |
| HELP | **SOCORRO** | sokoarroa |
| Get help quickly | **Busque ayuda rápido** | booskay ahyoodhah rahpeedhoa |
| I'm ill | **Estoy enfermo(a)** | aystoy aynfehrmoa(ah) |
| I'm lost | **Me he perdido** | may ay payrdeedhoa |
| Leave me alone | **Déjeme en paz** | daykhaymay ayn pahth |
| LOOK OUT | **CUIDADO** | kweedhahdhoa |
| POLICE | **POLICIA** | poaleetheeah |
| Quick | **Rápido** | rahpeedhoa |
| STOP | **DETENGASE** | daytayngahssay |
| Stop that man/ woman | **Detenga a ese(a) hombre/mujer** | daytayngah ah ayssay(ah) oambray/mookhehr |
| STOP THIEF | **AL LADRÓN** | ahl lahdron |

## Lost!    *¡Perdido!*

| | | |
|---|---|---|
| Where's the ...? | **¿Dónde está la ...?** | doanday aystah lah |
| lost property (lost and found) office | **oficina de objetos perdidos** | oafeetheenah day oabkhaytoass pehrdeedhoass |
| police station | **comisaría de policía** | koameessahryah day poaleetheeah |
| I want to report a theft. | **Quiero denunciar un robo.** | kyayroa daynoonthyahr oon roabhoa |
| My ... has been stolen. | **Me han robado mi ...** | may ahn roabhahdhoa mee |
| handbag | **bolso** | boalsoa |
| money | **dinero** | deenayroa |
| passport | **pasaporte** | passahportay |
| ticket | **billete** | beelyaytay |
| wallet | **cartera** | kahrtayrah |
| I've lost my ... | **He perdido mi ...** | ay pehrdeedhoa mee |
| I lost it in ... | **Lo perdí en ...** | loa pehrdee ayn |
| this morning | **esta mañana** | aystah mahñahnah |
| yesterday | **ayer** | ahyehr |

CAR ACCIDENTS, see page 78

## Conversion tables

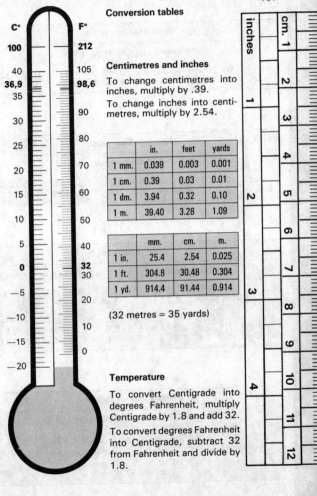

### Centimetres and inches

To change centimetres into inches, multiply by .39.

To change inches into centimetres, multiply by 2.54.

|  | in. | feet | yards |
|---|---|---|---|
| 1 mm. | 0.039 | 0.003 | 0.001 |
| 1 cm. | 0.39 | 0.03 | 0.01 |
| 1 dm. | 3.94 | 0.32 | 0.10 |
| 1 m. | 39.40 | 3.28 | 1.09 |

|  | mm. | cm. | m. |
|---|---|---|---|
| 1 in. | 25.4 | 2.54 | 0.025 |
| 1 ft. | 304.8 | 30.48 | 0.304 |
| 1 yd. | 914.4 | 91.44 | 0.914 |

(32 metres = 35 yards)

### Temperature

To convert Centigrade into degrees Fahrenheit, multiply Centigrade by 1.8 and add 32.

To convert degrees Fahrenheit into Centigrade, subtract 32 from Fahrenheit and divide by 1.8.

REFERENCE SECTION

Informaciones generales

## Kilometres into miles

1 kilometre (km.) = 0.62 miles

| km. | 10 | 20 | 30 | 40 | 50 | 60 | 70 | 80 | 90 | 100 | 110 | 120 | 130 |
|---|---|---|---|---|---|---|---|---|---|---|---|---|---|
| miles | 6 | 12 | 19 | 25 | 31 | 37 | 44 | 50 | 56 | 62 | 68 | 75 | 81 |

## Miles into kilometres

1 mile = 1.609 kilometres (km.)

| miles | 10 | 20 | 30 | 40 | 50 | 60 | 70 | 80 | 90 | 100 |
|---|---|---|---|---|---|---|---|---|---|---|
| km. | 16 | 32 | 48 | 64 | 80 | 97 | 113 | 129 | 145 | 161 |

## Fluid measures

1 litre (l.) = 0.88 imp. quarts = 1.06 U.S. quarts

1 imp. quart = 1.14 l.          1 U.S. quart = 0.95 l.
1 imp. gallon = 4.55 l.          1 U.S. gallon = 3.8 l.

| l. | 5 | 10 | 15 | 20 | 25 | 30 | 35 | 40 | 45 | 50 |
|---|---|---|---|---|---|---|---|---|---|---|
| imp. gal. | 1.1 | 2.2 | 3.3 | 4.4 | 5.5 | 6.6 | 7.7 | 8.8 | 9.9 | 11.0 |
| U.S. gal. | 1.3 | 2.6 | 3.9 | 5.2 | 6.5 | 7.8 | 9.1 | 10.4 | 11.7 | 13.0 |

## Weights and measures

1 kilogram or kilo (kg.) = 1000 grams (g.)

100 g. = 3.5 oz.          ½ kg. = 1.1 lb.
200 g. = 7.0 oz.          1 kg. = 2.2 lb.

1 oz. = 28.35 g.
1 lb. = 453.60 g.

# Basic Grammar

### Articles

Nouns in Spanish are either masculine or feminine. Articles agree in gender and number with the noun.

1. Definite article (the):

|  | singular | | plural |
|---|---|---|---|
| masc. | **el tren** | the train | **los trenes** |
| fem. | **la casa** | the house | **las casas** |

2. Indefinite article (a/an):

|  | | | |
|---|---|---|---|
| masc. | **un lápiz** | a pencil | **unos lápices** |
| fem. | **una carta** | a letter | **unas cartas** |

### Nouns

1. Most nouns which end in **o** are masculine. Those ending in **a** are generally feminine.

2. Normally, nouns which end in a vowel add **s** to form the plural; nouns ending in a consonant add **es**.

3. To show possession, use the preposition **de** (of).

| | |
|---|---|
| **el fin de la fiesta** | the end of the party |
| **el principio del\* mes** | the beginning of the month |
| **las maletas de los viajeros** | the travellers' suitcases |
| **los ojos de las niñas** | the girls' eyes |
| **la habitación de Roberto** | Robert's room |

\* (**del** is the contraction of **de** + **el**)

### Adjectives

1. Adjectives agree with the noun in gender and number. If the masculine form ends in **o** the feminine ends in **a**. As a rule, the adjective comes after the noun.

| | |
|---|---|
| **el niño pequeño** | the small boy |
| **la niña pequeña** | the small girl |

If the masculine form ends in **e** or with a consonant, the feminine keeps in general the same form.

| | |
|---|---|
| **el muro/la casa grande** | the big wall/house |
| **el mar/la flor azul** | the blue sea/flower |

2. Most adjectives form their plurals in the same way as nouns.

| | |
|---|---|
| **un coche inglés** | an English car |
| **dos coches ingleses** | two English cars |

3. Possessive adjectives: They agree with the thing possessed, not with the possessor.

| | sing. | plur. |
|---|---|---|
| my | **mi** | **mis** |
| your (fam.) | **tu** | **tus** |
| your (polite form) | **su** | **sus** |
| his/her/its | **su** | **sus** |
| our | **nuestro(a)** | **nuestros(as)** |
| your | **vuestro(a)** | **vuestros(as)** |
| their | **su** | **sus** |

| | |
|---|---|
| **su hijo** | *his* or *her* son |
| **su habitación** | *his* or *her* or *their* room |
| **sus maletas** | *his* or *her* or *their* suitcases |

4. Comparative and superlative: These are formed by adding **más** (more) or **menos** (less) and **lo más** or **lo menos,** respectively, before the adjective.

| | | | |
|---|---|---|---|
| **alto** | high | **más alto** | **lo más alto** |

### Adverbs

These are generally formed by adding **-mente** to the feminine form of the adjective (if it differs from the masculine); otherwise to the masculine.

| | | | |
|---|---|---|---|
| **cierto(a)** | sure | **fácil** | easy |
| **ciertamente** | surely | **fácilmente** | easily |

## Possessive pronouns

|  | sing. | plur. |
|---|---|---|
| mine | mío(a) | míos(as) |
| yours (fam. sing.) | tuyo(a) | tuyos(as) |
| yours (polite form) | suyo(a) | suyos(as) |
| his / hers / its | suyo(a) | suyos(as) |
| ours | nuestro(a) | nuestros(as) |
| yours (fam. pl.) | vuestro(a) | vuestros(as) |
| theirs | suyo(a) | suyos(as) |

## Demonstrative pronouns

|  | masc. | fem. | neut. |
|---|---|---|---|
| this | éste | ésta | esto |
| these | éstos | éstas | estos |
| that | ése/aquél | ésa/aquélla | eso/aquello |
| those | ésos/aquéllos | ésas/aquéllas | esos/aquellos |

The above masculine and feminine forms are also used as demonstrative adjectives, but accents are dropped. The two forms for "that" designate difference in place; **ése** means "that one", **aquél** "that one over there".

| **Esos libros no me gustan.** | I don't like those books. |
|---|---|
| **Eso no me gusta.** | I don't like that. |

## Personal pronouns

|  | subject | direct object | indirect object |
|---|---|---|---|
| I | yo | me | me |
| you | tú | te | te |
| you | usted | lo | le |
| he | él | lo | le |
| she | ella | la | le |
| it | él/ella | lo/la | le |
| we | nosotros(as) | nos | nos |
| you | vosotros(as) | os | os |
|  | ustedes | los | les |
| they | ellos(as) | los | les |

Subject pronouns are generally omitted, except in the polite form (**usted, ustedes**) which corresponds to "you". **Tú** (sing.) and **vosotros** (plur.) are used when talking to relatives, close friends and children and between young people; **usted** and the plural **ustedes** (often abbreviated to **Vd./Vds.**) are used in all other cases.

### Verbs

Here we are concerned only with the infinitive and the present tense.

|  | ser*<br>(to be) | estar*<br>(to be) | haber*<br>(to have) |
|---|---|---|---|
| yo | soy | estoy | he |
| tú | eres | estás | has |
| usted | es | está | ha |
| él/ella | es | está | ha |
| nosotros(as) | somos | estamos | hemos |
| vosotros(as) | sois | estáis | habéis |
| ustedes | son | están | han |
| ellos(as) | son | están | han |

* There are two verbs in Spanish for "to be". **Ser** is used to describe a permanent condition. **Estar** is used to describe location or a temporary condition.

** **haber** is used *only* in compound tenses.

Here are three of the main categories of regular verbs in the present tense:

|  | ends in **ar**<br>hablar<br>(to speak) | ends in **er**<br>comer<br>(to eat) | ends in **ir**<br>reír<br>(to laugh) |
|---|---|---|---|
| yo | hablo | como | río |
| tú | hablas | comes | ríes |
| usted | habla | come | ríe |
| él/ella | habla | come | ríe |
| nosotros(as) | hablamos | comemos | reímos |
| vosotros(as) | habláis | coméis | reís |
| ustedes | hablan | comen | ríen |
| ellos(as) | hablan | comen | ríen |

**Irregular verbs:** As in all languages, these have to be learned. Here are four you will find useful.

|  | poder<br>(to be able) | ir<br>(to go) | ver<br>(to see) | tener<br>(to have) |
|---|---|---|---|---|
| yo | puedo | voy | veo | tengo |
| tú | puedes | vas | ves | tienes |
| usted | puede | va | ve | tiene |
| él/ella | puede | va | ve | tiene |
| nosotros(as) | podemos | vamos | vemos | tenemos |
| vosotros(as) | podéis | vais | veis | tenéis |
| ustedes | pueden | van | ven | tienen |
| ellos(as) | pueden | van | ven | tienen |

### Negatives

Negatives are formed by placing **no** before the verb.

**Es nuevo.**   It's new.          **No es nuevo.**   It's not new.

### Questions

In Spanish, questions are often formed by changing the intonation of your voice. Very often, the personal pronoun is left out, both in affirmative sentences and in questions.

**Hablo español.**          I speak Spanish.
**¿Habla español?**          Do you speak Spanish?

Note the double question mark used in Spanish.
The same is true of exclamation marks.

**¡Qué tarde se hace!**          How late it's getting!

# Dictionary
and alphabetical index

## English–Spanish

*f* feminine                *m* masculine                *pl* plural

**a** un, una 159
**abbey** abadía *f* 81
**abbreviation** abreviatura *f* 154
**able, to be** poder 163
**about** *(approximately)* aproximadamente 153
**above** encima 15, 63
**abscess** flemón *m* 145
**absent** ausente 136
**absorbent cotton** algodón *m* 109
**accept, to** aceptar, 31, 62, 102
**accessories** accesorios *m/pl* 117, 125
**accident** accidente *m* 78, 139
**accommodation** alojamiento *m* 22
**account** cuenta *f* 131
**ache** dolor *m* 141
**acne cream** crema para el acné *f* 110
**adaptor** adaptador *m* 119
**address** señas *f/pl* 21, 102; dirección *f* 31, 76, 79
**address book** librito de direcciones *m* 104
**adhesive** adhesivo(a) 105
**admission** entrada *f* 82, 91, 155
**admit, to** admitir 149
**Africa** Africa *f* 146
**after** después de 77, 150; siguiente 150
**afternoon** tarde *f* 151
**after-shave lotion** loción para después del afeitado *f* 110
**age** edad *f* 149
**ago** hace 149, 151
**air conditioner** acondicionador de aire *m* 28

**air conditioning** aire acondicionado *m* 23
**airmail** por correo aéreo 133
**air mattress** colchón neumático *m* 92
**airplane** avión *m* 65
**airport** aeropuerto *m* 16, 21, 65
**air terminal** terminal aérea *f* 21
**alarm clock** despertador *m* 121
**alcohol** alcohol *m* 106
**Algeria** Argelia *f* 146
**allergic** alérgico(a) 141, 143
**almond** almendra *f* 53, 54
**alphabet** alfabeto *m* 9
**alter, to** *(garment)* arreglar 116
**a.m.** de la mañana 153
**amazing** asombroso(a) 84
**amber** ámbar *m* 122
**ambulance** ambulancia *f* 79
**American** americano(a) 105, 126
**American plan** pensión completa *f* 24
**amethyst** amatista *f* 122
**amount** cantidad *f* 62; suma *f* 131
**amplifier** amplificador *m* 119
**anaesthetic** anestésico *m* 144, 145
**anchovy** anchoa *f* 44
**and** y 15
**animal** animal *m* 85
**aniseed** anís *m* 51, 59
**ankle** tobillo *m* 139
**another** otro(a) 58
**answer** respuesta *f* 136
**antibiotic** antibiótico *m* 143
**antidepressant** antidepresivo 143
**antiques** antigüedades *f/pl* 83
**antique shop** tienda de antigüedades *f* 98

antiseptic antiséptico(a) 109
antiseptic antiséptico *m* 140
any alguno(a) 14
anyone alguien 11
anything algo 17, 25, 113
apartment *(flat)* apartamento *m* 22
aperitif aperitivo *m* 55
appendicitis apendicitis *f* 142
appetizer entremés *m* 41; tapa *f* 63
apple manzana *f* 54, 63
apple juice jugo de manzana *m* 60
appliance aparato *m* 119
appointment cita *f* 30, 131, 137, 145
apricot albaricoque *m* 54
April abril *m* 150
archaeology arqueología *f* 83
architect arquitecto *m* 83
area code indicativo *m* 134
arm brazo *m* 138, 139
arrival llegada *f* 16, 65
arrive, to llegar 65, 68, 130
art arte *m* 83
artery arteria *f* 138
art gallery galería de arte *f* 81, 98
artichoke alcachofa *f* 41, 44, 50
artificial artificial 114, 124
artist artista *m/f* 81, 83
ashtray cenicero *m* 36
Asia Asia *f* 146
ask for, to preguntar 36; pedir 24, 61, 136
asparagus espárrago *m* 41, 50
aspirin aspirina *f* 109
assorted variado(a) 41
asthma asma *m* 141
astringent astringente *m* 110
at a, en 15
at least por lo menos 24
at once ahora mismo 31
aubergine berenjena *f* 50
August agosto *m* 150
aunt tía *f* 94
Australia Australia *f* 146
automatic automático(a) 20, 122, 124
autumn otoño *m* 149
avocado aguacate *m* 41
awful horrible 84

B

baby bebé *m* 24, 111
baby food alimento para bebé *m* 111
babysitter niñera *f* 27

back espalda *f* 138
backache dolor de espalda *m* 141
bacon tocino *m* 38, 47
bacon and eggs huevos con tocino *m/pl* 38
bad malo(a) 11, 14
bag bolsa *f* 103
baggage equipaje *m* 18, 26, 31, 71
baggage car furgón de equipajes *m* 66
baggage cart carrito de equipaje *m* 18, 71
baggage check oficina de equipaje *f* 67, 71
baggage locker consigna automática *f* 18, 67, 71
baked al horno 46, 48
baker's panadería *f* 98
balance *(account)* balance *m* 131
balcony balcón *m* 23
ball *(inflated)* pelota *f* 128
ballet ballet *m* 87
ball-point pen bolígrafo *m* 104
banana plátano *m* 53, 63
bandage venda *f* 109
Band-Aid esparadrapo *m* 109
bangle esclava *f* 121
bangs flequillo *m* 30
bank *(finance)* banco *m* 98, 129, 130
banknote billete *m* 130
barber's barbería *f* 30, 98
basil albahaca *f* 51
basketball baloncesto *m* 90
bath *(hotel)* baño *m* 23, 25, 26
bathing cap gorro de baño *m* 117
bathing hut cabina *f* 92
bathing suit traje de baño *m* 117
bathrobe albornoz *m* 117
bath salts sales de baño *f/pl* 110
bath towel toalla de baño *f* 27
battery pila *f* 119, 121, 125; *(car)* batería *f* 75, 78
be, to ser, estar 13, 162
beach playa *f* 92
bean judía *f* 50
beard barba *f* 31
beautiful bonito(a) 14; hermoso(a) 84
beauty salon salón de belleza *m* 27, 30, 98
bed cama *f* 144
bed and breakfast habitación y desayuno *f* 24
bedpan silleta *f* 144

**beef** carne de buey f 47
**beef steak** biftec m 47
**beer** cerveza f 59
**beet(root)** remolacha f 50
**before** antes de 150; anterior 150, 151
**begin, to** empezar 80, 86, 88
**beginning** principio m 150
**behind** atrás 77
**bellboy** botones m 26
**below** debajo 14, 63
**belt** cinturón m 118
**bend** *(road)* curva f 79
**berth** litera f 66, 70, 71
**best** mejor 152
**better** mejor 14, 25, 101, 114
**between** entre 15
**bicycle** bicicleta f 74
**big** grande 14, 101
**bill** cuenta f 31, 62, 102; *(banknote)* billete m 130
**binoculars** binoculares m/pl 123
**bird** pájaro m 85
**birth** nacimiento m 25
**birthday** cumpleaños m 151, 152
**biscuit** *(Br.)* galleta f 54, 63; pasta f 54
**bitter** amargo(a) 61
**black** negro(a) 113
**blackberry** zarzamora f 53
**blackcurrant** grosella negra f 53
**bladder** vesícula f 138
**blanket** manta f 27
**blazer** blázer m 117
**bleach** aclarado m 30
**bleed, to** sangrar 139, 145
**blind** *(window)* persiana f 29
**blister** ampolla f 139
**block** *(paper)* bloc m 105
**blood** sangre f 142
**blood pressure** presión f 141, 142
**blood transfusion** transfusión de sangre f 144
**blouse** blusa f 113, 117
**blow-dry** modelado m 30
**blue** azul 113
**blueberry** arándano m 53
**blusher** colorete m 111
**boar** *(wild)* jabalí m 48
**boarding house** pensión f 19, 22
**boat** barco m 74
**bobby pin** horquilla de pinza f 111
**body** cuerpo m 138
**boil** furúnculo m 139

**boiled** cocido(a) 38; hervido(a) 48; en dulce 42
**boiled egg** huevo cocido m 38
**bone** hueso m 138
**bonfire** hoguera f 32
**book** libro m 11, 104
**book, to** reservar 69
**booking office** oficina de reservas f 19, 67
**booklet** taco m 72
**bookshop** librería f 98, 104
**boot** bota f 116
**born** nacido(a) 149
**botanical gardens** jardín botánico m 81
**botany** botánica f 83
**bottle** botella f 17, 58, 59
**bottle-opener** abridor de botellas m 106
**bourbon** whisky americano m 59
**bowels** intestinos m/pl 138
**bow tie** corbata de lazo f 117
**box** caja f 126
**boxing** boxeo m 90
**boy** niño m 112, 128
**boyfriend** amigo m 94
**bra** sostén m 117
**bracelet** pulsera f 121
**braces** *(suspenders)* tirantes m/pl 117
**braised** estofado(a) 48
**brake** freno m 78
**brake fluid** líquido de frenos m 75
**brandy** coñac m 59
**brawn** cabeza f 41
**bread** pan m 37, 38, 63
**break, to** romper 29, 119, 123, 139, 140, 145
**break down, to** estropear 78
**breakdown** avería f 78
**breakdown van** coche grúa m 78
**breakfast** desayuno m 24, 27, 34, 38
**breast** seno m 138
**breathe, to** respirar 141, 142
**bridge** puente m 85
**briefs** calzoncillos m/pl 117
**bring, to** traer 12
**bring down, to** bajar 31
**broken** roto(a) 29, 119, 139, 140, 145
**brooch** broche m 121
**brother** hermano m 94
**brown** marrón 113

DICTIONARY

**bruise** cardenal *m* 139
**brush** cepillo *m* 111
**Brussels sprouts** coles de bruselas *f/pl* 50
**bucket** cubo *m* 106, 128
**buckle** hebilla *f* 118
**build, to** construir 83
**building** edificio *m* 83, 85
**building blocks** cubos de construcción *m/pl* 128
**bulb** bombilla *f* 28, 75, 119
**bullfight** corrida *f* 89
**bullfighter's cap** montera *f* 127
**bullfight poster** cartel de toros *m* 127
**bullring** plaza de toros *f* 81
**burn** quemadura *f* 139
**burn out, to** *(bulb)* fundir 29
**bus** autobús *m* 18, 19, 65, 72, 73
**business** negocios *m/pl* 16, 131
**business trip** viaje de negocios *m* 94
**bus stop** parada de autobús *f* 72, 73
**busy** ocupado(a) 96
**butane gas** gas butano *m* 32, 106
**butcher's** carnicería *f* 98
**butter** mantequilla *f* 37, 38, 63
**button** botón *m* 29, 118
**buy, to** comprar 82, 104

# C

**cabbage** berza *f*, repollo *m* 50
**cabin** *(ship)* camarote *m* 74
**cable** telegrama *m* 133
**cable car** funicular *m* 74
**cable release** cable del disparador *m* 125
**caffein-free** descafeinado(a) 38, 60
**cake** pastel *m* 54, 63; bollo *m* 63
**cake shop** pastelería *f* 98
**calculator** calculadora *f* 105
**calendar** calendario *m* 104
**call** *(phone)* llamada *f* 135, 136
**call, to** llamar 10, 31, 71, 78, 136, 156
**cambric** batista *f* 114
**camel-hair** pelo de camello *m* 114
**camera** cámara *f* 124, 125
**camera shop** tienda de fotografía *f* 98
**camp, to** acampar 32
**campbed** cama de campaña *f* 106
**camping** camping *m* 32
**camping equipment** equipo de camping *m* 106

**camp site** camping *m* 32
**can** *(of peaches)* lata *f* 120
**can** *(to be able)* poder 12, 163
**Canada** Canadá *m* 146
**cancel, to** anular 65
**candle** vela *f* 106
**candy** caramelo *m* 63, 126
**candy store** bombonería *f* 98
**can opener** abrelatas *m* 106
**cap** gorra *f* 116
**caper** alcaparra *f* 51
**capital** *(finance)* capital *m* 131
**car** coche *m* 20, 75, 76, 78
**carafe** garrafa *f* 58
**carat** quilate *m* 121
**caravan** caravana *f* 32
**caraway** comino *m* 51
**carbon paper** papel carbón *m* 104
**carburetor** carburador *m* 78
**card** tarjeta *f* 131
**card game** juego de cartas *m* 128
**cardigan** chaqueta de punto *f* 117
**car hire** alquiler de coches *m* 20
**car park** estacionamiento *m* 77
**car radio** radio para coche *m* 119
**car rental** alquiler de automóviles *m* 20
**carrot** zanahoria *f* 50
**carry, to** llevar 21
**cart** carrito *m* 18
**carton** *(cigarettes)* cartón (de cigarrillos) *m* 17
**cartridge** *(camera)* cartucho *m* 124
**case** *(instance)* caso *m* 143; *(glasses etc.)* estuche *m* 123; funda *f* 125
**cash, to** cobrar 129, 130
**cash desk** caja *f* 155
**cashier** cajero(a) *m/f* 103
**cassette** casete *f* 119, 127
**castanets** castañuelas *f/pl* 127
**castle** castillo *m* 81
**catalogue** catálogo *m* 82
**cathedral** catedral *f* 81
**Catholic** católico(a) 84
**cauliflower** coliflor *f* 50
**caution** cuidado *m* 79, 155; atención *f* 79
**cave** cueva *f* 81
**celery** apio *m* 50
**cellophane tape** cinta adhesiva *f* 104
**cemetery** cementerio *m* 81
**centimetre** centímetro *m* 112
**centre** centro *m* 19, 21, 72, 76, 81
**century** siglo *m* 149

Diccionario

**ceramics** cerámica f 83
**cereal** cereales m/pl 38
**certificate** certificado m 144
**chain** *(jewellery)* cadena f 121
**chair** silla f 36, 106
**chamber music** música de cámara f 128
**champagne** champán m 56
**change** *(money)* suelto m 77; moneda f 130
**change, to** cambiar 18, 61, 65, 68, 73, 75, 123, 130; hacer transbordo 73
**chapel** capilla f 81
**charcoal** carbón m 106
**charge** precio m 32; tarifa f 136
**charge, to** cobrar 24, 124; *(commission)* cargar 130
**charm** *(trinket)* amuleto m 121
**charm bracelet** pulsera de fetiches f 121
**cheap** barato(a) 14, 24, 25, 101
**check** cheque m 129; *(restaurant)* cuenta f 62
**check, to** controlar 75, 123; *(luggage)* facturar 71
**check book** chequera f 131
**check in, to** *(airport)* presentarse 65
**check out, to** marcharse 31
**checkup** *(medical)* reconocimiento general m 142
**cheers!** ¡salud! 55
**cheese** queso m 52, 63
**cheesecake** pastel de queso m 54
**chemist's** farmacia f 98, 108
**cheque** cheque m 130
**cheque book** chequera f 131
**cherry** cereza f 53
**chervil** perifollo m 51
**chess** ajedrez m 128
**chest** pecho m 138, 141
**chestnut** castaña f 53
**chewing gum** chicle m 126
**chicken** pollo m 49, 63
**chicken breast** pechuga de pollo f 49
**chicken liver** higadito de pollo m 41, 48
**chickpea** garbanzo m 50
**chicory** *(Am.)* achicoria f 50
**chiffon** gasa f 114
**child** niño(a) m/f 24, 61, 92, 139, 149
**children's doctor** pediatra m/f 137
**chips** patatas fritas f/pl 63; (Am.) patatas fritas f/pl, chips m/pl 63

**chives** cebolleta f 51
**chocolate** chocolate m 54, 63, 126; *(hot)* chocolate (caliente) m 38, 60
**chop** chuleta f 47
**Christmas** Navidad f 152
**church** iglesia f 81, 84, 85
**cigar** puro m 126
**cigarette** cigarrillo m 17, 95, 126
**cigarette case** pitillera f 121
**cigarette lighter** encendedor m 121, 126
**cigarette paper** papel para cigarrillos m 126
**cine camera** cámara de filmar f 124
**cinema** cine m 86, 96
**cinnamon** canela f 51
**circle** *(theatre)* anfiteatro m 87
**city** ciudad f 81
**clam** almeja f 41, 45
**classical** clásico(a) 128
**clean** limpio(a) 61
**clean, to** limpiar 29, 76
**cleansing cream** crema limpiadora f 110
**cliff** acantilado m 85
**clip** clip m 121
**clock** reloj m 121, 153
**clog, to** atascar 28
**close** *(near)* cercano(a) 78, 98
**close, to** cerrar 11, 82, 108, 129, 132, 155
**closed** cerrado(a) 155
**clothes** ropa f 29, 117
**clothes peg** percha f 106
**clothing** prendas de vestir f/pl 112
**cloud** nube f 95
**clove** clavo m 50
**coach** *(bus)* autocar m 72, 80
**coat** abrigo m 117
**coconut** coco m 53
**cod** bacalao m 45
**coffee** café m 38, 60, 64
**coin** moneda f 83
**cold** frío(a) 14, 25, 38, 61, 95
**cold** *(illness)* resfriado m 108, 141
**cold cuts** fiambres m/pl 41, 64
**collar** cuello m 118
**collect call** llamada a cobro revertido f 135
**cologne** agua de colonia f 110
**colour** color m 103, 112, 124, 125
**colour chart** muestrario m 30
**colour fast** color fijo 113
**colourful** colorido(a) 101

**colour negative** negativo de color *m* 124

**colour rinse** reflejos *m/pl* 30

**colour shampoo** champú colorante *m* 111

**colour slide** diapositiva *f* 124

**comb** peine *m* 111

**come, to** venir 34, 61, 93, 95, 137, 146

**comedy** comedia *f* 86

**commission** comisión *f* 130

**compact disc** disco compacto *m* 127

**compartment** departamento *m* 71

**compass** brújula *f* 106

**complaint** reclamación *f* 61

**concert** concierto *m* 87

**concert hall** sala de conciertos *f* 81, 87

**condition** condición *f* 91

**conductor** *(orchestra)* director *m* 88

**confectioner's** confitería *f* 98

**confirm, to** confirmar 65

**confirmation** confirmación *f* 23

**congratulation** enhorabuena *f* 152

**connection** *(plane)* conexión *f* 65; *(train)* transbordo *m* 68

**constipated** estreñido(a) 140

**contact lens** lente de contacto *m* 123

**contain, to** contener 37

**contraceptive** contraceptivo *m* 109

**control** control *m* 16

**convent** convento *m* 81

**convention hall** palacio de convenciones *m* 81

**cookie** galleta *f* 54, 64; pasta *f* 54

**cool box** nevera portátil *f* 106

**copper** cobre *m* 122

**copperware** objetos de cobre *m/pl* 127

**coral** coral *m* 122

**corduroy** pana *f* 114

**cork** corcho *m* 61

**corkscrew** sacacorchos *m* 106

**corn** *(Am.)* maíz *m* 50

**corner** rincón *m* 36; *(street)* esquina *f* 21, 77

**corn plaster** callicida *m* 109

**correct** correcto(a) 11

**cost** precio *m* 131; coste *m* 135, 136

**cost, to** costar 10, 80

**cotton** algodón *m* 114

**cotton wool** algodón *m* 109

**cough** tos *f* 108, 141

**cough, to** toser 142

**cough drops** gotas para la tos *f/pl* 109

**counter** mostrador *m* 132

**countryside** campo *m* 85

**court house** palacio de justicia *m* 81

**courtyard** patio *m* 23, 36

**cousin** primo(a) *m/f* 94

**cover charge** cubierto *m* 62

**crab** cangrejo *m* 46

**cracker** galleta salada *f* 64

**cramp** calambre *m* 141

**crayfish** cangrejo *m* 46

**crayon** lápiz de color *m* 104

**cream** crema 113

**cream** nata *f* 54, 64; crema *f* 60, 110

**creamy** cremoso(a) 52

**credit** crédito *m* 130

**credit, to** acreditar 131

**credit card** tarjeta de crédito *f* 20, 31, 62, 102, 129, 130

**crepe** crepé *m* 114

**crisps** patatas fritas *f/pl*, chips *m/pl* 64

**crockery** vajilla *f* 106, 107

**cross** cruz *f* 121

**crossing** *(by sea)* travesía *f* 74

**crossroads** cruce *m* 77, 79

**cruise** crucero *m* 74

**crystal** cristal *m* 122

**cucumber** pepino *m* 42, 50, 64

**cuff link** gemelo *m* 121

**cuisine** cocina *f* 34

**cup** taza *f* 36, 60, 107

**cured** en salazón 46; serrano 42

**currency** moneda *f* 129

**currency exchange office** oficina de cambio *f* 18, 67, 129

**current** corriente *f* 92

**curtain** cortina *f* 28

**curve** *(road)* curva *f* 79

**customs** aduana *f* 16, 79, 102

**cut** *(wound)* cortadura *f* 139

**cut, to** cortar 139

**cut glass** cristal tallado *m* 122

**cuticle remover** quitacutículas *m* 110

**cutlery** cubiertos *m/pl* 106, 107, 121

**cycling** ciclismo *m* 90

**cystitis** cistitis *f* 142

**D**

**dairy** lechería f 98
**dance** baile m 88
**dance, to** bailar 88, 96
**danger** peligro m 79, 155, 156
**dangerous** peligroso(a) 79, 92
**dark** oscuro(a) 25, 101, 112, 113
**date** fecha f 25, 150; (fruit) dátil m 53
**daughter** hija f 94
**day** día m 16, 20, 24, 32, 80, 151
**daylight** luz del día f 124
**day off** día libre m 151
**death** muerte f 155
**decade** década f 149
**December** diciembre m 150
**decision** decisión f 24, 102
**deck** (ship) cubierta f 74
**deck-chair** silla de lona f 92, 106
**declare, to** declarar 16, 17
**deer** corzo m 48
**delay** demora f 69
**delicatessen** mantequería f 98
**deliver, to** enviar 102
**delivery** envío m 102
**denim** algodón asargado m 114
**dentist** dentista m/f 98, 145
**denture** dentadura f 145
**deodorant** desodorante m 110
**department** departamento m 83, 100
**department store** grandes almacenes m/pl 98
**departure** salida f 65, 80
**deposit** depósito m 20, 131
**deposit, to** (bank) depositar 131
**dessert** postre m 37, 54
**detour** (traffic) desviación f 79
**develop, to** revelar 124
**diabetic** diabético(a) 141
**diabetic** diabético(a) m/f 37
**dialling code** indicativo m 134
**diamond** diamante m 122
**diaper** pañal m 111
**diarrhoea** diarrea f 140
**dice** dado m 128
**dictionary** diccionario m 104
**diet** dieta f 37
**difficult** difícil 14
**difficulty** dificultad f 28, 102, 141
**dill** eneldo m 51
**dining-car** coche restaurante m 66, 68
**dining-room** comedor m 27
**dinner** cena f 34, 95

**dinner jacket** smoking m 117
**direct** directo(a) 68, 134
**direct, to** indicar 12
**direction** dirección f 76
**directory** (phone) guía de teléfonos f 134
**disabled** minusválido(a) 82
**disc** disco m 77, 127, 128
**disc film** disco-película m 124
**discotheque** discoteca f 88
**disease** enfermedad f 142
**dish** plato m 37
**dishwashing detergent** detergente para vajilla m 106
**disinfectant** desinfectante m 109
**dislocate, to** dislocar 140
**display case** vitrina f 100
**dissatisfied** descontento(a) 103
**district** (country) comarca f 76
**disturb, to** molestar 155
**diversion** (traffic) desviación f 79
**dizzy** mareado(a) 140
**doctor** doctor(a) m/f 79, 137, 145; médico(a) m/f 137, 144
**doctor's office** consultorio m 137
**dog** perro m 155
**doll** muñeca f 127
**dollar** dólar m 18, 102, 130
**door** puerta f 155
**dose** dosis f 143
**double** doble 59, 74
**double bed** cama matrimonial f 23
**double room** habitación doble f 19, 23
**down** abajo 15
**downstairs** abajo 15
**downtown** centro de la ciudad m 81
**dozen** docena f 148
**drawing paper** papel de dibujo m 104
**drawing pin** chincheta f 104
**dress** vestido m 117
**dressing gown** bata f 117
**drink** bebida f 60, 61; copa f 95
**drink, to** beber 13, 35, 36
**drinking water** agua potable f 32
**drip, to** (tap) gotear 28
**drive, to** conducir 76
**driving licence** permiso de conducir m 20, 79
**drop** (liquid) gota f 109
**drugstore** farmacia f 98, 108
**dry** seco(a) 30, 58, 111
**dry cleaner's** tintorería f 29, 98

**dry shampoo** champú seco *m* 111
**Dublin bay prawn** cigala *f* 41, 46
**duck** pato *m* 49
**dummy** chupete *m* 111
**during** durante 150, 151
**duty** *(customs)* impuestos *m/pl* 17
**duty-free shop** tienda libre de impuestos *f* 19
**dye** tintura *f* 30, 111

# E
**each** cada 149
**ear** oreja *f* 138
**earache** dolor de oídos *m* 141
**ear drops** gotas para los oídos *f/pl* 109
**early** temprano 14
**earring** pendiente *m* 121, 127
**earthenware** loza de barro *f* 127
**east** este *m* 77
**Easter** Pascua *f* 152
**easy** fácil 14
**eat, to** comer 13, 36, 144, 162
**eel** anguila *f* 41
**egg** huevo *m* 38, 42, 44, 64
**eggplant** berenjena *f* 50
**eight** ocho 147
**eighteen** dieciocho 147
**eighth** octavo(a) 148
**eighty** ochenta 147
**elastic** elástico(a) 109
**elastic** elástico *m* 118
**Elastoplast** esparadrapo *m* 109
**electrical** eléctrico(a) 119
**electrical appliance** aparato eléctrico *m* 119
**electrician** electricista *m* 98
**electricity** electricidad *f* 32
**electronic** electrónico(a) 125, 128
**elevator** ascensor *m* 27, 100
**eleven** once 147
**embarkation** embarco *m* 74
**embroidery** bordado *m* 127
**emerald** esmeralda *f* 122
**emergency** urgencia *f* 156
**emergency exit** salida de emergencia *f* 27, 99, 155
**emery board** lima de papel *f* 110
**empty** vacío(a) 14
**enamel** esmalte *m* 122
**end** final *m* 150
**endive** *(Br.)* achicoria *f* 50
**engagement ring** sortija de pedida *f* 121

**engine** *(car)* motor *m* 78
**England** Inglaterra *f* 146
**English** inglés(esa) 11, 80, 82, 84, 104, 105, 126
**enjoy, to** gustar 62
**enjoyable** agradable 31
**enjoy oneself, to** divertirse 96
**enlarge, to** amplificar 125
**enough** bastante 14
**enquiry** información *f* 68
**enter, to** entrar 155
**entrance** entrada *f* 68, 99, 155
**entrance fee** entrada *f* 82
**envelope** sobre *m* 27, 104
**equipment** equipo *m* 92, 106
**eraser** goma de borrar *f* 104
**escalator** escalera mecánica *f* 100
**espresso coffee** café exprés *m* 60
**estimate** estimación *f* 131
**Europe** Europa *f* 146
**evening** tarde *f* 9, 96, 151; noche *f* 86, 95
**evening dress** traje de noche *m* 88, 117
**everything** todo 31
**excellent** excelente 62
**exchange, to** cambiar 103
**exchange rate** cambio *m* 18, 130
**exclude, to** excluir 24
**excursion** excursión *f* 80
**excuse, to** perdonar 10
**exercise book** cuaderno *m* 104
**exhaust pipe** tubo de escape *m* 78
**exhibition** exhibición *f* 81
**exit** salida *f* 68, 79, 99, 155
**expect, to** esperar 130
**expensive** caro(a) 14, 19, 23, 101
**exposure** *(photography)* exposición *f* 124
**exposure counter** escala de exposición *f* 125
**express** urgente 133
**expression** expresión *f* 10
**expressway** autopista *f* 76, 79
**external** externo(a) 109
**extra** más 27, 36
**extract, to** *(tooth)* sacar 145
**eye** ojo *m* 123, 138, 139
**eye drops** gotas para los ojos *f/pl* 109
**eye liner** perfilador de ojos *m* 110
**eye pencil** lápiz de ojos *m* 110
**eye shadow** sombra de ojos *f* 110
**eye specialist** oculista *m/f* 137

# F

**face** cara *f* 138
**face powder** polvo de la cara *m* 110
**factory** fábrica *f* 79, 81
**fair** feria *f* 81
**fall** caída *f* 139; *(autumn)* otoño *m* 149
**family** familia *f* 94
**fan** ventilador *m* 28; *(folding)* abanico *m* 127
**fan belt** correa de ventilador *f* 75
**far** lejos 14, 100
**fare** tarifa *f* 21, 65, 67, 72
**farm** granja *f* 85
**fast** rápido(a) 124
**fat** *(meat)* grasa *f* 37
**father** padre *m* 94
**faucet** grifo *m* 28
**February** febrero *m* 150
**fee** *(doctor)* honorarios *m/pl* 144
**feeding bottle** biberón *m* 111
**feel, to** *(physical state)* sentirse 140
**felt** fieltro *m* 114
**felt-tip pen** rotulador *m* 114
**ferry** transbordador *m* 74
**fever** fiebre *f* 140
**few** pocos(as) 14; *(a)* (alg)unos(as) 14
**field** campo *m* 85
**fifteen** quince 147
**fifth** quinto(a) 148
**fig** higo *m* 53
**file** *(tool)* lima *f* 110
**fill in, to** llenar 25, 144
**filling** *(tooth)* empaste *m* 145
**filling station** gasolinera *f* 75
**film** película *f* 86, 124, 125; rollo *m* 124
**film winder** enrollador *m* 125
**filter** filtro *m* 125
**filter-tipped** con filtro 126
**find, to** encontrar 10, 12, 100, 137
**fine** *(OK)* muy bien 25
**fine arts** bellas artes *f/pl* 83
**finger** dedo *m* 138
**fire** fuego *m* 156
**first** primero(a) 68, 72, 148
**first class** primera clase *f* 66, 69
**first name** nombre (de pila) *m* 25
**fish** pescado *m* 45
**fish, to** pescar 91
**fishing** pesca *f* 91
**fishing tackle** aparejo de pesca *m* 106

**fishmonger's** pescadería *f* 98
**fit, to** quedar bien 115, 116
**fitting room** probador *m* 115
**five** cinco 147
**fix, to** arreglar 75, 145
**flannel** franela *f* 114
**flash** *(photography)* flash *m* 125
**flashlight** linterna *f* 106
**flat** plano(a) 116
**flat** *(apartment)* apartamento *m* 22
**flat tyre** pinchazo *m* 75, 78
**flea market** mercado de cosas viejas *m* 81
**flight** vuelo *m* 65
**flint** piedra de mechero *f* 126
**flippers** aletas para nadar *f/pl* 128
**floor** piso *m* 26
**floor show** atracciones *m/pl* 88
**flour** harina *f* 37
**flower** flor *f* 85
**flower shop** florería *f* 98
**flu** gripe *f* 142
**fluid** líquido *m* 75
**folding chair** silla plegable *f* 107
**folding table** mesa plegable *f* 107
**folk music** música folklórica *f* 128
**food** alimento *m* 37, 111; comida *f* 61
**food box** fiambrera *f* 106
**food poisoning** intoxicación *f* 142
**foot** pie *m* 138
**football** fútbol *m* 90
**foot cream** crema para los pies *f* 110
**footpath** sendero *m* 85
**for** por, para 15
**forbid, to** prohibir 155
**foreign** extranjero(a) 59
**forest** bosque *m* 85
**fork** tenedor *m* 36, 107
**form** *(document)* impreso *m* 133; ficha *f* 25
**fortnight** quincena *f* 151
**fortress** fortaleza *f* 81, 85
**forty** cuarenta 147
**foundation cream** maquillaje *m* 110
**fountain** fuente *f* 81
**fountain pen** pluma estilográfica *f* 104
**four** cuatro 147
**fourteen** catorce 147
**fourth** cuarto(a) 148
**France** Francia *f* 146
**free** libre 14, 71, 82, 96, 155
**french fries** patatas fritas *f/pl* 64
**fresh** fresco(a) 53, 61

**Friday** viernes *m* 151
**fried** frito(a) 46, 48
**fried egg** huevo frito *m* 38, 64
**friend** amigo(a) *m/f* 93, 95
**fringe** flequillo *m* 30
**frock** vestido *m* 117
**from** de, desde 15
**front** delantero(a) 23, 75
**fruit** fruta *f* 53
**fruit cocktail** ensalada de fruta *f* 53
**fruit juice** jugo de fruta *m* 38, 60;
  zumo de fruta *m* 42
**fruit stand** frutería *f* 98
**frying-pan** sartén *f* 106
**full** lleno(a) 14
**full board** pensión completa *f* 24
**full insurance** seguro a todo riesgo *m*
  20
**furnished** amueblado(a) 22
**furniture** muebles *m/pl* 83
**furrier's** peletería *f* 98

**G**

**gabardine** gabardina *f* 114
**gallery** galería *f* 81, 98
**game** juego *m* 128; *(food)* caza *f* 48
**garage** garaje *m* 26, 78
**garden** jardín *m* 85
**gardens** jardines públicos *m/pl* 81
**garlic** ajo *m* 51
**garment** prenda *f* 29
**gas** gas *m* 156
**gasoline** gasolina *f* 75, 78
**gastritis** gastritis *f* 142
**gauze** gasa *f* 109
**general** general 26
**general delivery** lista de correos *f* 133
**general practitioner** generalista *m/f*
  137
**gentleman** caballero *m* 155
**geology** geología *f* 83
**Germany** Alemania *f* 146
**get, to** *(find, call)* conseguir 10, 32,
  90, 134; coger 19, 21; llamar
  137; buscar 156; *(go)* llegar 100
**get back, to** volver 80; regresar 85
**get by, to** pasar 70
**get off, to** apear 73
**get to, to** llegar a 10, 70; ir a 19
**get up, to** levantarse 144
**gherkin** pepinillo *m* 42, 50, 64
**gift** *(present)* regalo *m* 120
**gin** ginebra *f* 59
**gin and tonic** ginebra con tónica *f* 60

**ginger** jengibre *m* 51
**girdle** faja *f* 117
**girl** niña *f* 112, 128
**girlfriend** amiga *f* 94
**give, to** dar 12, 136, 140
**give way, to** *(traffic)* ceder el paso 79
**glad** *(to know you)* tanto gusto 93
**gland** glándula *f* 138
**glass** vaso *m* 36, 58, 59, 61, 143
**glasses** gafas *f/pl* 123
**gloomy** lúgubre 84
**glossy** *(finish)* acabado de brillo 125
**glove** guante *m* 117
**glue** cola de pegar *f* 104
**go, to** ir 77, 96, 163
**go away, to** irse 156
**go back, to** regresar 77
**gold** oro *m* 121, 122
**golden** dorado(a) 113
**gold plate** lámina de oro *f* 122
**golf** golf *m* 91
**golf club** palo de golf *m* 91
**golf course** campo de golf *m* 91
**good** bueno(a) 14, 101
**good-bye** adiós 9
**Good Friday** Viernes Santo *m* 152
**goods** artículos *m/pl* 16
**goose** ganso *m* 48
**go out, to** salir 96
**gram** gramo *m* 120
**grammar book** libro de gramática *m*
  105
**grape** uva *f* 53, 64
**grapefruit** pomelo *m* 53
**grapefruit juice** jugo de pomelo *m*
  38, 60; zumo de pomelo *m* 42
**gray** gris 113
**graze** arañazo *m* 139
**greasy** graso(a) 30, 111
**great** *(excellent)* estupendo(a) 95
**Great Britain** Gran Bretaña *f* 146
**green** verde 113
**green bean** judía verde *m* 50
**greengrocer's** verdulería *f* 98
**green salad** ensalada de lechuga *f* 43
**greeting** saludo *m* 9
**grey** gris 113
**grilled** a la parrilla 46, 48;
  a la plancha 41
**grocery** tienda de comestibles *f* 98,
  120
**groundsheet** alfombra (de hule) *f* 106
**group** grupo *m* 82
**guide** guía *m/f* 80

**guidebook** guía f 82, 104, 105
**guitar** guitarra f 127
**gum** *(teeth)* encía 145
**gynaecologist** ginecólogo m/f 137

**H**

**hair** cabello m 30, 111
**hairbrush** cepillo para el pelo m 111
**haircut** corte de pelo m 30
**hairdresser's** peluquería f 27, 30, 98
**hair dryer** secador de pelo m 119
**hairgrip** horquilla de pinza f 111
**hairpin** horquilla f 111
**hairspray** laca para el pelo f 30, 111
**hake** merluza f 46
**half** mitad f 148
**half a day** medio día m 80
**half an hour** media hora f 153
**half board** media pensión f 24
**half price** *(ticket)* media tarifa f 69
**hall** *(large room)* sala f 81, 87
**hall porter** conserje m 26
**ham** jamón m 38, 42, 44, 47, 64
**ham and eggs** huevos con jamón m/pl 38
**hamburger** hamburguesa f 64
**hammer** martillo m 106
**hand** mano f 138
**handbag** bolso de mano m 117, 156
**hand cream** crema para las manos f 110
**handicrafts** artesanía f 83
**handkerchief** pañuelo m 117
**hand lotion** loción para las manos f 110
**handmade** hecho(a) a mano 113
**hanger** percha f 27
**hangover** resaca f 108
**happy** feliz 152
**harbour** puerto m 81
**hard** duro(a) 52, 123
**hard-boiled** *(egg)* duro 38, 42
**hardware shop** ferretería f 98
**hare** liebre f 49
**hat** sombrero m 117
**have, to** haber 162; tener 163
**hay fever** fiebre del heno f 108
**hazelnut** avellana f 53
**he** él 161
**head** cabeza f 138, 139
**headache** dolor de cabeza m 141
**headcheese** cabeza f 41
**headlight** luz f 79

**headphones** casco con auriculares m 119
**head waiter** jefe m 61
**health** salud f 55
**health food shop** tienda de alimentos dietéticos f 98
**health insurance** seguro m 144
**health insurance form** hoja de seguro f 144
**heart** corazón m 47, 138
**heart attack** ataque al corazón m 141
**heating** calefacción f 23, 28
**heavy** pesado(a) 14, 101
**heel** tacón m 116
**height** altura f 85
**helicopter** helicóptero m 74
**hello!** *(phone)* oiga 135
**help** ayuda f 156
**help!** ¡socorro! 156
**help, to** ayudar 12, 21, 71; atender 100; *(oneself)* servirse 120
**hen** gallina f 48
**her** su 160
**herbs** hierbas finas f/pl 51
**here** aquí 13, 15
**herring** arenque m 41, 45
**high** alto(a) 92, 141
**high season** alta estación f 149
**high-speed** rápido(a) 124
**high tide** marea alta f 92
**hill** colina f 85
**hire** alquiler m 20
**hire, to** alquilar 20, 91, 92, 119, 155
**his** su 160
**history** historia f 83
**hitchhike, to** hacer auto-stop 74
**hold on!** *(phone)* espere 136
**hole** hoyo m 29
**holiday** día festivo m 151
**holidays** vacaciones f/pl 16, 151
**home address** domicilio m 25
**honey** miel f 38
**hope, to** esperar 94
**hors d'œuvre** entremés m 41
**horse riding** equitación f 90
**hospital** hospital m 98, 144
**hot** caliente 14, 24, 38, 60, 95
**hotel** hotel m 19, 21, 22, 80
**hotel guide** guía de hoteles f 19
**hotel reservation** reserva de hotel f 19
**hot water** agua caliente f 23, 28

**hot-water bottle** botella de agua caliente f 27
**hour** hora f 153
**house** casa f 83, 85
**hovercraft** aerodeslizador m 74
**how** cómo 10
**how far** a qué distancia 10, 76
**how long** cuánto tiempo 10
**how many** cuántos(as) 10
**how much** cuánto 10
**hundred** cien, ciento 147
**hungry, to be** tener hambre 13, 35
**hunt, to** cazar 91
**hurry (to be in a)** tener prisa 21
**hurry up!** ¡dése prisa! 13
**hurt, to** doler 139, 140, 145
**husband** marido m 94
**hut** cabaña f 85
**hydrofoil** hidroplano m 74

**I**
**I** yo 161
**ice-cream** helado m 54, 64
**ice cube** cubito de hielo m 27
**ice pack** elemento congelable m 106
**iced tea** té helado m 60
**ill** enfermo(a) 140, 156
**illness** enfermedad f 140
**immediately** inmediatamente 137
**important** importante 13
**in** en 15
**include, to** incluir 20, 24, 31, 62, 80
**indigestion** indigestión f 141
**indoor (swimming pool)** cubierto(a) 91
**inexpensive** barato(a) 35, 124
**infect, to** infectar 140
**infection** infección f 141
**inflammation** inflamación f 142
**inflation** inflación f 131
**inflation rate** tasa de inflación f 131
**influenza** gripe f 142
**information** información f 67, 80
**injection** inyección f 142, 144
**injure, to** herir 139
**injured** herido(a) 79, 139
**injury** herida f 139
**ink** tinta f 105
**inn** fonda f, posada f 33
**inquiry** información f 68
**insect bite** picadura de insecto f 108, 139
**insect repellent** repelente para insectos m 109

**insect spray** spray para insectos m 109
**inside** dentro 15
**instead** en lugar de 37
**insurance** seguro m 20, 79, 144
**insurance company** compañía de seguros f 79
**interest** interés m 80, 131
**interested, to be** interesarse 83
**interesting** interesante 84
**international** internacional 132, 134
**interpreter** intérprete m 131
**intersection** cruce m 77, 79
**introduce, to** presentar 93
**introduction** presentación f 93; for-mulario de presentación m 130
**investment** inversión f 131
**invitation** invitación f 94
**invite, to** invitar 94
**invoice** factura f 131
**iodine** yodo f 109
**Ireland** Irlanda f 146
**iron (laundry)** plancha f 119
**iron, to** planchar 29
**ironmonger's** ferretería f 99
**Italy** Italia f 146
**its** su 160
**ivory** marfil m 122

**J**
**jacket** chaqueta f 117
**jade** jade m 122
**jam** mermelada f 38
**jam, to** atrancar 28, 125
**January** enero m 150
**jar** tarro m 120
**jaundice** ictericia f 142
**jaw** mandíbula f 138
**jeans** tejanos m/pl 117
**jersey** jersey m 117
**jewel box** joyero m 121
**jeweller's** joyería f 99, 121
**jewellery** joyas f/pl 127
**joint** articulación f 138
**journey** viaje m 73
**juice** jugo m 38, 40, 60; zumo m 42
**July** julio m 150
**June** junio m 150
**just (only)** sólo 16, 100

**K**
**kerosene** petróleo m 106
**ketchup** salsa de tomate f 37, 64

**key** llave f 26
**kid** (goat) cabrito m 47
**kidney** riñón m 47, 48, 138
**kilogram** kilogramo m 120
**kilometre** kilómetro m 20, 79
**kind** amable 95
**kind** (type) clase f 140
**knee** rodilla f 138
**knife** cuchillo m 36, 107
**knock, to** llamar 155
**know, to** saber 16, 24; conocer 114

**L**

**label** etiqueta f 105
**lace** encaje m 114, 127
**lady** señora f 155
**lake** lago m 85, 91
**lamb** cordero m 47
**lamp** lámpara f 29, 106, 119
**lamprey** lamprea f 46
**landmark** punto de referencia m 85
**large** grande 101, 116
**last** último(a) 14, 68, 72, 74; pasa-
   do(a) 149, 150
**late** tarde 14
**later** más tarde 135
**laugh, to** reír 11, 162
**launderette** launderama f 99
**laundry** (place) lavandería f 29, 99;
   (clothes) ropa f 29
**laundry service** servicio de lavado m
   23
**laxative** laxante m 109
**lead, to** llevar 76
**leap year** año bisiesto m 149
**leather** cuero m 114, 116
**leather goods store** tienda de artículos de cuero f 99
**leave, to** marcharse 31, 95; salir 68,
   74; (deposit) dejar 27, 71
**leek** puerro m 50
**left** izquierdo(a) 21, 63, 69, 77
**left-luggage office** oficina de equipaje f 67, 71
**leg** pierna f 47, 138
**lemon** limón m 37, 38, 53, 60, 64
**lemonade** limonada f 60
**lemon juice** jugo de limón m 60
**lens** (glasses) lente m 123; (camera)
   objetivo m 125
**lens cap** capuchón para el objetivo m
   125
**lentil** lenteja f 50

**less** menos 14
**let, to** (hire out) alquilar 155
**letter** carta f 132
**letter box** buzón m 133
**letter of credit** carta de crédito m 130
**lettuce** lechuga f 50, 64
**level crossing** paso a nivel m 79
**library** biblioteca f 81, 99
**licence** (permit) permiso m 20, 79
**lie down, to** acostarse 142
**life belt** cinturón salvavidas m 74
**life boat** bote salvavidas m 74
**lifeguard** vigilante m 92
**lift** ascensor m 27, 100
**light** luz f 28, 124; (cigarette)
   lumbre f 95
**light** ligero(a) 14, 54, 101, 128;
   liviano(a) 58; (colour) claro(a)
   101, 112, 113
**light, to** (fire) encender 32
**lighter** encendedor m 126
**lighter fluid** gasolina para encendedor m 126
**lighter gas** gas para encendedor m
   126
**light meter** exposímetro m 125
**like, to** querer 12, 20, 23; gustar 24,
   27, 93, 102, 112
**lime** (fruit) lima f 53
**line** línea f 73
**linen** (cloth) hilo m 114
**lip** labio m 138
**lipsalve** cacao para los labios m 110
**lipstick** lápiz de labios m 110
**liqueur** licor m 59, 60
**listen, to** escuchar 128
**litre** litro m 58, 75, 120
**little** (a) un poco 14
**live, to** vivir 83
**liver** hígado m 47, 138
**lobster** (spiny) langosta f 42, 46
**local** local 36, 43, 59
**long** largo(a) 30, 116, 117
**long-sighted** présbite 123
**look, to** mirar 100; ver 123
**look for, to** buscar 13
**look out!** ¡cuidado! 156
**lose, to** perder 123, 156
**loss** pérdida f 131
**lost** perdido(a) 13, 156
**lost and found office** oficina de objetos perdidos f 67, 156
**lost property office** oficina de objetos perdidos f 67, 156

**lot** *(a)* mucho 14
**lotion** loción *f* 110
**lovely** bonito(a) 94
**low** bajo(a) 92,
**lower** inferior 70
**low season** baja estación *f* 149
**low tide** marea baja *f* 92
**luck** suerte *f* 135, 152
**luggage** equipaje *m* 18, 26, 31, 71
**luggage locker** consigna automática *f* 18, 67, 71
**luggage trolley** carrito de equipaje *m* 18, 71
**luggage van** furgón de equipajes *m* 66
**lump** *(bump)* chichón *m* 139
**lunch** almuerzo *m* 34, 80
**lunch, to** almorzar 95
**lung** pulmón *m* 138

**M**

**machine** máquina *f* 113
**mackerel** caballa *f* 45
**magazine** revista *f* 105
**magnificent** magnífico(a) 84
**maid** camarera *f* 26
**mail, to** mandar por correo 28
**mail** correo *m* 28, 133
**mailbox** buzón *m* 133
**main** principal 80
**make, to** hacer 104
**make up, to** hacer 28, 71; preparar 108
**make-up remover pad** toallita de maquillaje *f* 110
**man** caballero *m* 115; hombre *m* 156
**manager** director *m* 26
**manicure** manicura *f* 30
**many** muchos(as) 14
**map** mapa *m* 76, 105
**March** marzo *m* 150
**marinated** en escabeche 46
**market** mercado *m* 81, 99
**marmalade** mermelada amarga de naranjas *f* 38
**married** casado(a) 94
**mascara** pintura de pestañas *f* 110
**mass** *(church)* misa *f* 84
**mat** *(finish)* mate 125
**match** cerilla *f* 106, 126; *(sport)* partido *m* 90
**match, to** *(colour)* hacer juego 112
**material** *(cloth)* tejido *m* 113
**matinée** sesión de la tarde *f* 87

**mattress** colchón *m* 106
**mauve** malva 113
**May** mayo *m* 150
**may** *(can)* poder 12, 163
**meadow** prado *m* 85
**meal** comida *f* 24, 34, 35, 62, 143
**mean, to** querer decir 11, 25
**means** medio *m* 74
**measles** sarampión *m* 142
**measure, to** medir 114
**meat** carne *f* 47, 61
**mechanic** mecánico *m* 78
**mechanical pencil** lapicero *m* 121
**medical** médico(a) 144
**medicine** medicina *f* 83, 143
**medium** *(meat)* regular 48
**meet, to** encontrar 96
**melon** melón *m* 42, 53, 64
**mend, to** arreglar 75; *(clothes)* remendar 29
**menthol** *(cigarettes)* mentolado(a) 126
**menu** menú *m* 37, 39; *(printed)* carta *f* 36, 40
**message** recado *m* 28, 136
**methylated spirits** alcohol de quemar *m* 106
**metre** metro *m* 112
**mezzanine** *(theatre)* anfiteatro *m* 87
**middle** medio 69, 87, 150
**midnight** medianoche *f* 153
**mild** suave 52
**mileage** kilometraje *m* 20
**milk** leche *f* 38, 60, 64
**milkshake** batido *m* 60
**million** millón *m* 148
**minced meat** carne picada *f* 47
**mineral water** agua mineral *f* 60
**minister** *(religion)* ministro *m* 84
**mint** menta *f* 51
**minute** minuto *m* 153
**mirror** espejo *m* 115, 123
**miscellaneous** diverso(a) 127
**Miss** señorita *f* 9
**miss, to** faltar 18, 29, 61
**mistake** error *m* 61; *(to make a mistake)* equivocarse 31, 62, 103
**modified American plan** media pensión *f* 24
**moisturizing cream** crema hidratante *f* 110
**moment** momento *m* 136
**monastery** monasterio *m* 81
**Monday** lunes *m* 151

money dinero *m* 129, 156
money order giro postal *m* 132
month mes *m* 150
monument monumento *m* 81
moped velomotor *m* 74
more más 14
morning mañana *f* 151
Morocco Marruecos *m* 146
mortgage hipoteca *f* 131
mosque mezquita *f* 81
mosquito net red para mosquitos *f* 106
mother madre *f* 94
motorbike motocicleta *f* 74
motorboat motora *f* 92
motorway autopista *f* 76, 79
mountain montaña *f* 85
moustache bigote *m* 31
mouth boca *f* 138
mouthwash gargarismo *m* 109
move, to mover 139, 140
movie película *f* 86
movie camera cámara de filmar *f* 124
movies cine *m* 86, 96
Mr. Señor *m* 9
Mrs. Señora *f* 9
much mucho 14
mug taza alta *f* 107
muscle músculo *m* 138, 139
museum museo *m* 81
mushroom seta *f* 44, 50; champiñon *m* 41, 50
music música *f* 83, 128
mussel mejillón *m* 42
must, to deber 31, 37, 61; tener que 23, 95
mustard mostaza *f* 37, 51, 64
mutton carnero *m* 47
my mi 160
myself mismo(a) 120

**N**

nail *(human)* uña *f* 110
nail clippers alicates de uñas *m/pl* 110
nail file lima de uñas *f* 110
nail polish esmalte de uñas *m* 110
nail polish remover acetona quita-esmalte de uñas *f* 110
nail scissors tijeras de uñas *f/pl* 110
name nombre *m* 23, 25, 79, 93
napkin servilleta *f* 36, 105
nappy pañal *m* 111
narrow estrecho(a) 116

nationality nacionalidad *f* 25
natural natural 83
natural history historia natural *f* 83
nausea náusea *f* 140
near cerca 14
near to cerca de 15
nearby cerca de aquí 77, 84
nearest más cercano(a) 78, 98
necessary necesario(a) 88
neck cuello *m* 30, 138
necklace collar *m* 121
need, to necesitar 29, 116
needle aguja *f* 27
negative negativo *m* 124
nephew sobrino *m* 94
nerve nervio *m* 138
nervous nervioso(a) 138
nervous system sistema nervioso *m* 138
Netherlands Países Bajos *m/pl* 146
never nunca 15
new nuevo(a) 14
newspaper periódico *m* 104, 105
newsstand quiosco de periódicos *m* 19, 67, 99, 104
New Year Año Nuevo *m* 152
New Zealand Nueva Zelandia *f* 146
next próximo(a) 14, 68, 73, 76, 149, 151
next to junto a 15, 77
niece sobrina *f* 94
night noche *f* 24, 26, 151
nightclub centro nocturno *m* 88
night cream crema de noche *f* 110
nightdress camisón *m* 117
nine nueve 147
nineteen diecinueve 147
ninety noventa 147
ninth noveno(a) 148
nipple *(feeding bottle)* tetina *f* 111
no no 9
noisy ruidoso(a) 25
nonalcoholic sin alcohol 60
none ninguno(a) 15
nonsmoker no fumadores *m/pl* 36, 69, 70
noon mediodía *m* 153
normal normal 30
north norte *m* 77
North America América del Norte *f* 146
nose nariz *f* 138
nosebleed hemorragia nasal *f* 141
not no 15, 163

**note** *(banknote)* billete *m* 130
**notebook** cuaderno *m* 105
**note paper** papel de cartas *m* 105
**nothing** nada 15, 17
**notice** *(sign)* indicación *f* 155
**November** noviembre *m* 150
**now** ahora 15
**number** número *m* 26, 65, 134, 136, 147
**nurse** enfermera *f* 144
**nutmeg** nuez moscada *f* 51

## O

**occupation** ocupación *f* 94
**occupied** ocupado(a) 14, 70, 155
**October** octubre *m* 150
**octopus** pulpo *m* 46
**office** oficina *f* 19, 67, 99, 132, 156
**oil** aceite *m* 30, 37, 75, 111
**oily** graso(a) 30, 111
**old** viejo(a) 14
**old town** ciudad vieja *f* 81
**olive** aceituna *f* 41
**olive oil** aceite de oliva *m* 37
**omelet** tortilla *f* 44
**on** sobre, en 15
**once** una vez 148
**one** uno(a) 147
**one-way** *(ticket)* ida 65, 69
**one-way street** dirección única *f* 79
**onion** cebolla *f* 50
**only** sólo 80, 109
**on request** a petición 73
**on time** a la hora 68
**onyx** ónix *m* 122
**open** abierto(a) 14, 82, 155
**open, to** abrir 11, 17, 82, 108, 129, 131, 132, 142
**open-air** al aire libre 91
**opera** ópera *f* 87
**opera house** teatro de la ópera *m* 87
**operation** operación *f* 144
**operator** telefonista *m/f* 134
**operetta** opereta *f* 87
**opposite** enfrente 77
**optician** óptico *m* 99, 123
**or** o 15
**orange** naranja 113
**orange** naranja *f* 53, 64
**orange juice** jugo de naranja *m* 38, 60; zumo de naranja *m* 42
**orangeade** naranjada *f* 60
**orchestra** orquesta *f* 88; *(seats)* platea *f* 87

**order, to** *(meal)* pedir 36, 61; *(goods)* encargar 102, 103
**oregano** orégano *m* 51
**ornithology** ornitología *f* 83
**our** nuestro(a) 160
**out of order** estropeado(a) 78; averiado(a) 155
**out of stock** agotado(a) 103
**outlet** *(electric)* enchufe *m* 26
**outside** fuera 15, 36
**overdone** demasiado hecho(a) 61
**overheat, to** *(engine)* calentar demasiado 78
**overtake, to** adelantar 79
**owe, to** deber 144
**oxtail** rabo de buey *m* 47
**oyster** ostra *f* 42, 46

## P

**pacifier** chupete *m* 111
**packet** paquete *m* 120; *(cigarettes)* cajetilla *f* 126
**page** *(hotel)* botones *m* 26
**pail** cubo *m* 128
**pain** dolor *m* 140, 141, 144
**painkiller** analgésico *m* 140, 144
**paint** pintura *f* 155
**paint, to** pintar 83
**paintbox** caja de pinturas *f* 105
**painter** pintor *m* 83
**painting** pintura *f* 83
**pair** par *m* 116
**pajamas** pijama *m* 118
**palace** palacio *m* 81
**palpitation** palpitación *f* 141
**panties** bragas *f/pl* 117
**pants** *(trousers)* pantalón *m* 117
**panty girdle** faja braga *f* 117
**panty hose** leotardos *m/pl* 117
**paper** papel *m* 104, 105
**paperback** rústica *f* 105
**paper napkin** servillete de papel *f* 105
**paraffin** *(fuel)* petróleo *m* 106
**parcel** paquete *m* 132
**pardon** perdone 10
**parents** padres *m/pl* 94
**park** parque *m* 81
**park, to** aparcar 26, 77
**parking** aparcamiento *m* 77; estacionamiento *m* 79
**parking disc** disco de aparcamiento *m* 77
**parking meter** parquímetro *m* 77

**parliament** cortes *f/pl* 81
**parsley** perejil *m* 51
**parsnip** chirivía *f* 50
**part** parte *f* 138; *(hair)* raya *f* 30
**parting** raya *f* 30
**partridge** perdiz *f* 48, 49
**pass** *(rail, bus)* pase *m* 72
**pass, to** *(car)* adelantar 79
**passport** pasaporte *m* 16, 17, 25, 156
**passport photo** foto para pasaporte *f* 124
**pass through, to** estar de paso 16
**pasta** pastas *f/pl* 42
**paste** *(glue)* engrudo *m* 105
**pastry** pastel *m* 64
**pastry shop** pastelería *f* 33, 99
**path** sendero *m* 155
**patient** paciente *m/f* 144
**pay, to** pagar 17, 62, 100, 102
**payment** pago *m* 131
**pea** guisante *m* 50
**peach** melocotón *m* 53, 54
**peanut** cacahuete *m* 53
**pear** pera *f* 53
**pearl** perla *f* 122
**people** gente *f* 79
**pedestrian** peatón *m* 79
**peg** *(tent)* estaca *f* 107
**pen** pluma *f* 105
**pencil** lápiz *m* 105
**pencil sharpener** sacapuntas *m* 105
**pendant** medallón *m* 121
**penicilline** penicilina *f* 143
**penknife** cortaplumas *m* 106
**pensioner** jubilado(a) *m/f* 82
**pepper** pimienta *f* 37, 38, 51, 64
**peppers** pimientos *m/pl* 42, 48, 50
**per cent** por ciento 148
**perch** perca *f* 46
**per day** por día 20, 32, 91
**performance** *(session)* función *f* 86
**perfume** perfume *m* 110
**perfume shop** perfumería *f* 108
**perhaps** quizá, tal vez 15
**per hour** por hora 77, 91
**period** *(monthly)* reglas *f/pl* 141
**period pains** dolores menstruales *m/pl* 141
**permanent wave** permanente *f* 30
**permit** permiso *m* 91
**per night** por noche 24
**per person** por persona 32
**person** persona *f* 32

**personal** personal 17
**personal call** llamada personal *f* 135
**personal cheque** cheque personal *m* 130
**person-to-person call** llamada personal *f* 135
**per week** por semana 20, 24
**peseta** peseta *f* 129
**petrol** gasolina *f* 75, 78
**pewter** peltre *m* 122
**pheasant** faisán *m* 48
**phone** teléfono *m* 28, 134
**phone, to** telefonear 134
**phone booth** cabina de teléfono *f* 134
**phone call** llamada 135, 136
**phone number** número de teléfono *m* 96
**photo** foto(grafía) *f* 82, 124, 125
**photocopy** fotocopia *f* 104
**photograph, to** fotografiar, tomar fotografías 82
**photographer** fotógrafo *m* 99
**photography** fotografía *f* 124
**phrase** expresión *f* 11
**pickles** pepinillos *m/pl* 50, 64
**pick up, to** recoger 80
**picnic** merienda *f* 63
**picnic basket** bolsa para merienda *f* 106
**picture** cuadro *m* 83; *(photo)* fotografía *f* 82
**piece** *(slice)* trozo *m* 52, 120
**pigeon** pichón *m* 49
**pill** píldora *f* 141, 143
**pillow** almohada *f* 27
**pin** alfiler *m* 121
**pineapple** piña *f* 53
**pineapple juice** zumo de piña *m* 42
**pink** rosa 113
**pipe** pipa *f* 126
**pipe cleaner** limpiapipas *m* 126
**pipe tobacco** tabaco para pipa *m* 126
**pipe tool** utensilios para pipa *m/pl* 126
**pitcher** botijo *m* 127
**place** lugar *m* 25
**place of birth** lugar de nacimiento *m* 25
**plane** avión *m* 65
**plaster** yeso *m* 140
**plastic** plástico *m* 107
**plastic bag** bolsa de plástico *f* 107
**plate** plato *m* 36, 61, 107
**platform** *(station)* andén *m* 67, 68, 69, 70

platinum platino *m* 122
play *(theatre)* pieza *f* 86
play, to jugar 90; *(music)* tocar 88
playground campo de juego *m* 32
playing card naipe *m* 105
please por favor 9
plimsolls zapatos de lona *m/pl* 116
plug *(electric)* clavija de enchufe *f* 29, 119
plum ciruela *f* 53
p.m. de la tarde 133
pneumonia neumonía *f* 142
poached hervido(a) 46
pocket bolsillo *m* 118
pocket watch reloj de bolsillo *m* 121
point punto *m* 80
point, to *(show)* señalar 11
poison veneno *m* 109
poisoning intoxicación *f* 142
police policía *f* 78, 156
police station comisaría de policía *f* 99, 156
pomegranate granada *f* 53
poplin popelín *m* 114
popular popular 80
pork cerdo *m* 47
port puerto *m* 74; *(wine)* oporto *m* 60
portable portátil 119
porter mozo *m* 18, 26, 71
portion porción *f* 61; ración *f* 54
Portugal Portugal *m* 146
possible posible 137
post *(letters)* correo *m* 133
post, to mandar por correo 28
postage franqueo *m* 132
postage stamp sello *m* 28, 126, 132
postcard tarjeta postal *f* 105, 126, 132
poste restante lista de correos *f* 133
post office oficina de correos *f* 99, 132
potato patata *f* 50, 64
pottery alfarería *f* 83
poultry aves *f/pl* 48
pound *(money)* libra *f* 18, 102, 130; *(weight)* libra *f* 120
powder polvo *m* 110
powder compact polvera *f* 121
prawn gamba *f* 41, 43; quisquilla *f* 42, 46; langostino *m* 42, 46
preference preferencia *f* 101
pregnant embarazada 141
premium *(gasoline)* super 75

prescribe, to recetar 143
prescription receta *f* 108, 143
present *(gift)* regalo *m* 120
press, to *(iron)* planchar 29
press stud broche de presión *m* 118
pressure presión *f* 75
price precio *m* 24
priest sacerdote *m* 84
print *(photo)* copia *f* 125
print, to imprimir 124
private privado(a) 155; particular 80, 92, 155
private toilet water particular *m* 23
processing *(photo)* revelado *m* 124
profession profesión *f* 25
profit ganancia *f* 131
programme programa *m* 87, 88
prohibit, to prohibir 32, 79, 92, 155
pronunciation pronunciación *f* 6, 11
propelling pencil lapicero *m* 121
Protestant protestante 84
provide, to conseguir 131
prune ciruela pasa *f* 53
public holiday día festivo *m* 152
pull, to tirar 155
pullover pullover *m* 117
puncture pinchazo *m* 75
purchase compra *f* 131
pure puro(a) 113
purple purpúreo(a) 113
push, to empujar 155
pyjamas pijama *m* 118

**Q**
quail codorniz *f* 48
quality calidad *f* 103, 114
quantity cantidad *f* 14, 103
quarter cuarto *m* 148; *(part of town)* barrio *m* 81
quarter of an hour cuarto de hora *m* 153
quartz cuarzo *m* 122
question pregunta *f* 10, 76
quick rápido(a) 14, 156
quickly rápidamente 137
quiet tranquilo(a) 23, 25

**R**
rabbi rabino *m* 84
rabbit conejo *m* 48, 49
race course/track pista de carreras *f* 91
racket *(sport)* raqueta *f* 91
radiator radiador *m* 78

**radio** *(set)* radio f 23, 28, 119
**radish** rábano m 42, 50
**railroad crossing** paso a nivel m 79
**railway** ferrocarril m 154
**railway station** estación (de ferroca-rril) f 19, 21, 67, 70
**rain, to** llover 94
**rain boot** bota par la lluvia f 116
**raincoat** impermeable m 118
**raisin** pasa f 53
**rangefinder** telémetro m 125
**rare** *(meat)* poco hecho(a) 48
**rash** sarpullido m 139
**raspberry** frambuesa f 53
**rate** tarifa f 20; tasa f 131
**razor** máquina (navaja) de afeitar f 111
**razor blade** hoja de afeitar f 111
**reading-lamp** lámpara para leer f 27
**ready** listo(a) 29, 116, 123, 125
**real** auténtico(a) 121
**rear** trasero(a) 75
**receipt** recibo m 103, 144
**recent** reciente 149
**reception** recepción f 23
**receptionist** recepcionista m/f 26
**recommend, to** recomendar 35, 80, 86, 88, 137, 145; aconsejar 36, 41, 43, 50, 54
**record** *(disc)* disco m 127, 128
**record player** tocadiscos m 119
**rectangular** rectangular 101
**red** rojo(a) 113; *(wine)* tinto 58
**redcurrant** grosella roja f 53
**red mullet** salmonete m 46
**reduction** descuento m 24, 82
**refill** recambio m 105
**refund, to** devolver 103
**regards** recuerdos m/pl 152
**register, to** facturar 71
**registered mail** registrado(a) 133
**registration** inscripción f 25
**registration form** ficha f 25
**regular** *(petrol)* normal 75
**religion** religión f 83
**religious service** servicio religioso m 84
**rent, to** alquilar 20, 91, 92, 119, 155
**rental** alquiler m 20
**repair** reparación f 125
**repair, to** arreglar 29, 119, 121, 123, 145; reparar 116, 125
**repeat, to** repetir 11
**report, to** denunciar 156

**reservation** reserva f 19, 23, 65, 69
**reservation office** oficina de reser-vas f m 19, 67
**reserve, to** reservar 19, 23, 35, 86
**restaurant** restaurante m 19, 32, 34, 35, 67
**return** *(ticket)* ida y vuelta 65, 69
**return, to** *(give back)* devolver 103
**reversed charge call** llamada a cobro revertido f 135
**rheumatism** reumatismo m 141
**rhubarb** ruibarbo m 53
**rib** costilla f 138
**ribbon** cinta f 105
**rice** arroz m 45, 50, 54
**ride, to** *(horse)* montar a caballo 74
**right** derecho(a) 21, 63, 69, 77; *(correct)* correcto(a) 14
**ring** *(on finger)* sortija f 121
**ring, to** tocar el timbre 155; telefo-near 134
**river** río 85, 91
**road** carretera f 76, 77, 79, 85
**road map** mapa de carreteras m 105
**road sign** señal de circulación f 79
**roast** asado(a) 48, 49
**roll** *(bread)* panecillo m 37, 64
**roller skate** patín de ruedas m 128
**roll film** carrete m, rollo m 124
**roll-neck** cuello vuelto m 117
**room** habitación f 19, 23, 24, 25, 27; *(space)* sitio m 32
**room number** número de la habita-ción m 26
**room service** servicio de habitación m 23
**rope** cuerda f 107
**rosary** rosario m 122, 127
**rosé** rosé 58
**rosemary** romero m 51
**rouge** colorete m 111
**round** redondo(a) 101
**round** *(golf)* juego m 91
**round-neck** cuello redondo m 117
**roundtrip** *(ticket)* ida y vuelta 65, 69
**rowing-boat** barca f 92
**royal palace** palacio real m 82
**rubber** *(eraser)* goma de borrar f 105
**ruby** rubí m 122
**rucksack** mochila f 107
**ruin** ruina f 82
**ruler** regla f 105
**rum** ron m 44, 60
**running water** agua corriente f 23

# S

safe *(not dangerous)* sin peligro 92
safe caja fuerte f 27
safety pin imperdible m 111
saffron azafrán m 51
sage salvia f 51
sailing-boat velero m 92
salad ensalada f 43, 64
salami salchichón m 42, 64
sale venta f 131; *(bargains)* rebajas f/pl 101
sales tax impuesto m 102
salmon salmón m 42, 46
salt sal f 37, 38, 51, 64
salty salado(a) 61
sand arena f 91
sandal sandalia f 116
sandwich bocadillo m 64
sanitary towel/napkin paño higiénico m 109
sapphire zafiro m 122
sardine sardina f 42, 46
satin raso m 114
Saturday sábado m 151
sauce salsa f 49
saucepan cazo m 107
saucer platillo m 107
sausage salchicha f 47, 64
sautéed salteado(a) 46, 48
scallop venera f 46
scarf bufanda f 118
scarlet escarlata 113
school escuela f 79
scissors tijeras f/pl 107, 110
scooter escúter m 74
Scotch whisky escocés m 60
Scotland Escocia f 146
scrambled egg huevo revuelto m 38, 44
screwdriver destornillador m 107
sculptor escultor m 83
sculpture escultura f 83
sea mar m 23, 85
sea bream besugo m 45
seafood mariscos m/pl 45
season estación f 149
seasoning condimento m 37
seat asiento m 69, 70, 87; *(theatre, etc.)* localidad f, entrada f 86, 87, 89
seat belt cinturón de seguridad m 75
second segundo(a) 148
second segundo m 153,
second class segunda clase f 66, 69

second hand segundero manecilla m 122
second-hand de segunda mano 104
secretary secretario(a) m/f 27, 131
see, to ver 12, 163
sell, to vender 100
send, to mandar 31, 78, 102, 132, 133; enviar 103
send up, to subir 26
sentence frase f 11
separately separadamente 62
September septiembre m 150
serge estameña f 114
serious serio(a) 139
service servicio m 24, 62, 98, 100; *(religion)* servicio m 84
serviette servilleta f 36
set *(hair)* marcado m 30
set menu plato combinado m 36, 39
setting lotion fijador m 30, 111
seven siete 147
seventeen diecisiete 147
seventh séptimo(a) 148
seventy setenta 147
sew, to coser 29
shade sombra f 89; *(colour)* tono m 112
shampoo lavado m 30; champú m 30, 111
shape forma f 103
sharp *(pain)* agudo(a) 140
shave, to afeitar 30
shaver máquina de afeitar (eléctrica) f 26, 119
shaving cream crema de afeitar f 111
she ella 161
shelf estante m 120
sherry jerez m 43, 48, 55, 60
ship embarcación f 74
shirt camisa f 118
shirt-maker's camisería f 99
shiver escalofrío m 140
shoe zapato m 116
shoelace cordón (para zapato) m 116
shoemaker's zapatero m 99
shoe polish crema para zapatos f 116
shoe shop zapatería f 99
shop tienda f, comercio m 98, 99; *(big)* almacén m 98
shopping compras f/pl 97
shopping area zona de tiendas f 82, 100

**shopping centre** centro comercial *m* 99

**short** corto(a) 30, 116, 117

**shorts** pantalón corto *m* 118

**short-sighted** miope 123

**shoulder** espalda *f* 138

**shovel** pala *f* 128

**show** *(theatre)* función *f* 86; *(night-club)* atracciones *f/pl* 88

**show, to** enseñar 12, 13, 76, 100, 124; mostrar 119

**shower** ducha *f* 23, 32

**shrimp** quisquilla *f* 42, 46; gamba *f* 41, 43; langostino *m* 42, 46

**shrink, to** encoger 113

**shut** cerrado(a) 14

**shutter** *(window)* postigo *m* 29; *(camera)* obturador *m* 125

**sick** *(ill)* enfermo 140, 156

**sickness** *(illness)* enfermedad *f* 140

**side** lado *m* 30

**sideboards/burns** patillas *f/pl* 31

**sightseeing tour** recorrido turístico *m* 80

**sign** *(notice)* letrero *m* 155; *(road)* señal *f* 79

**sign, to** firmar 25

**signature** firma *f* 25

**signet ring** sortija de sello *f* 121

**silk** seda *f* 114

**silver** plateado(a) 113

**silver** plata *f* 121, 122

**silver plate** plata chapada *f* 122

**silverware** objetos de plata *m/pl* 122

**simple** sencillo(a) 124

**since** desde 15, 150

**sing, to** cantar 88

**single** soltero(a) 94; *(ticket)* ida 65, 69

**single room** habitación sencilla *f* 19, 23

**sister** hermana *f* 94

**sit down, to** sentarse 96

**six** seis 147

**sixteen** dieciséis 147

**sixth** sexto(a) 148

**sixty** sesenta 147

**size** tamaño *m* 124; *(clothes, shoes)* talla *f* 114, 115, 116

**sketching block** bloc de dibujo *m* 105

**ski, to** esquiar 91

**skiing** esquí *m* 90

**ski lift** telesquí *m* 91

**skin** piel *f* 138

**skin-diving** natación submarina *m* 92

**skirt** falda *f* 118

**sleep, to** dormir 71, 144

**sleeping bag** saco de dormir *m* 107

**sleeping-car** coche cama *m* 66, 68, 71

**sleeping pill** somnífero *m* 109, 143, 144

**sleeve** manga *f* 117

**slice** rebanada *f* 120

**slide** *(photo)* diapositiva *f* 124

**slip** combinación *f* 118

**slipper** zapatilla *f* 116

**slow** lento(a) 14; *(slowly)* despacio 11, 21, 79, 135

**small** pequeño(a) 14, 25, 54, 61, 101, 116

**smoke, to** fumar 155

**smoked** ahumado(a) 41, 42, 46

**smoker** fumadores *m/pl* 69, 70

**snack** tentempié *m* 63

**snail** caracol *m* 41

**snap fastener** broche de presión *m* 118

**sneakers** zapatos de lona *m/pl* 116

**snorkel** espantasuegras *m/pl* 128

**snow, to** nevar 94

**snuff** rapé *m* 126

**soap** jabón *m* 27, 111

**soccer** fútbol *m* 90

**sock** calcetín *m* 118

**socket** *(outlet)* enchufe *m* 26

**soda water** soda *f* 60

**soft** blando(a) 52; suave 123

**soft-boiled** *(egg)* pasado por agua 38

**sold out** *(theatre)* agotado(a) 87

**sole** suela *f* 116; *(fish)* lenguado *m* 46

**solution** solución *f* 123

**some** unos(as) 14

**someone** alguien 96

**something** algo 36, 54, 108, 112, 114, 125, 139

**son** hijo *m* 94

**soon** pronto 15

**sore throat** angina *f* 141

**sorry** *(I'm)* lo siento 10, 16, 87

**sort** clase *f* 52, 120

**soup** sopa *f* 43

**south** sur *m* 77

**South Africa** Africa del Sur *f* 146

**South America** América del Sur *f* 146

**souvenir** recuerdo *m* 127

**souvenir shop** tienda de objetos de regalo *f* 99

**Soviet Union** Unión Soviética f 146
**spade** pala f 128
**spaghetti** espaguetis m/pl 64
**Spain** España f 146
**Spanish** español(a) 11, 114, 104
**spare tyre** rueda de repuesto f 75
**sparking plug** bujía f 75
**sparkling** (wine) espumoso(a) 58
**spark plug** bujía f 75
**speak, to** hablar 11, 135, 162
**speaker** (loudspeaker) altavoz m 119
**special** especial 20, 37
**special delivery** urgente 133
**specialist** especialista m/f 142
**speciality** especialidad f 40, 43, 59
**specimen** (medical) muestra f 142
**spectacle case** estuche para gafas m
123
**spend, to** gastar 101
**spice** especia f 51
**spinach** espinaca f 50
**spine** espina dorsal f 138
**spiny lobster** langosta f 46
**sponge** esponja f 111
**spoon** cuchara f 36, 107
**sport** deporte m 90
**sporting goods shop** tienda de
artículos de deporte f 99
**sprain, to** torcer 140
**spring** (season) primavera f 149
**square** cuadrado(a) 101
**squid** calamar m 41, 46
**stadium** estadio m 82
**staff** personal m 26
**stain** mancha f 29
**stainless steel** acero inoxidable m
107, 122
**stalls** (theatre) platea f 87
**stamp** (postage) sello m 28, 126, 132
**staple** grapa f 105
**start, to** empezar 80, 86, 88; (car)
arrancar 78
**starter** entremés m 41; tapa f 63
**station** (railway) estación (de ferrocarril) f 21, 67, 70; (underground,
subway) estación de metro f 73
**stationer's** papelería f 99, 104
**statue** estatua f 82
**stay** estancia f 31, 93
**stay, to** quedarse 16, 24, 25; hospe-
darse 93
**steak** filete m 47
**steal, to** robar 156
**steamed** cocido(a) al vapor 46

**stewed** estofado(a) 48
**stew pot** cacerola f 107
**stiff neck** tortícolis f 141
**sting** picadura f 139
**sting, to** picar 139
**stock exchange** bolsa f 82
**stocking** media f 118
**stomach** estómago m 138
**stomach ache** dolor de estómago m
141
**stools** heces f/pl 142
**stop** (bus) parada f 72, 73
**stop!** alto 79; deténgase 156
**stop, to** parar 21, 68, 70; detenerse
74
**stop thief!** al ladrón 156
**store** tienda f 98, 99; (big) almacén
m 98
**straight ahead** (todo) derecho 21,
77
**strange** extraño(a) 84
**strawberry** fresa f 53, 54
**street** calle f 25, 76
**street map** mapa de la ciudad m 105
**string** cuerda f 105
**strong** fuerte 52, 143
**student** estudiante m/f 82, 94
**stuffed** relleno(a) 41
**subway** metro m 73
**suede** ante m 114, 116
**sufficient** suficiente 68
**sugar** azúcar m 37, 64
**suit** (man) traje m 118; (woman)
vestido m 118
**suitcase** maleta f 18
**summer** verano m 149
**sun** sol m 89, 94
**sunburn** quemadura de sol f 108
**Sunday** domingo m 151
**sunglasses** gafas de sol f/pl 123
**sunny** soleado(a) 94
**sunshade** (beach) sombrilla f 92
**sunstroke** insolación f 141
**sun-tan cream** crema solar f 111
**super** (petrol) súper 75
**superb** soberbio(a) 84
**supermarket** supermercado m 99
**suppository** supositorio m 109
**surcharge** suplemento m 69
**sure** (fact) cierto(a) 160
**surfboard** plancha de deslizamiento f
92
**surgery** (consulting room) consulta f
137

**surgical dressing** hilas *f/pl* 109
**suspenders** *(Am.)* tirantes *m/pl* 118
**sweater** suéter *m* 118
**sweatshirt** suéter de tela de punto *m* 118
**sweet** dulce 58, 61
**sweet** caramelo *m* 64, 126
**sweet corn** maíz *m* 50
**sweetener** edulcorante *m* 37, 64
**sweet shop** bombonería *f* 99
**swell, to** hinchar 139
**swelling** hinchazón *f* 139
**swim, to** nadar 91, 92; bañarse 92
**swimming** natación *f* 90
**swimming pool** piscina *f* 32, 91
**swimming trunks** bañador *m* 118
**swimsuit** traje de baño *m* 118
**switch** interruptor *m* 29
**switchboard operator** telefonista *m/f* 26
**switch on, to** *(light)* encender 79
**swollen** hinchado(a) 139
**swordfish** pez espada *m* 46
**synagogue** sinagoga *f* 84
**synthetic** sintético(a) 114
**system** sistema *m* 138

**T**

**table** mesa *f* 35, 36, 107
**tablet** tableta *f* 109
**taffeta** tafetán *m* 114
**tailor's** sastre *m* 99
**take, to** llevar 18, 21, 67, 102; tomar 25, 72
**take away, to** *(carry)* llevar 63, 103
**take off, to** *(plane)* despegar 65
**talcum powder** polvo de talco *m* 111
**tambourine** pandereta *f* 127
**tampon** tampón higiénico *m* 109
**tangerine** mandarina *f* 53
**tap** *(water)* grifo *m* 28
**tape recorder** magnetófono *m* 119
**tarragon** estragón *m* 51
**tart** tarta *f* 54; tartaleta *f* 42
**tax** impuesto *m* 24, 102
**taxi** taxi *m* 19, 21, 31, 67
**tea** té *m* 38, 50, 64
**tear, to** desgarrar 140
**tearoom** salón de té *m* 34
**teaspoon** cucharilla *f* 107, 143
**teat** *(feeding bottle)* tetina *f* 111
**telegram** telegrama *m* 133
**telephone** teléfono *m* 28, 134

**telephone, to** telefonear 134
**telephone booth** cabina de teléfonos *f* 134
**telephone call** llamada *f* 135, 136
**telephone directory** guía de teléfonos *f* 134
**telephone number** número de teléfono *m* 96, 134, 136
**telephoto lens** lente de acercamiento *f* 125
**television** televisión *f* 23; *(set)* televisor *m* 28
**telex** télex *m* 133
**telex, to** mandar un télex 130
**tell, to** decir 12, 73, 76, 135, 136, 153
**temperature** temperatura *f* 92, 140, 142
**temporary** temporal 145
**ten** diez 147
**tendon** tendón *m* 138
**tennis** tenis *m* 91
**tennis court** pista de tenis *f* 91
**tennis racket** raqueta de tenis *f* 91
**tent** tienda (de campaña) *f* 32, 107
**tent peg** estaca *f* 107
**tent pole** mástil *m* 107
**tenth** décimo(a) 148
**term** *(word)* expresión *f* 131
**terminus** terminal *f* 72
**terrible** terrible 84
**terrycloth** tela de toalla *f* 114
**tetanus** tétanos *m* 140
**than** que 14
**thank you** gracias 10
**that** ése(a), aquél(lla) 161
**the** el, la 159
**theatre** teatro *m* 86
**theft** robo *m* 156
**their** su 160
**then** entonces 15
**there** allí 14
**thermometer** termómetro *m* 109, 144
**these** éstos(as) 161
**they** ellos(as) 161
**thief** ladrón *m* 156
**thigh** muslo *m* 138
**thin** tenue 114
**think, to** *(believe)* creer 62, 95
**third** tercero(a) 148
**third** tercio *m* 148
**thirsty, to be** tener sed 13, 35
**thirteen** trece 147

**thirty** treinta 147
**this** éste(a) 161
**those** ésos(as), aquéllos(as) 161
**thousand** mil 148
**thread** hilo m 27
**three** tres 147
**throat** garganta f 138
**throat lozenge** pastilla para la garganta f 109
**through train** tren directo m 68, 69
**thumb** pulgar m 138
**thumbtack** chincheta f 105
**Thursday** jueves m 151
**thyme** tomillo m 51
**ticket** billete m 65, 69, 72, 156; *(theatre, etc.)* localidad f, entrada f 86, 87, 90
**ticket office** taquilla f 67
**tide** marea f 92
**tie** corbata f 118
**tie clip** sujetador de corbata m 122
**tight** ajustado(a) 116
**tights** leotardos m/pl 118
**time** tiempo m 80; *(clock)* hora f 137, 153; *(occasion)* vez f 143
**timetable** *(railway guide)* guía de ferrocarriles f 68
**tin** *(can)* lata f 120
**tinfoil** papel de estaño m 107
**tin opener** abrelatas m 107
**tint** tinte m 111
**tinted** ahumado(a) 123
**tire** neumático m 75
**tired** cansado(a) 13
**tissue** *(handkerchief)* pañuelo de papel m 111
**tissue paper** papel de seda m 105
**to** a, para 15
**toast** tostada f 38, 64
**tobacco** tabaco m 126
**tobacconist's** tabacos m/pl 99, 126; estanco m 99
**today** hoy 29, 151
**toe** dedo del pie m 138
**toilet paper** papel higiénico m 111
**toiletry** artículos de tocador m/pl 110
**toilets** servicios m/pl 27, 28, 32, 67
**toll** peaje m 79
**tomato** tomate m 50, 64
**tomato juice** zumo de tomate m 42; jugo de tomate m 60
**tomb** tumba f 82
**tomorrow** mañana 29, 151
**tongue** lengua f 138

**tonic water** tónica f 60
**tonight** esta noche 29, 86, 87, 96
**tonsil** amígdala f 138
**too** demasiado 14; *(also)* también 15
**tool kit** caja de herramientos f 107
**tooth** diente m 145
**toothache** dolor de muelas m 145
**toothbrush** cepillo de dientes m 111, 119
**toothpaste** pasta de dientes f 111
**topaz** topacio m 122
**torch** *(flashlight)* linterna f 107
**torn** desgarrado(a) 140
**touch, to** tocar 155
**tough** duro(a) 61
**tourist information** información turística f 67
**tourist office** oficina de turismo f 80
**towel** toalla f 27
**tower** torre f 82
**town** ciudad f 21, 76, 105
**town hall** ayuntamiento m 82
**tow truck** grúa f 78
**toy** juguete m 128
**toy shop** juguetería f 99
**tracing paper** papel transparente m 105
**tracksuit** chandal de entrenamiento m 118
**traffic** *(car)* tráfico m 76
**traffic light** semáforo m 77
**trailer** caravana f 32
**train** tren m 66, 68, 69, 70, 73
**tranquillizer** sedante m 109
**transfer** *(bank)* transferencia f 131
**transformer** transformador m 119
**translate, to** traducir 11
**transport** transporte m 74
**travel agency** agencia de viajes f 99
**traveller's cheque** cheque de viajero m 18, 62, 102, 129, 130
**travel sickness** mareo m 108
**treatment** tratamiento m 143
**tree** árbol m 85
**tremendous** tremendo 84
**trim, to** *(beard)* recortar 31
**trip** viaje m 73, 94, 152
**tripe** callos m/pl 41, 47
**trolley** carrito m 18, 71
**trousers** pantalón m 118
**trout** trucha f 46
**truffle** trufa f 50
**try, to** probar 115; intentar 135
**T-shirt** camiseta f 118

**tube** tubo *m* 120
**Tuesday** martes *m* 151
**tulle** tul *m* 114
**tuna** atún *m* 41, 45
**Tunisia** Túnez *m* 146
**tunny** atún *m* 41, 45
**turbot** rodaballo *m* 46
**turkey** pavo *m* 48
**turn, to** *(change direction)* doblar 21, 77
**turquoise** turquesa 113
**turquoise** turquesa *f* 122
**turtleneck** cuello vuelto *m* 117
**tuxedo** smoking *m* 117
**tweezers** pinzas *f/pl* 111
**twelve** doce 147
**twenty** veinte 147
**twice** dos veces 148
**twin bed** dos camas *f/pl* 23
**two** dos 147
**type** *(kind)* clase *f* 140
**typewriter** máquina de escribir *f* 27
**typewriter ribbon** cinta para máquina *f* 105
**typical** típico(a) 35
**typing paper** papel de máquina *m* 105
**tyre** neumático *m* 75

**U**

**ugly** feo(a) 14, 84
**umbrella** paraguas *m* 118; *(beach)* sombrilla *f* 92
**uncle** tío *m* 94
**unconscious** inconsciente 139
**under** debajo 15
**underdone** *(meat)* poco hecho(a) 48, 61
**underground** *(railway)* metro *m* 73
**underpants** calzoncillos *m/pl* 118
**undershirt** camiseta *f* 118
**understand, to** comprender 12, 16; entender 12
**undress, to** desvestir 142
**United States** Estados Unidos *m/pl* 146
**university** universidad *f* 82
**unleaded** sin plomo 75
**until** hasta 150
**up** arriba 15
**upper** superior 70
**upset stomach** molestias de estómago *f/pl* 108
**upstairs** arriba 15, 69
**urgent** urgente 13, 145

**urine** orina *f* 142
**use** uso *m* 17, 109
**use, to** usar 134
**useful** útil 15

**V**

**vacancy** habitación libre *f* 23
**vacant** libre 14, 155
**vacation** vacaciones *f/pl* 151
**vaccinate, to** vacunar 140
**vacuum flask** termo *m* 107
**vaginal** vaginal 141
**valley** valle *m* 85
**value** valor *m* 131
**vanilla** vainilla *f* 51, 54
**veal** ternera *f* 47
**vegetable** verdura *f*, legumbre *f* 50
**vegetable store** verdulería *f* 99
**vegetarian** vegetariano(a) 37
**vein** vena *f* 138
**velvet** terciopelo *m* 114
**venereal disease** enfermedad venérea *f* 142
**venison** venado *m* 49
**vermouth** vermut *m* 55, 60
**very** muy 15
**vest** camiseta *f* 118; *(Am.)* chaleco *m* 118
**veterinarian** veterinario *m* 99
**video cassette** video-cassette *f* 119, 127
**video-recorder** video-grabadora *f* 119
**video tape** cinta video *f* 124
**view** vista *f* 23, 25
**village** pueblo *m* 76, 85
**vinegar** vinagre *m* 37
**vineyard** viñedo *m* 85
**visit** visita *f* 144
**visit, to** visitar 84
**visiting hours** horas de visita *f/pl* 144
**V-neck** cuello en forma de V *m* 117
**volleyball** balonvolea *m* 90
**voltage** voltaje *m* 119
**vomit, to** vomitar 140

**W**

**waistcoat** chaleco *m* 118
**wait, to** esperar 21, 96, 108
**waiter** camarero *m* 26, 36
**waiting-room** sala de espera *f* 67
**waitress** camarera *f* 26, 36
**wake, to** despertar 27; llamar 71
**Wales** País de Gales *m* 146

**walk, to** caminar 74; ir a pie 85
**wall** muro *m* 85
**wallet** cartera *f* 156
**walnut** nuez *f* 53
**want, to** *(wish)* desear, querer 12
**wash, to** lavar 29
**washable** lavable 113
**wash-basin** lavabo *m* 28
**washing powder** jabón en polvo *m* 107
**watch** reloj *m* 121, 122
**watchmaker's** relojería *f* 99, 121
**watchstrap** correa de reloj *f* 122
**water** agua *f* 23, 28, 32, 38, 75, 92
**waterfall** cascada *f* 85
**water flask** cantimplora *f* 107
**watermelon** sandía *f* 53
**water-ski** esquí acuático *m* 92
**wave** ola *f* 92
**way** camino *m* 76
**we** nosotros(as) 161
**weather** tiempo *m* 94
**wedding ring** anillo de boda *m* 121
**Wednesday** miércoles *m* 151
**week** semana *f* 16, 20, 24, 151
**weekday** día de la semana *m* 151
**weekend** fin de semana *m* 151
**well** *(healthy)* bien 10, 140
**well-done** *(meat)* muy hecho(a) 48
**west** oeste *m* 77
**western** *(film)* película del Oeste *f* 86
**what** qué 10; cómo 11; cuál 20
**wheel** rueda *f* 78
**when** cuándo 10
**where** dónde 10
**which** cuál 10
**whisky** whisky *m* 17, 60
**white** blanco(a) 58, 113
**whitebait** boquerón *m* 45
**whiting** pescadilla *f* 46
**who** quién 10
**why** por qué 10
**wick** mecha *f* 126
**wide** ancho(a) 116
**wide-angle lens** gran angular *m* 125
**wife** mujer *f* 94
**wild boar** jabalí *m* 49
**wind** viento *m* 95
**windmill** molino de viento *m* 85
**window** ventana *f* 28, 36, 69;
   *(shop)* escaparate *m* 100, 112
**windscreen/shield** parabrisas *m* 76
**wine** vino *m* 17, 56, 58, 61
**wine list** carta de vinos *f* 58

**wine merchant's** tienda de vinos *f*, bodega *f* 99
**wine skin** bota *f* 127
**winter** invierno *m* 149
**wiper** limpiaparabrisas *m* 75
**wish** deseo *m* 152
**with** con 15
**withdraw, to** *(bank)* retirar 131
**without** sin 15
**woman** señora *f* 115; mujer *f* 141, 156
**wood alcohol** alcohol de quemar *m* 107
**woodcarving** talla en madera *f* 127
**woodcock** becada *f* 48
**wool** lana *f* 114
**word** palabra *f* 11, 15, 133
**work, to** *(function)* funcionar 28, 119
**working day** día laborable *m* 151
**worse** peor 14
**wound** herida *f* 139
**wrap, to** envolver 102
**wrapping paper** papel de envolver *m* 105
**wristwatch** reloj de pulsera *m* 122
**write, to** escribir 11, 101
**writing pad** bloc de papel *m* 105
**writing-paper** papel de escribir *m* 27
**wrong** incorrecto(a) 14; equivo-
   cado(a) 77, 136

## X

**X-ray** *(photo)* radiografía *f* 140

## Y

**year** año *m* 149
**yellow** amarillo(a) 113
**yes** sí 9
**yesterday** ayer 151
**yet** todavía 15
**yield, to** *(traffic)* ceder el paso 79
**yoghurt** yogur *m* 64
**you** tú, usted 161
**young** joven 14
**your** tu, su, vuestro(a) 160
**youth hostel** albergue de juventud *m* 22

## Z

**zero** cero *m* 147
**zip(per)** cremallera *f* 118
**zoo** zoo(lógico) *m* 82
**zoology** zoología *f* 83
**zucchini** calabacín *m* 50

# Índice en español

| | | | | |
|---|---|---|---|---|
| Abreviaturas | 154 | Compras, guía de | 97 |
| Accidentes | 78, 139 | Concierto | 87 |
| Aduana | 16 | Conversión, tablas de | |
| Aeropuerto | 16, 65 | capacidad | 158 |
| Alfabeto | 8 | millas en km | 158 |
| Alimentación | 63, 120 | peso | 158 |
| Amigos, haciendo | 93 | tallas | 114 |
| Año | 149 | temperatura | 157 |
| Aparatos eléctricos | 119 | Correos, oficina de | 132 |
| Aparcamiento | 77 | Cubiertos | 107 |
| Aperitivos | 55 | Cuerpo, partes del | 138 |
| Autobús | 72 | Dentista | 145 |
| Autocar | 72 | Deportes | 90 |
| Aves | 48 | Desayuno | 38 |
| Avión | 65 | Diabéticos | 37, 141 |
| | | Días de la semana | 151 |
| Ballet | 87 | Días festivos | 152 |
| Banco | 129 | Dinero | 18, 129 |
| Barcos | 74 | Direcciones | 76 |
| Bebidas | 55 | Discos | 127 |
| sin alcohol | 60 | Discoteca | 88 |
| Billetes | | Diversiones | 86 |
| concierto | 87 | | |
| corrida | 89 | Edad | 149 |
| fútbol | 90 | Electricista | 119 |
| tren | 69 | Enfermedad | 140 |
| | | Ensaladas | 43 |
| Cambio | 18, 129 | Entremeses | 41 |
| Camping | 32 | Equipaje | 18, 71 |
| Campo | 85 | Especias | 51 |
| Carne | 47 | Estación | 66 |
| Cassettes | 127 | Estaciones | 149 |
| Caza, carne de | 48 | Expresiones generales | 9 |
| Centros nocturnos | 88 | | |
| Cerveza | 59 | Familia | 94 |
| Cines | 86 | Fechas | 150 |
| Citas | 95 | Fotografía | 124 |
| Coche | 75 | Fruta | 53 |
| accidentes | 78 | | |
| alquiler | 20 | Gasolinera | 75 |
| aparcamiento | 77 | Gramática | 159 |
| averías | 78 | | |
| Color | 112 | Herida | 139 |
| Comercios | 98 | Hora | 153 |
| Comestibles, tienda de | 120 | Hospital | 144 |

| | |
|---|---|
| Hotel | 22 |
| correo | 28 |
| despedida | 31 |
| dificultades | 28 |
| recepción | 23 |
| reserva | 19 |
| Iglesia | 84 |
| Invitaciones | 95 |
| Joyería | 121 |
| Juguetes | 128 |
| Lavandería | 29 |
| Letreros | 155 |
| Librería | 104 |
| Mariscos | 45 |
| Médico | 137 |
| Menú | 39 |
| Meriendas | 63, 120 |
| Meses | 150 |
| Metro | 73 |
| Música | 87, 127 |
| Negocios, expresiones de | 131 |
| Números | 147 |
| Objetos perdidos | 156 |
| Oficina de turismo | 80 |
| Ópera | 88 |
| Óptico | 123 |
| Paella | 45 |
| Países | 146 |
| Papelería | 104 |
| Pasaporte | 16 |
| Peluquería | 30 |
| Perfumería | 110 |
| Periódicos | 104 |
| Personal del hotel | 26 |
| Pesca | 91 |
| Pescado | 45 |
| Playa | 92 |
| Policía | 78, 156 |
| Prendas de vestir | 112 |
| Presentaciones | 93 |
| Provisiones | 63 |

| | |
|---|---|
| Queso | 52 |
| Relojería | 121 |
| Restaurante | 33 |
| carta | 39 |
| cuenta | 62 |
| pidiendo | 36 |
| reclamaciones | 61 |
| Robo | 156 |
| Salsas | 49 |
| Saludos | 152 |
| Sellos | 132 |
| Señales de circulación | 79 |
| Servicios religiosos | 84 |
| Sopas | 43 |
| Tabacos | 126 |
| Tallas | 114 |
| Tapas | 63 |
| Taxi | 21 |
| Teatro | 86 |
| Tejidos | 113 |
| Teléfonos | 134 |
| Telegramas, télex | 133 |
| Tiempo | 94 |
| Tintorería | 29 |
| Tocador, artículos de | 110 |
| Tortillas | 44 |
| Transportes | |
| autobús | 72 |
| avión | 65 |
| barco | 74 |
| billetes | 69 |
| información | 68 |
| metro | 73 |
| tren | 66 |
| Urgencias | 156 |
| Vajilla | 107 |
| Vegetarianos | 37 |
| Verduras | 50 |
| Vino | 56 |
| Visitas turísticas | 80 |
| Vivienda | 22 |
| Zapatos | 116 |

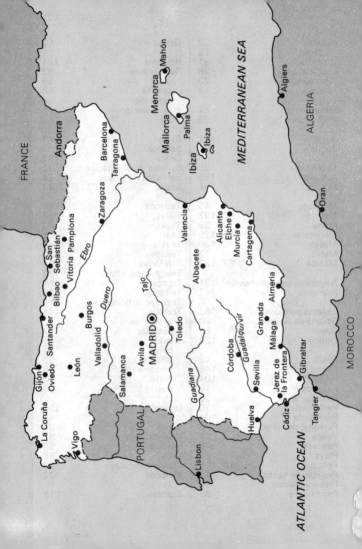

# Say BERLITZ®

... and most people think of outstanding language schools. But Berlitz has also become the world's leading publisher of books for travellers – Travel Guides, Phrase Books, Dictionaries – plus Cassettes and Self-teaching courses.

Informative, accurate, up-to-date, Books from Berlitz are written with freshness and style. They also slip easily into pocket or purse – no need for bulky, old-fashioned volumes.

Join the millions who know how to travel. Whether for fun or business, put Berlitz in your pocket.

# BERLITZ®

Leader in
Books and Cassettes
for Travellers

A Macmillan Company

# BERLITZ® Books for travellers

## TRAVEL GUIDES

They fit your pocket in both size and price. Modern, up-to-date, Berlitz gets all the information you need into 128 lively pages with colour maps and photos throughout. What to see and do, where to shop, what to eat and drink, how to save.

| | | |
|---|---|---|
| **ASIA, MIDDLE EAST** | China (256 pages) Hong Kong India (256 pages) Japan (256 pages) Nepal* Singapore Sri Lanka Thailand Egypt Jerusalem and the Holy Land Saudi Arabia |
| **AUSTRAL-ASIA** | Australia (256 pages) New Zealand |
| **AFRICA** | Kenya Morocco South Africa Tunisia | **BRITISH ISLES** | Channel Islands London Ireland Oxford and Stratford Scotland |
| *in preparation | | **BELGIUM** | Brussels |

## PHRASE BOOKS

World's bestselling phrase books feature all the expressions and vocabulary you'll need, and pronunciation throughout. 192 pages, 2 colours.

| | | |
|---|---|---|
| Arabic | Hebrew | Russian |
| Chinese | Hungarian | Serbo-Croatian |
| Danish | Italian | Spanish (Castilian) |
| Dutch | Japanese | Spanish (Lat. Am.) |
| Finnish | Korean | Swahili |
| French | Norwegian | Swedish |
| German | Polish | Turkish |
| Greek | Portuguese | European Phrase Book |
| | | European Menu Reader |